Painting, Patching, and Wallcovering Toolbox Manual

Painting, Patching, and Wallcovering Toolbox Manual

David Tenenbaum

Prentice Hall

New York   London   Toronto
Sydney   Tokyo   Singapore

Prentice Hall General Reference
15 Columbus Circle
New York, New York, 10023

An Arco Book

Arco, Prentice Hall and colophons are
registered trademarks of Simon&Schuster, Inc.

Manufactured in the United States of America

10 9 8 7 6 5 4 3 2 1

Library of Congress Cataloging in Publication Data

Tenenbaum, David.
    The painting, patching, and wallcovering toolbox manual/David Tenenbaum.
       p.   cm.
    ISBN: 0-13-647025-4
    1. House painting. 2. Paperhanging. I. Title.
TT323.T46   1991
698—dc20   91-31255
                                           CIP

Table of Contents

Part C—Color

Part D—The ABCs of Painting

Part E—Patching

Section F—Wallcovering

Part G—Health and Safety

Introduction

A paint job is too often taken for granted—open the can, splash on the paint, clean the brush, and walk away while it dries. Unfortunately, painting is not that simple—not if you want a top-quality, long-lasting coating at the lowest reasonable price. To get optimum protection and decoration from any paint job, you must prepare the surface diligently, then select and apply the right coating in the approved manner. Each of these steps—preparing, selecting, and applying—is covered in detail in this book. Other tasks of the painting and decorating contractor, including drywall installation and repair, patching surfaces, and applying wallcovering, are also described.

The book was written for painting contractors and sophisticated do-it-yourselfers doing residential and commercial painting, patching, and paperhanging.

Part A: Tools and Equipment describes the tools and equipment needed for painting, patching, and wallcovering. Personal protective equipment is described in some detail.

Part B: Materials presents the materials used in the decorating trade. The varieties of paints are detailed, with the emphasis on viewing paint selection and application as a system, not as a group of individual elements. Patching and wallcovering materials are also reviewed.

Part C: Color explains the color wheel, the Munsell system, color matching, color mixing, and the psychological impact of various color schemes.

Part D: The ABCs of Painting covers surface preparation and coating application by brush, roller, and spray. Troubleshooting tables for paint, and for air-atomization and airless sprayers, are included. Special techniques, including staining, wood-graining, and stenciling, are briefly described.

Part E: Patching covers patching of wood, drywall, plaster, and masonry. An extensive list of patching techniques for drywall and plaster is included.

Part F: Wallcovering covers estimating, designing, surface preparation, and application of various types of wallcovering.

Part G: Health and Safety reviews these vital concerns of the painting trade. A detailed explanation of the health hazards of solvents and other paint chemicals is included. The book concludes with a glossary for the painting and decorating trade.

My five years' experience as a mason and plasterer helped me to write some parts of this book, but I am grateful for the expert assistance of Donald Linstroth, a veteran of the painting and wallcovering trades, a teacher of apprentices, and apprentice administrator at Madison (Wis.) Area Technical College.

William Feist, a research chemist in wood finishing at the U.S. Forest Service's Forest Products Laboratory, contributed greatly to the accuracy of this manuscript. John Bernardi and Brendan Foley of U.S. Gypsum helped me sort out the universe of gypsum products. And Jerry Hund of Binks Manufacturing Company helped keep me on the mark in describing spray finishing equipment.

TOOLS AND EQUIPMENT

Professional painters and decorators require a good assortment of top-quality brushes, other tools, and equipment. The selection of these items depends on the user's preferences and the nature of the job.

1

Painting Tools

BRUSH

Brushes should be chosen according to the type of paint and the job. Brushes have these virtues:

- force paint into crevices and surface irregularities (particularly valuable for prime coats)
- are excellent for painting trim and corners
- produce smooth, attractive surfaces

• suited for small jobs that do not justify the masking needed for a spray or roller application

Brushing does have some disadvantages: brush marks make a series of valleys and ridges, and these valleys become the thinnest and weakest part of the coating. For large areas, brushing is slower and more tiring than rolling or spraying.

Brush quality varies enormously. Good quality brushes carry more paint, cut truer lines, coat more smoothly, drip and spatter less, and give better paint control. They also last longer and are considerably more expensive than cheap brushes.

Bristles are set into a chemically inert compound like epoxy in the heel. In a cheap brush, a large plug in the center can leave a hollow between the two rows of bristle, reducing paint capacity. A ferrule, usually made of stainless steel in professional brushes, fastens the bristles to the handle. In good brushes, ring-shank nails affix the ferrule to the handle. The handle should be large and comfortable to hold.

Bristles are the biggest single factor in brush quality. Bristles vary in length, straightness, stiffness, diameter, and composition. Harder bristles are used in wall brushes, and softer ones in sash tools. The greater the quantity of bristle, the more paint a brush can carry and distribute. Fewer passes will be needed to coat a given area, and the brush is likely to last longer.

Bristles may be of natural and synthetic origin. Natural bristle is better for solvent-based paint, but it can soften in water-based paint. *Bristle* gets its name from the traditional brush material, the bristle from a hog. The highest grade of bristle is named, after its country of origin, *China* bristle. Horsehair, another natural bristle, is used in cheap brushes, but it does not stay stiff or carry much paint. Horsehair is also used in painter's dusters.

Synthetic bristle, usually nylon or polyester, holds less paint than natural bristle, but it wears longer. Nylon can be softened by paints containing methyl or ethyl alcohol. If this happens, boil the brush in water for thirty minutes and let it dry overnight. Nylon is good for water-based paint because it does not soften in water. Polyester bristle offers the benefits of nylon, but does not remain soft in hot conditions.

Bristles should taper somewhat from the root to tip; this increases springiness and speeds application. Some synthetic bristles are shaped in various ways to increase paint capacity; shaped bristles are harder to clean than round bristles.

The nature of the tip determines how much paint a brush can hold, and how well it will apply paint. Hog bristle has a "flag end" with many fine hairs spreading out from the tip. The flag end allows the brush to carry a lot of paint and minimizes brush marks. Synthetic bristles may be "exploded" (shaped or split) to give similar benefits.

A brush should feel full and springy to the hand, have good balance, and contain varying lengths of bristle. When the longer ones wear, the flag ends of the shorter ones become available to spread the paint. Test for varying bristle lengths by flexing the brush with your hand. The shorter bristles should spring free before the longer ones.

BRUSH TERMINOLOGY

Angular—bristles as a group are angled when seen from the side; usually for painting trim and sash.

Butt end—the end of a bristle that was embedded in the hog's hide; placed in the heel.

Chiseled edge—bristles as a group are cut to a V-shape when seen from the end.

Ferrule—the binding around the bristles; attaches bristles to the handle.

Flag end—the tip of each bristle is divided into tiny "flags" to increase paint capacity, application speed, and coating smoothness.

Heel—the end of the brush near the ferrule.

Heeled up—a brush whose heel is clogged with drying or dried paint.

Length out—the length of bristles, measured from ferrule to tip.

Solid—each bundle of bristle contains more long than short bristles.

Square edge—brush is cut off at a right angle, when seen from the side.

Taper—the change in diameter of natural bristle from a wide root to a narrow tip; also a brush with an overall tapered shape.

Texture—the feel of a brush; can be altered by changing the bristle material or proportion of stiff to soft bristles.

BRUSH TYPES

- A square-end trim brush can be used for cutting-in and other small areas.

- Angular trim brushes are between 1 and 3 inches wide; length out is 1 1/2 to 3 inches; good for painting sash and trim.

- Round or oval sash brushes range from 1/2- to 2-inch diameter.

- A chiseled brush is used for trim; width can range from 1 to about 3 inches. A "sashtool" is a chiseled sash-and-trim brush with a width between 1 and 2 inches.

- A wall brush is designed for large, flat areas. Width ranges from 3 to 6 inches, and length out from 2 to 7 inches long. Brush thickness ranges from 3/4 to 1 1/2 inches. The brush is usually square-ended.

- A fiber masonry brush is about 5 to 6 inches wide; length out is 4 to 6 inches. The brush may be made of bristle, nylon, or fiber. It is used for rough surfaces, including concrete, concrete block, stucco, and brick.

- Varnish brushes are made in various shapes. Short, fine natural bristle is used to spread viscous finishes into a good film. Some are chiseled to help distribute varnish and to prevent lap marks. Others have a slight oval shape when viewed from the bristle end.

- A calcimine brush is used to apply water-based paint to large areas. Long, tough hog bristle is used; width is 5 to 8 inches.

- A stippling brush is used to stipple surfaces. The block is about 3 1/2 × 9 inches; groups of bristle are placed in rows.

- A roofing brush is used to paint large areas of shingle roof. Three bunches of bristle are bound to a block that can be attached to a long handle.

- A painter's duster can be made of various types of bristle. The duster, used to remove dust before painting, can be flat or round.

Figure A1 Paint brushes

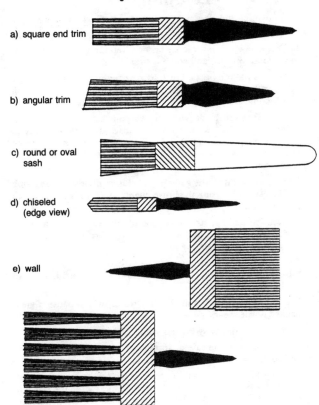

a) square end trim

b) angular trim

c) round or oval sash

d) chiseled (edge view)

e) wall

f) fiber masonry

CARE AND CLEANING

The following guidelines will help you get the longest life from your brushes:

- Inspect a new brush for loose bristles. Tap the brush, twirl it, remove loose bristles, and comb it straight.

- Break in a natural bristle brush by suspending it in linseed oil or oil paint for up to 72 hours. The bristles absorb the linseed oil and become sealed against moisture and solvents.

- Never draw a brush edgewise across a paint can to remove excess paint. Draw it flat. Some authorities insist that the only way to remove excess paint is to tap the brush against the rim. Tapping removes less paint, is gentler to the bristles, and leaves little paint in the rim.

- Prevent "fingering," the gathering of clumps of bristles. Fingering can be caused by using the brush edgewise. Use a brush comb to prevent clumps.

- Prevent "fishtailing," the separation of bristles into groups at opposite ends of the brush. Paint pipes with a brush no wider than the pipe, or use a painting mitt.

- Do not jab a brush into corners, because this bends or mats the bristles. Use a vibrating side-to-side motion to persuade paint to get into tight corners.

- Use an old brush to paint rough surfaces, which cause a great deal of bristle wear.

- Occasionally trim stray bristles with knife or scissors.

- Store a brush on the side or suspended from a hook. Storing on end ruins the bristles.

- For long-term storage, remove thinner with water and detergent. When dry (water will eventually ruin bristles) wrap the brush in stiff paper to prevent bristles from spreading. For winter storage, moth balls may be needed to protect against moths.

Clean brushes immediately after use, in the proper solvent for the paint. Make sure the solvent gets into the heel, especially if the brush was used for a long time. Press the brush against the side of the container and flex the bristles. Squeeze thinner from the brush, starting from the heel. Flick out the solvent, or use a brush spinner, and repeat until the solvent comes out clear. For water-based paints, add a bit of detergent to the water to speed the cleaning. Use a steel comb to clean bristles near the heel. Hang the brush to dry.

Select the correct brush-cleaning thinner:

- Water is used for all water-based paints, casein, portland cement paint, and calcimine. Detergent may be necessary for cleaning, or just to speed up the process.
- Mineral spirits can be used if mineral spirits or turpentine can thin the paint.
- If turpentine is used, rinse it out with naptha or mineral spirits.
- Alcohol is used for shellac or spirit (alcohol-based) stains.
- Lacquer thinner is used for lacquer brushes. A specific type of lacquer thinner may be indicated on the container.

Many thinners can be salvaged and reused, which offers both economic and environmental benefits. After the paint particles settle, pour off the thinner for reuse. Some painters prefer to suspend oil-paint brushes in oil instead of cleaning them. This works well, especially for overnight storage, as long as the brush will be used in the same paint the next day.

A brush can be "renovated" if it becomes filled with dried paint, but it's best to clean it properly in the first place. The solvent that thins the paint may work if the paint is not completely hard. To renovate a hard brush, soak in paint remover or brush cleaner. When the paint softens, use a brush comb and plenty of elbow grease, then wash out the sludge with detergent and water. Use care because solvents or brush cleaner can damage the ferrule, bristle binding material, or heel.

ROLLER

Rollers create a good deal of spatter and leave a slight stippling effect. The degree of stippling depends on the nap and the nature of the paint and substrate. Rollers greatly speed up application to large flat surfaces:

- rough and hard-to-reach surfaces
- jobs that would require a great deal of masking before spraying
- jobs where spraying would create drift, fire, toxic fumes, or explosion hazards

Rollers range in width from 1 to 18 inches, with the most common being 9 inches. A 7-inch width is handy for rolling narrow siding. Narrow rollers are suitable for cutting in, trim, and small areas. The widest rollers are suitable for floors and large walls.

A roller can be filled from a pan or a frame placed inside a 5-gallon bucket. Pressure-feed rollers eliminate trips to the roller pan, but are much harder to clean. The center of a "fountain-style" roller holds paint, eliminating the use of the roller pan.

A roller extension is a pole that screws into the roller handle. Some extensions telescope. Extensions are handy for rolling ceilings without staging. They also enable you to roll down to the baseboard and fill the roller without leaning over. And by allowing the use of two hands, they significantly reduce hand strain.

Roller covers should be chosen on the basis of paint type, substrate roughness, and desired surface finish. Use synthetic fiber for water-based paints. Use natural fibers (mohair or wool) for oils, alkyds, and varnishes.

The longer the nap, the greater the paint delivery and the fewer the trips to the roller pan, but the greater the stippling effect. The rougher the surface, the longer the nap needed. (See Table A1.) If several naps are listed for a substrate, select according to the surface texture you want: the finer the nap, the smoother the surface.

Clean a cover by rolling in a tray containing the appropriate solvent. A curved scraper or a roller spinner can speed up the process. If you will use the same paint the next day, add some thinner to the tray, place the cover in it, then wrap the tray securely inside two plastic bags. Often, roller covers are just discarded. Paper-core covers can only be washed a few times before they "melt away."

TABLE A1
Roller cover selection

Material/substrate	nap length			
	3/16"	3/8"	3/4"	1 1/2"
Varnish	X			
Wallboard or plaster	X	X	X	
Wood or hardboard	X	X		
Cement block or brick			X	X
Stucco			X	X
Ceiling tile		X	X	
High-gloss enamel	X			
Shingle, shakes, and rough siding			X	X
Textured ceiling		X	X	X

BRUSH AND ROLLER SPINNER

A spinner is used to clean brushes and roller covers. The rotary action is created by a spiral mechanism like the one found in a yankee drill. Centrifugal force flings the dirty solvent out of the tool and speeds up the cleaning. Pump the handle up and down while holding the tool in a 5-gallon bucket to catch spray.

MITT

A painter's mitt can be used to apply paint to odd-shaped objects, such as pipes, pipe fittings, and railings. A mitt may be faster and cleaner than spray or brush for coating such objects. Mitts are available with a thumb or a square end. The best quality mitts are made of lambskin. If the mitt does not have a liner, wear a glove to protect your hand from paint.

FOAM PAD AND BRUSH

Synthetic foam pads or brushes can be substituted for brush, roller, or spray applicators. A foam block holds the paint, and the napped fabric on the surface applies it. Some pads have a small roller to guide against a straightedge or trim to simplify cutting a true edge. When selecting a foam applicator, make sure solvent in the paint cannot dissolve the foam. These tools may be cleaned, but many are cheap enough to discard.

Pad applicators have these advantages:

- less spatter than a roller
- can cut a straighter line than a brush
- have no stray bristles
- low cost

MOISTURE METER

A moisture meter electronically measures the moisture percentage in a substrate to determine when a surface is ready to paint. A meter can eliminate guesswork and is especially helpful in damp climates, where it can a) prevent the loss of work time due to a mistaken impression that a surface is too wet, and b) prevent painting over damp substrate.

PAINT-THICKNESS GAUGE

A paint-thickness gauge measures the thickness of a dry film of paint on a metal substrate. The gauge works on the principle that magnetic attraction falls off with distance. The thicker the film, the lower the magnetic attraction between the meter and the substrate. This gauge is helpful for government specification work or for whenever a certain dry film thickness is required to withstand abrasion, corrosion, or weathering.

Figure A2 Brush or roller spinner

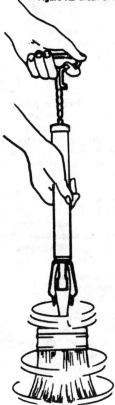

Courtesy of Hyde Tool Company

2

Spray-Finishing Equipment

Spray-finishing equipment is necessary on some jobs, and can greatly increase productivity on many others. Although spray equipment can quickly and smoothly apply paint, it is subject to equipment failure or operator error and is relatively expensive and complicated. For architectural jobs, spray equipment is most suitable for large areas where the time saved exceeds the time and expense needed to mask surfaces and clean equipment.

The two major types of spray painting, as far as trade painters and homeowners are concerned, are air-atomization and airless. Air-atomization sprayers use air pressure to atomize the paint and propel it at the substrate. Airless sprayers create extremely high pressure in the paint, forcing it to atomize as it passes through the orifice. They do not need air pressure, although some airless pumps are powered by air.

Industrial painters use a third type of equipment, the electrostatic sprayer. In this device, electrical attraction "pulls" the paint toward the substrate. The process reduces waste, especially for cylindrical shapes and some openwork. Electrostatic equipment can work with either air-atomization or airless equipment.

VISCOSITY

Paint viscosity helps determine spray equipment selection and operating pressure. Viscosity, the rate at which paint can flow, varies according to paint's temperature, particle size, and proportion of thinner. Viscosity can be measured by many methods, but the

TABLE A2
Air-atomization vs airless spraying

Factor	Airless spraying	Air-atomization spraying
Means of atomization	High-velocity of fluid using hydraulic pressure through small orifice	Fluid stream torn apart by jets of compressed air
Pattern control	Nozzle shape and size—must change nozzle to change pattern	Control of air and fluid pressure provides complete control of pattern
Air volume	About 1/4 to 1/2 of conventional spray system (only for air-powered pump)	4 to 20 cfm
Air pressure requirement	High pressure (100 psi)	Medium to low pressure best (50 to 75 psi)
Fluid pressure requirements	600 to 4,000 psi	Low pressure—generally to 18 psi at nozzle
Fluid delivery	Medium to high delivery. Provides fastest application speeds. Excellent for large areas	Low to medium delivery. Usually not more than 32 oz. per minute. Less speed than airless—more control
Air contamination	More overspray (material that misses the object) but less fog and rebound (material that bounces back from the surface)	Less overspray. More fog and rebound. Proportional to the atomizing pressure. Higher pressure increases fog
Materials	Not all materials can be sprayed. Requires uniform fine grinds (particle size 0-.008). Heavy-pigmented, fiber-filled,	Materials that can flow can be sprayed

TABLE A2 (continued)

Factor	Airless spraying	Air-atomization spraying
	abrasive, or cohesive materials will not work	
Material preparation	Requires considerable care to ensure proper patterns with no tip plugging	Less care required. Follow material supplier's instructions
Maintenance	More required because higher pressure pumping equipment and smaller fluid tip orifices are required	Less care required because equipment is more basic
Product contamination	No contamination from air-line impurities	Impurities in air line can spoil the finish
Spraying advantage	Material can be sprayed into cavities and corners with little rebound from the opening	Difficult to spray into cavities and corners because air cushion inhibits paint deposition
Atomization	Generally coarser atomization	Fine atomization for all high-quality finishes

COURTESY BINKS MANUFACTURING CO.

most common are the Zahn and Ford cups. Use this procedure with a Zahn cup:

1. Submerge the cup to fill it with paint.

2. Remove the cup from the coating, and note the time on a watch.

3. Note how long it takes for the stream to break, indicating that the cup is empty.

4. Express the results in terms of time and cup size (for example, 15 seconds, #2 Zahn cup).

It may be necessary to thin paint before applying it, but it's usually best to spray paint as packaged. Thinning can reduce hiding power and increase sags and runs. An alternative method for reducing viscosity is to warm paint in a portable heater.

AIR-ATOMIZATION SPRAY SYSTEMS

Air-atomization (conventional) spray systems create a fog of paint by mixing it with pressurized air. The air is supplied by a compressor powered by electricity or gasoline. Specific spray systems are rated by air pressure (in psi) and quantity (in cfm) requirements.

Air-atomization systems are categorized according to: a) type of gun—bleeder or nonbleeder; b) type of feed to the gun—suction or pressure; c) type of air cap—internal or external mix.

GUN

A bleeder-type gun allows some air to escape even if the trigger is closed. The gun has a fluid valve, but no air valve. A bleeder gun is useful for a system fed directly from a small compressor because it allows the compressor to start without load.

The trigger on a nonbleeder gun controls both air and paint flow. Atomization air is present whenever paint flows through the gun. The compressor needs a control to stop its pumping when pressure reaches the maximum safe level.

Special guns are used to spray two-component materials to promote drying, deaden noise, or resist corrosion.

The action of an air spray gun may be controlled by these components:

• The trigger can be used to make slight adjustments in the paint flow (not to regulate fan shape). The trigger operates a) only the

Figure A3 Basic air-atomization gun

Parts:

A) Air nozzle

B) Fluid nozzle

C) Needle assembly

D) Side port control

E) Fluid control assembly

F) Spray gun body handle

G) Air inlet

H) Trigger

I) Air valve

J) Fluid inlet

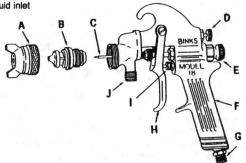

Courtesy of Binks Manufacturing Co.

fluid needle on a bleeder gun; b) the fluid needle and air flow on a nonbleeder gun. The trigger on a nonbleeder gun should be adjusted to open the air valve before the fluid valve.

- The fluid control knob adjusts fluid flow by regulating the open position of the needle.

- The size of the fluid nozzle orifice regulates the rate of paint flow.

- In an external-mix air cap, the side port control valve regulates fan size and shape.

TABLE A3

Air-atomization delivery
(ounces per minute)

Fluid pressure	8 psi	12 psi	18 psi
Orifice			
.040	12.5	15.0	19.0
.046	17.0	21.0	27.0
.052	20.5	25.5	33.0
.059	24.0	30.0	40.0
.070	28.0	36.0	48.0

COURTESY BINKS MANUFACTURING CO.

FLUID NOZZLE

The fluid nozzle has three functions: a) to regulate the flow rate, b) to direct the fluid from the gun, and c) to provide a seat for the needle valve. The higher the viscosity of the material, the larger the orifice (opening size) needed.

Choose a fluid nozzle for a pressure-feed system so the gun operates at a maximum of about 18 psi fluid pressure at the gun inlet. If the fluid nozzle is too small, excess pressure will be needed; and a) overall efficiency will be reduced, and b) paint will flow too fast for it to atomize completely.

In pressure- and siphon-feed systems, flow can be increased by:

• using a larger fluid orifice

• reducing viscosity

• opening the fluid control knob

In pressure-feed systems, fluid flow can also be increased by raising fluid pressure.

AIR NOZZLE

The air nozzle, or "air cap," is fastened to the front of the fluid nozzle. Its function is to atomize the paint by introducing com-

Figure A4 Air-atomization nozzle details

a) internal-mix nozzle

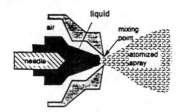

b) external-mix nozzle

c) external-mix nozzle face detail

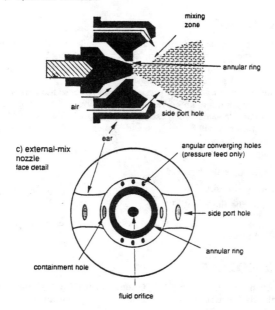

pressed air into the paint stream. Mixing occurs inside an "internal-mix" air cap. Mixing occurs outside an "external-mix" cap.

Internal-mix air caps produce large patterns with a high rate of fluid output and are suited to coarse spraying, heavy application, and slow-drying materials. This design must be used with a pressure-feed paint supply. Air and paint pressures must be about equal.

Internal-mix caps require less air volume and lower air pressure than external-mix caps. Both of these factors reduce overspray and bounce-back from the surface. However, the caps give relatively little control of the fan shape, are prone to plugging by fast-drying fluids, and cannot produce as fine a finish as external-mix caps.

External-mix air caps are better suited for fine work and fast-drying materials. They may be used with suction- or pressure-feed systems. Suction-feed guns must use suction air caps, but pressure-feed systems can use either type. The fluid nozzle protrudes slightly from a suction-feed, external-mix cap. Some companies place an "S" in the designation to indicate suction feed, and a "P" for pressure feed.

External-mix air caps create atomization in stages (see Figure A4):

- The "annular" ring surrounding the fluid orifice produces the first air stream and the first stage of atomization.

- Air from "containment holes" helps direct the air stream away from the ears.

- Further atomization in a pressure-feed cap may be produced by "angular converging holes."

- Finally, air streams from side port holes in the horns (wings or ears) control spreading of the fan. Air flow through these ports is regulated by the side port control valve.

Having several air holes in the air cap gives these advantages:

- good atomization and patterns at the high pressures needed for viscous paint

- better atomization at low pressure

- greater pattern uniformity

Figure A5 Air cap identification

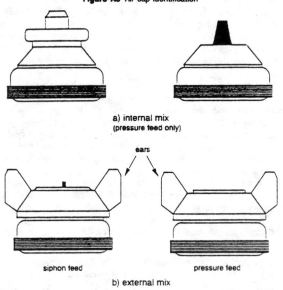

a) internal mix
(pressure feed only)

ears

siphon feed

pressure feed

b) external mix

The key elements of the spraying system—air and fluid pressure, air cap, and fluid nozzle and needle—must be compatible. Consider these factors when choosing:

- air volume in cfm and pressure in psi (smaller compressors need a smaller air cap to prevent the gun from being starved)

- material feed—suction or pressure

- type, viscosity, and amount of paint to be applied

- size and shape of object to be sprayed (using the largest possible spray pattern will reduce the number of passes and speed up the work)

Figure A6 Nozzle position—external-mix air cap

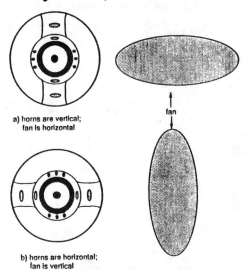

a) horns are vertical;
fan is horizontal

b) horns are horizontal;
fan is vertical

If the air pressure is too high, the paint may be atomized excessively and dry too fast. This wastes paint and harms the finish. If the fluid nozzle is too large, paint flow may be excessive, atomization will not be adequate, and you may lose control. It's best to regulate the spray volume by adjusting fluid pressure or changing the orifice, not by holding the fluid needle valve partly open.

PAINT CONTAINER

The paint container holds paint before it is sprayed. Two types of feed mechanisms can be used to supply paint from the container to the gun. Suction- (siphon-) feed systems store paint in a container (siphon cup) attached to the spray gun. Pressure-feed guns can be fed by a remote cup, tank, or pump.

TABLE A4
Air-atomization orifices and pressure

Types of coating materials	Fluid pressure (psi)	Atomizing air pressure (psi)	Fluid nozzle size (inches)	Air cap volume (cfm at 50 psi)
Acrylics	5-10	50-60	.040-.052	14-15
Alkyds	25-30	30-40	.070-.086	12-14
Chlorinated rubber	8-12	50-65	.070-.078	12-14
Coal tar epoxies	80-100	70-90	.187-.375	16-20
Epoxies	20-30	50-70	.059-.070	12-14
Epoxy-esters	25-30	30-40	.070-.086	12-14
Neoprene & hypalon	10-20	50-70	.046-.070	12-14
Phenolics	25-30	30-40	.070-.086	12-14
Phenolics catalysed	20-30	50-70	.059-.070	12-14
Polyesters	40-70	20-40	.086-.110	14-16
Polyurethanes	10-25	30-50	.040-.052	12-14
Silicones	10-20	40-70	.040-.052	13-15
Vinyls	15-25	60-90	.059-.030	14-16
Water-based coatings	15-30	30-45	.070-.086	14-15
Zinc-rich coatings	15-25	40-60	.070-.086	15-18

COURTESY BINKS MANUFACTURING CO.

Suction-feed systems create a vacuum at the air cap to "pull" finish from the container to the gun. The fast-moving air at the cap makes a low-pressure area in the paint stream. This reduction in pressure allows atmospheric pressure to push paint from the container, through the fluid nozzle, and into the air stream. Only an air hose is needed.

The suction-feed container is connected directly to the gun. Because the usual capacity is 1 to 2 quarts, the system is suited to small jobs and frequent changes of paint. Suction feed is good for spraying light-bodied materials, such as shellac, stain, varnish, synthetic enamels, and stain. To keep the vent holes in the suction container open, clean them occasionally with a straw or other nonmetallic object.

Paint is pushed to the gun in a *pressure-feed* system by air pressure in the container. The system needs one hose for air and another for paint. Pressure feed is suited to heavy paints, such as epoxies, enamels and alkyds, and is preferable for large painting jobs because the container can be much bigger.

COMPRESSOR

The compressor for a spray system must be chosen on the basis of output in pressure (psi) and volume (cfm), whether electric power will be available at all operating sites, and convenience features. A single-stage compressor may have multiple cylinders, but the air goes through only one piston on its trip through the machine. In a double-stage compressor, air exits the first cylinder, is cooled, and enters a second piston. This technique increases output pressure and efficiency.

The *displacement* of a compressor is the volume of the cylinder. Calculate displacement with this formula:

area of piston in square inches × stroke length in inches
= displacement in cubic inches

Output is the theoretical pumping capacity, measured in cfm. Calculate output with this formula:

(cylinder radius in inches)² ×
0.001818 × stroke × rpm × no. cylinders
= output in cfm

The *delivery* of a compressor—the actual amount of air supplied—must be measured.

Volumetric efficiency is the ratio of air delivered to output: volumetric efficiency = delivery/output. Volumetric efficiency generally decreases as operating pressure increases.

A compressor must have a device to prevent over-pressure (unless the gun is a bleeder type). This can be a) a pressure-controlled switch that shuts off electricity when pressure in the pressure tank reaches the set point, or b) an automatic unloader. An unloader does not stop the compressor. Instead, it holds the intake valve open to prevent the compressor from pumping air. When pressure in the receiver drops below the set point, the unloader closes and the compressor resumes pumping. The pressure setting can be adjusted with a screw. Unloaders are most suitable when the compressor's output is slightly higher than the gun's demand, and it is difficult to shut down the compressor frequently.

AIR TANK AND REGULATOR

Compressors generally feed compressed air to a pressure tank. This tank (receiver) can range in size from 2 to 50 gallons. Air is usually fed from the receiver into a regulator on the paint container. By ensuring constant air pressure, consistent atomization, and a reliable fan, the regulator makes the painter's job easier.

Pressure-feed systems can have a single or double regulator. In a single-regulated system, air pressure to the container is regulated, but the gun receives full pressure from the compressor. (A pressure-adjusting valve can be added at the gun air inlet.) In a double-regulated system, air pressure is regulated to the container and the gun. Because this system offers greater control, it is common on portable spray equipment.

HOSE

Hoses connect the various components of an air-atomization spray system. Hoses are chosen by whether they will carry air or paint, the type of paint, the operating pressure, cfm needed at the gun, and length. Do not use an air hose for solvent-based paints, as the solvent might dissolve the hose. Double-braided hoses can operate

Figure A7 Single and double air regulators (pressure feed)

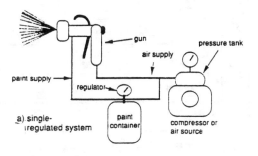

a) single-regulated system

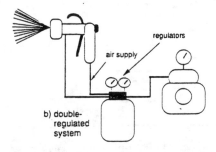

b) double-regulated system

at higher pressure than single-braided hoses. Suction systems need only an air hose; pressure-feed systems also require a paint hose.

Hoses are identified by inside diameter (I.D.). I.D. can range from 1/4 to 3/4 inch. Residential and commercial painters usually use 3/8- or 1/2-hoses.

Pressure drop between the compressor and gun is a crucial factor in choosing hose diameter. Pressure drop is caused by friction against the hose wall and fittings. Excess pressure drop will starve the gun and decrease paint flow rate and atomization.

Table A5
Air hose selection guide
Based on Pressure Drop At 90 PSI Input

Average Compressor H.P. Requirements Gas Powered	Tool CFM Requirements	5/16" I.D. Hose (71-131)			3/8" I.D. Hose (71-132)				1/2" I.D. Hose (71-133)		3/4" I.D. Hose (71-134)	
		25 Feet	50 Feet	100 Feet	50 Feet	50 Feet + 10 Ft. 5/16" ID	100 Feet	100 Feet + 10 Ft. 5/16" ID	100 Feet	100 Feet + 10 Ft. 5/16" ID	100 Feet	100 Feet + 10 Ft. 3/8" ID
4 to 6 HP	7-9	2.0	4.0	8.0		2.5	3.0	4.0				
6 to 8 HP	9-10	2.5	5.0			3.9	5.8	6.8				
6 to 8 HP	10-11	3.0	6.0		3.0	4.6	6.0	7.6	1.4	3.0		
	11-12	3.5	7.0		3.5	5.2	7.0	8.7	1.6	3.3		
	12-13	4.0	8.0		4.0	6.3	8.0	10.0	1.8	4.0		
8 to 12 HP	13-14	5.0	10.0		5.0	7.6	10.0		2.0	4.6		
	14-15	6.3			6.0	8.8			2.6	5.6		
	15-16	7.4			7.1	9.9			3.2	6.3		
	16-18	8.3			8.2				4.0	8.2		
	18-20	9.5			10.0				4.8	9.6		
	20-25								6.0			
12 to 18 HP	25-30										.9	
	30-35										1.3	
	35-40										1.7	
	40-50										2.5	
25 to 60 HP	50-60								8.2		3.5	5.1
	60-70								10.6		5.0	6.6
	70-80										6.5	10.1
	80-90										9.0	

Note: Pressure loss exceeding 10 PSI is excessive and unacceptable for normal conditions.
The specific pressure loss through a hose is relative to the pressure and C.F.M. usage of the tool.

Courtesy Binks Manufacturing Co.

These steps decrease pressure drop:

- shortening the hose
- increasing hose diameter
- decreasing paint viscosity
- decreasing working pressure

Hoses must be protected against such abuse as kinking, abrasion, and running over by vehicles. Clean paint hoses after use. A device called a hose cleaner forces solvent through the hose. A valve on the device stops the solvent flow and allows an air stream to purge solvent from the hose.

ACCESSORIES

An *extractor* (condenser) traps oil, dirt, and moisture on the way to the paint container. Open the drain occasionally to remove contaminants—more frequently in humid weather or during heavy use.

A *filter* removes particles from the air stream.

An *air transformer* has several functions: air regulator, extractor, air gauge (for outlet or outlet and input pressure), shutoff valve for outlet air, and drain.

An *agitator* in the paint container stirs the paint. Used primarily on paints with a tendency to settle, such as pigmented lacquers, it may be powered by hand, air pressure, or electric motor.

A *low-pressure pump* is used to move paint through a long hose or to painters located high above the compressor. This pump is especially useful for heavy-bodied paint, such as asphalts and other roof coatings. It is usually powered by compressed air.

AIRLESS SPRAY SYSTEM

Airless spray guns offer a number of advantages over air-atomization sprayers (see Table A2, pages 13–14)—they require less energy, can spray more paint per minute, and produce less fog and overspray. Due to their increased volume, the gun moves faster than a conventional gun and is held farther from the work—about 10 to 15 feet.

The pump in an airless system creates extremely high pressure (1,000 to 4,500 psi) at the gun. The pump may be powered by a gasoline engine, electric motor, or by air pressure. (An air-powered airless sprayer uses air only to operate the pump, not to atomize the paint.)

Atomization occurs in an airless gun when the pressurized paint exits the nozzle and is exposed to atmospheric pressure. The same principle allows a garden hose nozzle to create a fog of water.

Note: Airless systems operate at extreme pressures and can cause considerable injury if used improperly. Never aim the gun at anyone. Remove the tip on a clogged gun only after the system is shut down and pressure is bled off. Observe the other safety precautions listed in Part D.

The angle of delivery is determined by the nozzle; it can range from 10° to 80°. If operated at the same pressure, tips (with whatever angle) with the same orifice size will deliver the same amount of material per minute. A tip with a wider angle will distribute paint more broadly, and deposit less on each square foot.

These factors affect the rate of paint flow from an airless gun: paint viscosity, pressure, and orifice size. Viscosity can be reduced by thinning paint (or by heating, but this is usually done only in industry). Adjust pressure at the pump—it should be lower for low-viscosity paint than for thick paint. The orifice on an airless nozzle can range from .007-inch to .072-inch. It may help to experiment with the orifice—if you are losing control of the operation, try a smaller orifice.

Clogging is a major problem with airless systems. When the tip clogs, pressure buildup inside the gun makes it dangerous to clean out the clog. Most manufacturers sell reversible tip assemblies—when you move a control on the gun, the flow reverses and cleans out the dirt.

An optional pole on an airless system can extend the operator's reach. Some airless pumps can feed a paint roller.

Figure A8 Airless nozzle angles

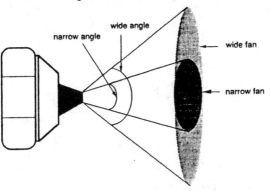

AIRLESS PUMP

The airless pump can pressurize the paint with pistons, turbines, or rotors. The pump may receive paint through a hose from the material supply container, or it may be located on top of the container. The pump must be selected on the basis of the type and volume of material to be sprayed, and the power source available (gasoline, electricity, or compressed air).

Altering pressure is one of the two major operating adjustments in an airless system, so the pump must be designed to create various pressures. The pump must also have a pressure-relief valve to prevent overpressure.

A fluid filter on the pump helps prevent particles from clogging the tip. The screen size in the filter must match the paint. (A separate filter may be located on the gun.)

Normal screen spacing

material to spray	spacing
metallics and primers	.009"
solid colors	.005" to .009"
sealers and solvents	.003"

Table A6
Airless tip selector

Type of Paints	Viscosity* (seconds)	Tip No.	Orifice Size (inches)	Spray Angle (degrees)	Spray Width▪ (inches)
Lacquers, Sealers, Stains	20–25	9-1140	.011	40	7.5
		9-1330	.013	25	5.5
		9-1350*	.013	50	9.0
Automotive Primers, Lacquers, Enamels	20–25	9-1540	.015	40	8.5
		9-1580	.015	80	13.0
Aluminums, Iso-Alkyds, Primers, Plastic Enamels, Alkyd Flats, Road Stripping	30–35	9-1540*	.015	40	8.5
		9-1580	.015	80	13.0
		9-1840	.018	40	10.0
		9-1860*	.018	65	13.5
Latex, Rustic & Shakes Mill Whites	35–45	9-1540*	.015	40	8.5
		9-1580	.015	80	13.0
		9-1840	.018	40	10.0
		9-1860*	.018	65	13.0
		9-2180*	.021	80	17.0
		9-2660	.026	65	17.0
		9-3170	.031	65	15.0

*No. 4 Ford Cup.   ▪With nozzle tip at 12 inches from work surface.   *Most frequently used.

Figure A9 Dead-end, air-powered airless system

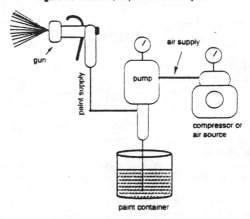

The most common airless equipment for trade painters is called the dead-end system. The pump forces a stream of paint through a hose to the gun. When the gun is not operating, the pump automatically stalls or shuts down. Hand-held, electric-powered airless sprayers are also available for homeowner use or small jobs.

A circulating-type system can be used for certain finishes. The system may also heat the paint to between 120° and 160°F to decrease viscosity. Heated systems have several advantages, particularly for spraying thick paint:

• Little or no thinner is needed.

• Build is higher per coat, so production rate is increased.

• Reduces tack time, power, paint and air, orange peel, and sag.

3

Scrapers

Scrapers are used to remove various surface contaminants, primarily deteriorated paint and rust. Take care—scrapers can gouge the surface. Holding the tool with the handle near the surface will scrape most effectively, but also pose the greatest danger of gouging.

Scrapers range in width from 1 to 4 inches. Blades should be removable for sharpening. Some scrapers have a long-life tungsten carbide blade. Scrapers with a curved handle, or a second handle atop the blade, are easier to operate. For scraping walls, use a blade between 3 and 4 inches wide. It's a good idea to keep a file handy for dressing blades.

Window scrapers remove paint from glass, generally with a single-edge razor blade. To avoid damaging the seal between the paint and the glass, scrape the area before it sets up too much, and keep the blade about 1/16 inch away from the sash.

Power scrapers and chisels can be used to remove rust and scale from metal. Wire brushes, preferably electric, and electric disc sanders are also effective at removing surface contaminants.

Figure A10 Scrapers

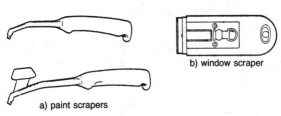

b) window scraper

a) paint scrapers

Courtesy of Hyde Tool Company

4

Knives

A variety of knives are used to apply drywall compound, patching material, or caulking:

- A *putty knife* is used to apply putty and do minor scraping. Widths range from 1 1/4 to 2 inches. A glazing knife is a variety of putty knife with a bent blade; it can glaze windows in an easy stroke.

- A *patching knife* is used for filling and finishing drywall. Width ranges from 3 to 6 inches.

- A *taping knife* is used to apply and embed drywall tape. Width ranges from 4 to 6 inches. The edges are at right angles to the blade end so the knife can apply compound into square corners. The knife should have a brass butt for driving nails below the

Figure A11 Knives

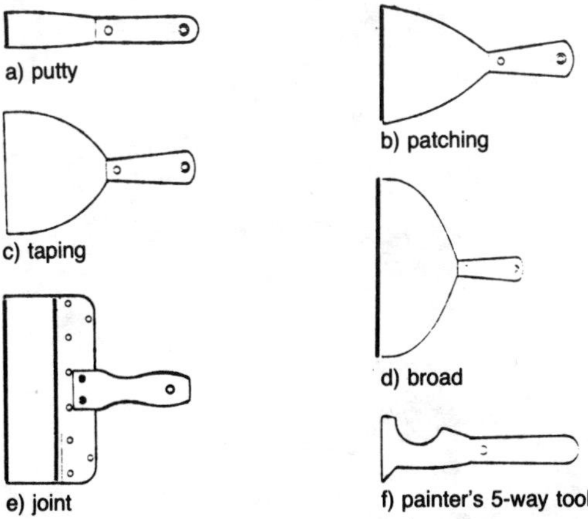

a) putty

b) patching

c) taping

d) broad

e) joint

f) painter's 5-way tool

Courtesy of Hyde Tool Company

surface. This knife is not generally used to cover the tape—use a broad knife instead.

- A *broad knife* ranges from 6 to 14 inches wide. The knife is used to fill and finish drywall, and to patch wide holes in plaster or other substrates.

- A *joint knife* can substitute for a broad knife.

- The *painter's 5-way tool* is a versatile tool used to clean roller covers, scrape paint from contoured surfaces, gouge, remove putty, and spread patching compound.

5

Mason's Tools

The following mason's tools are especially useful for patching:

- A *margin trowel* is handy for mixing into the bottom of a bucket and making small repairs in masonry, plaster, and drywall. It can substitute for a pointing trowel.

- A *tuckpointing trowel* has a narrow blade for forcing mortar into joints between bricks and concrete blocks.

- A *pointing trowel* is a good all-around repair tool for many of the same tasks as the margin trowel.

- A *concrete float* is used to float the surface of concrete after screeding. The tool can be homemade from a slightly convex 6 × 14 inch piece of 3/4-inch lumber. Nail a 2 × 4 handle to the middle of the concave side.

- A *jointer* is used to shape, or "tool," a joint after the mortar has taken its initial set. Various sizes and shapes are available. A piece of rubber hose or a large dowel will serve in an emergency.

Figure A12 Mason's Tools

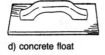

a) margin trowel   b) tuckpointing trowel

c) pointing trowel

d) concrete float   e) jointer

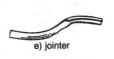

Courtesy of Hyde Tool Company

35

6

Drywall and Plaster Tools

What follows are some of the basic tools of the drywall and plastering trades (see also "Knives" and "Mason's Tools," above):

- A *plaster trowel* can be used to apply and smooth plaster, joint compound, or filler. It can also substitute as a finishing trowel for small concrete jobs. One version of this tool has a convex blade to leave a slightly mounded surface; shrinkage of the patching material should bring the patch down to the surface.

Figure A13 Drywall and plaster tools

a) plaster trowel

b) hawk

c) angle plow

d) mud box

e) drywall saw

f) utility knives

g) drywall square

h) drywall hatchet

i) circular cutter

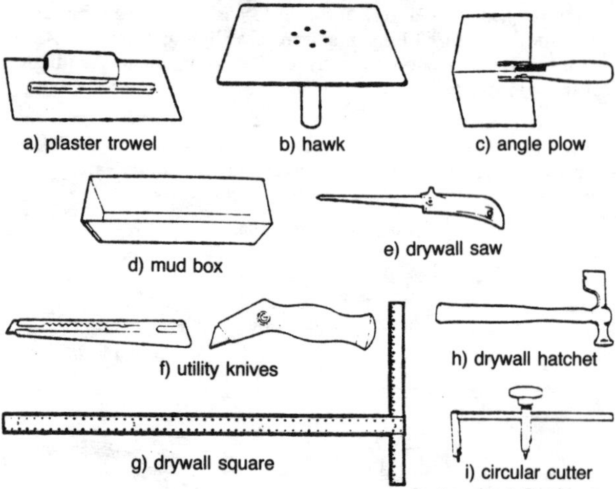

Courtesy of Hyde Tool Company

- A *hawk* is used with a plastering trowel to apply mortar, joint compound, or plaster. Size ranges from 10 × 10 inch to 13 × 13 inch.

- An *angle plow* presses drywall compound into 90° inside corners. The tool can be used before and after applying drywall tape.

- A drywaller's *mudbox* is handy for applying joint- or quick-setting compound. Mudboxes are available in plastic, and galvanized or stainless steel.

- A *drywall saw* is shaped like a keyhole saw; it is used to cut angles, curves, and cutouts for electrical boxes.

- A *utility knife* with replaceable blades is commonly used to cut drywall. Cut through the paper on one side, bend the sheet away from the cut, and cut through the remaining paper. A utility knife with snap-off blades is excellent for cutting wallcovering.

- A *drywall square* has a 48-inch blade and rulers along both blades. The square is handy for cutting drywall, plywood, paneling, and other sheet goods.

- A *drywall hatchet* is used to hammer nails and to cut drywall.

- A *circle cutter* makes circular cutouts for fixtures in drywall.

- A *rectangular cutout tool* is best for making cutouts for electrical boxes. A drywall saw can be substituted.

- An *open-bladed rasp*, sold under the brand name "Surform," is handy for smoothing and trimming cuts in drywall. A piece of wire lath nailed to a block of wood can be substituted—but watch your fingers on sharp wire lath.

- A *screw gun* is used to install drywall screws. Most models have an adjustable, automatic clutch to stop the rotation when the screw reaches the proper depth.

7

Wallcovering Tools

- A *chalk box* is used to mark straight lines and plumb lines. To prevent guidelines from showing through the seams, use a) light-colored chalk, or b) charcoal (which is easier to wash off).

- A *plumb bob* can be used to draw plumb lines.

- A *straightedge* is used to trim selvage on the table and to mark straight lines on the wall. A 6- or 7-foot straightedge is a handy length.

- A *pasting table* is used to cut and paste wallcovering. The table should have brackets to hold the straightedge out of the way when not in use.

- A *razor knife* is used to remove selvage and trim strips on the wall.

- A *30/30 trimmer* or 30/30 knife is used to cut heavyweight vinyl.

- *Scissors* are used for many cutting purposes, though a razor knife is usually preferable for trimming.

- A *water box*, or water tray, is used to immerse prepasted covering to activate the paste.

- A *pasting brush* (about 6 to 8 inches wide) is used to apply paste to the back of wallcovering or the wall. A *paste roller* can be substituted.

- A *smoothing brush* is used to press covering against the wall for removing air bubbles. For stiff vinyl, the bristles should be about 3/4 inch long; for softer material, about 2 inches long.

- A *smoothing tool* can be used to smooth heavy coverings.

- A *seam roller* is used to press adhesive out of seams. Both flat and oval (rounded) rollers are used.

- A *spirit level* is used to mark out level and plumb lines on the wall. Both 2- and 6-foot models are handy.

Figure A14 Wallcovering tools

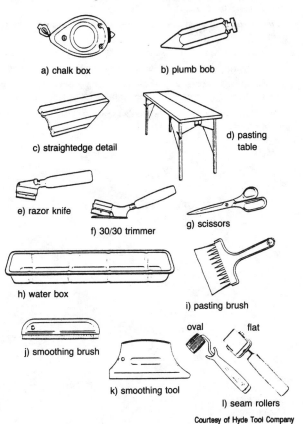

a) chalk box

b) plumb bob

c) straightedge detail

d) pasting table

e) razor knife

f) 30/30 trimmer

g) scissors

h) water box

i) pasting brush

j) smoothing brush

k) smoothing tool

oval   flat

l) seam rollers

Courtesy of Hyde Tool Company

- A *sponge* is used to smooth covering on the wall and to remove excess paste from seams.
- A *tape measure* or rigid metal ruler is handy for planning installations.
- A *paste bucket* is used to mix paste.
- *Colored pencils* are used to color and hide slight gaps in seams.
- The *broad knife* is used to peel old paper and to serve as a guideline for trimming material on the wall.

Miscellaneous tools include stepladders, pencils, plastic pails, and detergent.

8

Ladders

Ladders are an expensive and dangerous necessity for the decorating trades. Proper selection, care, and use of this equipment will increase productivity and decrease hazards. Ladders are made of wood, aluminum, and fiberglass.

TABLE A7

Ladder material comparison

Material	Advantages	Disadvantages
Wood	Does not conduct electricity, can be repaired.	Subject to rot, relatively heavy.
Aluminum	Lightweight, does not rot or rust, repairable, low cost.	Good conductor of electricity—do not use near powerlines.
Fiberglass	Does not conduct electricity, more durable than wood, strong.	Expensive, almost impossible to repair.

Ladders are rated by weight capacity and/or suitability for industrial, commercial, or household use. See Part G for ladder safety information.

- A *stepladder* is a fixed-height, self-supporting ladder with a flat top. The top is not a platform for standing, nor is the pail shelf (if present). A locking spreader holds the legs open. Rungs on the brace side of an ordinary stepladder are not intended to carry weight. Stepladders must not be over 20 feet high. Stepladders (and trestles) should have a 5 1/2-inch spread per foot of height.

- A *double-sided stepladder* has steps on both sides. It is the strongest self-supporting ladder and can be used as a trestle for scaffold, because rungs on both sides can bear weight.

41

- A *platform* stepladder has a standing work platform with guard rails.

- A trestle resembles a double stepladder in that both sets of rungs can support staging. An *extension trestle* has an adjustable vertical section that can be raised to support scaffold planks. A standard trestle has no adjustable section.

- The *combination* ladder can be used as a stepladder, double stepladder, short extension ladder, or stairway ladder. It can also be separated into two short, straight ladders.

An *extension* ladder has two or three straight sections that can slide past each other for height adjustment. Steel brackets fastened to the rails on one section of a wood extension ladder guide the other section. On aluminum extension ladders, channels formed into the side rails secure the sections.

Overlap the sections of an extension ladder at least 15 percent of the height. Do not use a ladder longer than 60 feet without providing an intermediate landing. It's better to use several ladders with independent supports for runs this long.

Ladder accessories increase the safety and utility of ladders:

- A pail hook (pot hook) is designed to suspend a paint can from a rung or rail in a convenient position.

- Nonskid feet prevent foot slippage. Toothed feet should be used for icy surfaces.

- Adjustable feet are used to level a ladder set up on a sloping surface.

- Ridge (roof) hooks grab the peak of the roof to temporarily fasten a ladder to a pitched roof.

- Pole straps can be used to grab a pole or to lean a ladder against a building corner.

- A standoff stabilizer holds a ladder away from a building so you can paint directly in front of you. Standoffs may be fixed or adjustable.

Figure A15 Ladder types

a) stepladder　　b) double-sided ladder　　c) platform stepladder

d) extension trestle　　　　e) combination ladder

LADDER JACK

A ladder jack is a fixture that can be fastened to straight or extension ladders to make a simple, quick scaffolding. Ladder jacks are legal up to 20 feet above ground. No more than two workers are allowed to work on a ladder jack scaffold. The scaffold must have a hand rail.

Figure A16 Pail hook

Courtesy of Hyde Tool Company

Figure A17 Ladder jack

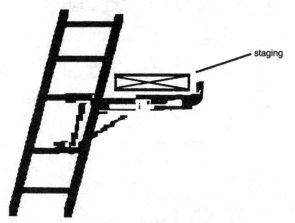

staging

9

Scaffold

Painters and decorators use many types of scaffolds, and it is only possible to survey the topic here. Scaffolds are categorized as follows:

- Rigid (built-up) scaffold is made of steel or wood.

- Pole scaffold uses fixtures attached to metal poles that are fastened to the building.

- Hanging scaffold is suspended at a fixed elevation.

- Swinging scaffold is suspended at an adjustable height from cable or rope.

- Outrigger scaffold rests on a beam protruding from the structure.

Scaffold is no better than the staging, or planking, used on it. Staging must be sound, free of defects, nonslip, and sufficiently strong. The two categories of staging are a) wood planks, and b) manufactured staging.

The Occupational Safety and Health Administration (OSHA) regulations contain the following requirements for wood plank staging:

- Planks shall be free of defects and of scaffold grade, or equivalent.

- All planking of platforms shall be overlapped (minimum 12 inches), or secured from movement.

- Scaffold planks shall extend over their end supports not less than 6-inches and not more than 12-inches.

- Inspect planks regularly. Do not paint planks, as this could hide defects. Damaged members must be repaired or replaced immediately.

The dimension of staging depends on the weight to be carried and the span between supports. Observe the following span requirements for wood planking:

	Full thickness undressed lumber			Nominal thickness lumber	
Working load (lb./sq.ft.)	25	50	75	25	50
Permissible span (ft.)	10	8	6	8	6

Manufactured staging includes wood extension planking, plywood supported by aluminum, and aluminum decking. Extension planking is handy because it can adapt to various jobs. Aluminum decking is sold in widths from 8 to 24 inches. The depth of side rail can vary from 3 1/2 to 7 inches. See Part G for further safety information.

TRESTLE SCAFFOLD

Trestle scaffold is made of planks supported by standard or adjustable trestles. The supports should be located as needed. Consult the plank manufacturer for weight capacity and sizes.

STEEL SCAFFOLD

Steel scaffold is a flexible system for building scaffold up to 125 feet high. The welded end frames are stacked on top of each other. Cross-braces link and support the end frames. Various types of patented connector devices join the braces and the end frames.

The key to setting up steel scaffold is to establish a sound, level base. Base plates may be used to distribute the load on soft ground. Adjusting screws are needed to establish a plumb scaffold on uneven ground. Bracing to the building may be required at 30-foot intervals horizontally and 26-foot intervals vertically.

Various accessories can be used with steel scaffold. Clamp-on ladders or stairways give easy access to the working platform. Material hoists can be suspended from pulleys that are attached to end frames.

Figure A18 Staging

a) wood extension

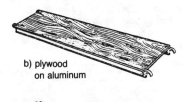

b) plywood
on aluminum

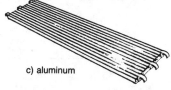

c) aluminum

10

Ropes

Ropes are used for safety lines, hoisting, and fastening. Rope should be chosen carefully and treated as a lifesaving device. Use only #1 grade for safety ropes. Manufacturers often insert a colored marker cord in premium grades of rope. Manila, nylon, and wire rope can be used for hoisting. For safety lines, nylon is the rope of choice due to its strength and elasticity. Each type of rope has certain advantages and disadvantages:

Rope type	Advantages	Disadvantages
Manila	Coarse, grabs metal Low stretch	Relatively weak Rots Subject to acid, alkali, or sunlight attack Deteriorates with age Heavy Low stretch
Nylon	Strong Rot-proof Easy to whip Lightweight Shock-resistant and elastic Undamaged by most chemicals	Slippery Elastic Can produce dangerous snap-back
Wire	Strong Durable	Tough to work Stiff Rusts if coating is damaged

ROPE STRENGTH AND DYNAMIC LOAD

Rope is rated by working or breaking strength. Working strength is the load a rope can safely carry day after day. Breaking strength is the load that will break a rope. Breaking strength is usually several times the working strength.

When deciding whether a rope will be adequate for a certain job, consider not only the weight of the load, but also the "dynamic load." Dynamic load is placed on a rope by the inertia of the load when hoisting starts. The faster the acceleration and greater the weight, the greater the dynamic load. Long ropes, and ropes made of elastic materials have higher resistance to dynamic load than short, nonelastic ropes. Accelerate slowly when a rope is operating near its working load, especially if the rope is inelastic.

Because manufacturers rate their ropes differently, be sure to consult data on the actual rope you are using. Wear, knots, splices, and bending all reduce a rope's capacity. Working strength is only relevant for rope:

- in good condition
- having appropriate splices (knots greatly reduce strength)
- used in noncritical applications
- used under normal service conditions

ROPE SAFETY

Rope is fragile and must be used and stored correctly. Observe these precautions:

1. Store rope (especially manila) in a dry place with good air circulation. Store away from chemicals and sunlight.
2. Keep rope clean. Dirt can penetrate a rope and abrade its fibers.
3. Replace rope approximately every 2 to 4 years.

4. Inspect occasionally for signs of deterioration. Look for broken or frayed strands or powder. Replace this rope.

5. Do not allow sharp bends. Use a collar to prevent sharp bends. Use thimbles in eye splices for the same reason.

6. Avoid sudden jerks and kinks.

7. Never stand in line with a rope under tension. If it fails, it can snap back with considerable force. This is especially true of nylon and wire rope.

8. Pay close attention to working strength. Reduce the load if it must be swung, picked up, or jerked.

9. Avoid knotting ropes that operate near their working load. Use a splice instead.

KNOTS

Painters need only a few basic knots, but it's better to learn them right rather than fumble around or tie a dangerous knot. A good knot is easy to tie, can be untied when needed, and cannot slip (unless designed to do so). A "hitch" connects a rope to another object. A "bend" connects two ropes.

All knots reduce the strength of a rope. Splices are stronger than knots, but weaker than plain rope. Anyone who uses safety lines, or hoists with rope should master these elementary knots:

a) The half hitch is commonly used in combination with another half hitch or other knot.

b) Two half hitches are a simple and effective means of tying to a post or beam. It is not good for hoisting a pipe or post, as it is likely to slip. Use a timber hitch or a round turn with two half hitches instead.

c) A round turn with two half hitches is an excellent all-around hitch because it does not slip, grabs an object well, and can be untied easily.

d) A figure-eight prevents unraveling and stops an end from passing through a pulley. The knot can be untied easily.

e) The square knot is used to join two ropes of equal diameters and composition. Both parts of one rope pass through the same side of the loop in the other rope.

f) The clove hitch is used to fasten to a post (a half hitch may be added for security). For hoisting, use a timber hitch or a round turn with two half-hitches.

g) The timber hitch is simple to tie, cannot jam, and will grab a fairly smooth object. A half hitch can be placed on the upper end of a load to hold it upright.

h) A bowline is the best way to tie a loop in the end of a line. It can be used for a running noose (just pass the "bight," a segment of rope away from either end, through the loop).

i) The sheet bend is used to join the ends of ropes of different sizes. (Note the difference between this knot and the square knot, which is only for ropes of equal diameter.)

j) The cat's paw temporarily fastens a rope to a hook.

k) The rolling (magnuson) hitch is used to fasten the running end of a rope to another rope.

EYE SPLICE

Splicing is stronger than knotting for permanently joining two ropes or for making an eye. The skill is not widely practiced, but it is relatively simple. The splicing technique shown below will only work for stranded rope. Braided rope cannot be spliced. Making an eye splice in hollow rope is simple if you have a fid (a tool for passing the rope through its own center). Do not make an *end* splice in hollow rope.

Insert a thimble in the eye splice to hold a pulley or other metal object. The thimble protects the fibers from abrasion and retains the eye's shape.

Figure A19 Common knots

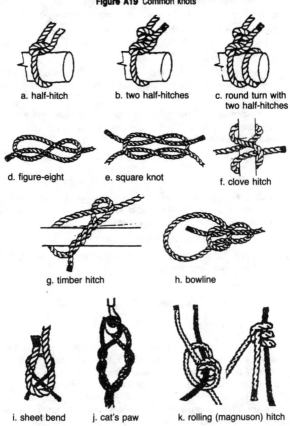

a. half-hitch

b. two half-hitches

c. round turn with two half-hitches

d. figure-eight

e. square knot

f. clove hitch

g. timber hitch

h. bowline

i. sheet bend

j. cat's paw

k. rolling (magnuson) hitch

d through h courtesy of VSI Fasteners, Inc.

Figure A20 Eye splice

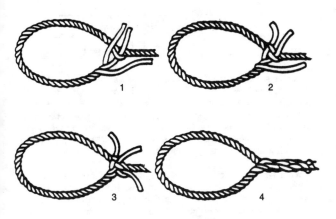

Follow these directions to make an eye splice in three-strand rope. Adapt the procedure to make an end splice.

1. Unlay the end a short distance. Double the end back across the bight so they cross at about 90°.

2. Tuck the center unlaid strand under a strand in the bight where you want the eye to start. The loop should be slightly larger than the completed eye will be.

3. Run the second unlaid strand over the strand that the center strand passes under, then under the next strand in the bight.

4. Tuck the last unlaid strand under the remaining strand of the bight, making sure it parallels the first two unlaid strands.

5. Pull each strand snug against the bight. Continue to make a total of three tucks with each strand (four for smooth rope).

6. Cut off the strands, but not too close to the rope. Roll the splice under your foot on a hard surface to shape it.

Power Washer
and Steam Cleaner

A power washer directs an intense stream of water against a surface. The machines can spray a) water with or without detergent or abrasive, or b) steam with or without detergent. Power washers can strip peeling paint and clean the substrate in one operation. To strip paint, hold the gun close to the substrate so the water gets beneath the paint. Unless they spray abrasive, water washers do not etch a surface, so they cannot increase the "tooth" for the new coating.

Wear waterproof clothing for a large washing job. If you use detergent in the solution, make sure to rinse the wall while it is still wet. Allow several days' drying after blasting. If in doubt, check the surface with a moisture meter. Blasting will not remove all degraded paint, so you may have to sand afterward to remove remaining paint and feather its edges.

Protective Equipment

Many types of protective equipment are required to protect painters against such hazards as toxic solvents and heavy metals. According to OSHA, protective equipment should only be used when substitution of less hazardous materials, engineering controls, and administrative controls cannot eliminate the danger. Unfortunately, the reality is that commercial painters must rely on protective equipment because it's too expensive to install engineering controls at most job sites. Taking care may seem expensive, unpleasant, and time-consuming—but if your health is not important, what is? See Part G, Health and safety, for more information.

RESPIRATORS

Respirators supply purified air to the operator. They are needed because painters often work around hazardous mists, dusts, or fumes. In rare cases, the air lacks sufficient oxygen for breathing. Both the physical and chemical properties of contaminants must be considered when selecting protective equipment.

The basic categories of respirator are supplied-air and air-purifying. A supplied-air respirator supplies clean air from a remote source. An air-purifying respirator uses a filter, cartridge, or canister to trap the hazardous substance and prevent you from inhaling it. Each design has strengths and weaknesses.

Respirators may be approved by either the National Institute of Occupational Health and Safety in the Department of Labor, or the Mine Safety and Health Administration in the Department of Health and Social Services.

Unfortunately, the industry and OSHA have yet to devise a simple system for specifying exactly which respirator is needed in a given situation. (See Table A8.)

RESPIRATOR TYPES

SUPPLIED-AIR

A *supplied-air respirator* gets air from a pressurized hose or tank. This design has several advantages: a) positive pressure inside the mask reduces the chance of leakage; b) light weight and low breathing effort both increase comfort and allow the device to be used for extended periods; and c) the respirator can be used in highly contaminated atmospheres, even where oxygen is not adequate. However, the hose restricts mobility; the operator is in immediate danger if the hose is damaged or disconnected or the tank runs empty; and the system is expensive, complicated, and fallible.

Air can be supplied by a compressor, tank, or blower. A reservoir on the compressor should hold a safety supply of air so you can escape the danger zone if the compressor fails. An alarm must be in place to indicate compressor overheating or failure. The supply air must be clean, and the hose must be protected from injury. Make sure connections are air-tight.

A *self-contained breathing apparatus* resembles the familiar scuba tank used by divers. Breathing time is limited by the tank size and the wearer's rate of exertion. The device is heavy and expensive, and rarely used by painters.

A *hose-mask respirator* gets its air through a large hose. A short hose can be used without a blower, although this can require a good deal of lung power. With a power blower, the hose can be as long as 300 feet.

An *airline respirator* accepts high-pressure air from a compressor. A regulator on the respirator reduces pressure before the air enters the facemask.

AIR-PURIFYING

An *air-purifying respirator* uses a filter, canister, or cartridge to remove contaminants from air. Keep these points in mind when selecting and using an air-purifying respirator:

- Sufficient oxygen must be present—the respirator cannot produce it.

- A plugged canister increases leakage and is uncomfortable. Increased breathing resistance indicates plugging. Stop and replace the canister rather than risk a loss of protection.

- Choose the filter or canister according to the material in the air. Gas and vapor cartridges are designed to protect against specific chemical agents. Consult Material Safety Data Sheets (MSDS) to determine the correct filter or cartridge.

- Particulate-removing filters are designed to remove dust and metal fumes. The filter size is determined by the size of particles present. PARTICULATE-REMOVING FILTERS ABSOLUTELY CANNOT PROTECT AGAINST VAPORS AND SOLVENTS.

- Minimize leakage by using the proper size respirator, changing canisters when necessary, and strapping the respirator on tightly.

- Due to the effort required to pull air through the cleaning element, air-purifying respirators place an additional strain on the heart. People with heart or lung problems should not use them.

RESPIRATOR PROGRAM

If employees are exposed to airborne hazardous chemicals, OSHA requires that the employer establish a respirator program with these components:

- written standard operating procedures for safe and proper use of respirators, and their limitations

- the program must be evaluated at least annually to check that the equipment is doing its job

- selection must be based on the chemical and physical properties of the contaminant, the amount of oxygen present, the nature of the work, and conditions in the workplace

- employee training must cover these topics:

    1. nature of the respiratory hazard, and the effects of breathing untreated air

    2. engineering and administrative controls used to reduce the hazard

TABLE A8
Selecting a respirator

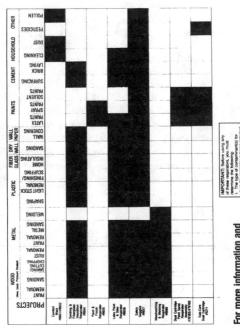

Courtesy of 3M Co.

For more information and assistance on 3M Personal Safety Products, call OH&ESD Technical Service, toll free 1-800-243-4630.

3. reasons for selecting the specific type of respirator, and contaminants and levels that the equipment can protect against

4. limitations of the selected respirator in terms of contaminants and/or service life

5. methods of donning the respirator, checking its fit, and wearing

6. maintenance and storage

7. emergency procedures

8. warning properties of the contaminants

- fit testing (see below)
- inspection, cleaning, maintenance, and storage (see below)
- periodic medical examinations are required to make sure that employees are not harmed by exposure to airborne contaminants. Laboratory tests may cover blood, urine, and fecal analysis. Tests of physical capabilities may also be specified by the employee's or employer's physician.
- work area surveillance
- air-quality standards
- approved respirators

FACEPIECES

Several types of face masks can be used with respirators:

style	coverage	comments
quarter-facepiece	nose and mouth, but not chin	least effective style
half-facepiece	also covers chin	twice as effective as quarter facepiece
full-facepiece	also covers eyes	twice as effective as half-facepiece
air-fed helmet	protects against flying abrasive	necessary for blasters

RESPIRATOR FIT AND MAINTENANCE

A respirator that fits poorly provides a false sense of security and could be worse than no respirator at all. Take the time to size and leak-check the respirator. Custom-fit respirators are available for faces of unusual size or shape. Because beards, sideburns, and stubble prevent a good seal, they should be shaved unless a hood is worn.

If eyeglasses prevent a good seal on the facepiece, a qualified person can mount corrective lenses in it. OSHA prohibits wearing contact lenses when using a respirator in a contaminated atmosphere.

To ensure that a respirator works well and continues working well, you must inspect, leak-check, clean and disinfect, and store it properly.

INSPECT

Before using a respirator, examine the condition of facepiece, headbands, valves, connecting tube, and filter, cartridge, or canister. Check that connections are tight and rubber parts still elastic. Massage rubber parts to keep them pliable.

LEAK-CHECK

Use negative and positive pressure tests to check the fit of the facepiece. First strap the respirator on your face. Make the negative pressure test by covering the air intake with your palm and inhaling. If the facepiece caves in and does not bounce back, you have a good seal. If not, readjust and repeat until the facepiece caves in and stays caved in. Then make the positive pressure test. With the respirator still strapped on, cover the air outlet and exhale. The facepiece should balloon out. Continue adjusting until the mask consistently passes both tests.

CLEAN AND DISINFECT

After each use of the respirator:

1. Remove all filters, canisters, and cartridges.

2. Wash facepiece and breathing tube in the solution suggested by the manufacturer.

3. Rinse completely in warm water.

4. Air dry in a clean area.

5. Clean other parts per manufacturer's suggestions. If information is not available, use soap and water or alcohol. Do not put a respirator in lacquer thinner.

6. Inspect for damage. Replace damaged parts with parts approved for that respirator. Only someone trained to repair the respirator should make the repair.

7. Install new filter, cartridge, or canister if needed.

8. Make a record of all cleaning, maintenance, and repair operations.

STORAGE

Store the clean respirator in a plastic bag or approved container away from heat, cold, sunlight, dust, chemicals, or excessive moisture.

CLOTHING, ETC.

Employees should wear and use OSHA-approved safety equipment. Use steel-toe shoes to protect feet from falling objects. Nonsparking shoes are required if a buildup of explosive gases is possible, as when painting tanks.

Long sleeves and pants protect against spatter. Taping cuffs helps keep arms and legs clean.

Neoprene gloves are impenetrable to most chemicals. Use polyvinyl alcohol gloves to handle chlorinated hydrocarbon solvents, including methylene chloride. Abrasive blaster operators should use gauntlet gloves.

HEAD

Protective helmets must be worn in areas where head injuries could be caused by flying or falling objects, impact, electrical shock, or burns. Helmets for impact protection must meet the requirements of ANSI Z89.1—1969. If hard hats are required, a sign at the workplace should so indicate.

EYE AND FACE

Eye and face protection is required whenever there is a danger of injury. This equipment must meet the requirements of ANSI Z87.1—1968 "Practice for Occupational and Educational Eye and Face Protection." Goggles are needed for many painting applications, such as spraying, abrasive blasting, and overhead work. If there is so much overspray that your goggles mist up, try changing equipment, adjustment, or technique to reduce or eliminate the overspray.

EARS

OSHA sets standards for maximum noise at job sites. If noise surpasses these levels, engineering and administrative efforts must be taken to reduce the noise. If these efforts fail, workers must wear hearing protection (not plain cotton). Exposure to impact noise must not exceed 140 dB peak sound pressure level.

Duration per day in hours	Maximum sound level (dBA slow response)
8	90
6	92
4	95
3	97
2	100
1 1/2	102
1	105
1/2	110
1/4 or less	115

HANDS

Use any commercial hand cleaner with a conditioner in it. Do not clean hands in solvent—many solvents can be absorbed through the skin and cause disease.

If desired, coat exposed parts of face with theatrical cream, which is similar to cold cream.

MATERIALS

Section 1: Paint

▬▬▬

PAINT AND COATINGS OVERVIEW

Two basic categories of paint and coatings are used to decorate and protect surfaces from weathering: a) "film-formers," including paints, varnishes, and lacquers; and b) materials that seep into the surface, including penetrating finishes, water repellents, stains, and other chemical treatments. Wood can be protected by either type; metal is usually protected by a film-former.

Coatings can also be categorized by whether they carry colored pigment (paint, some varnishes, and stain) or not (clear varnish and lacquer, some preservatives, and many sealers). While paint is strictly speaking a pigmented coating, the term is often used to refer to many other types of coatings.

Coatings adhere to a substrate by molecular attraction and/or mechanical bond. To improve adhesion, surface preparation allows:

• the paint to bond chemically to the molecules on the surface

• the paint to get close to the substrate so the short-range forces of adhesion can operate

• the surface to be rough enough (have adequate "tooth") so the paint can bond mechanically

Coating durability is affected by conditions, paint type, and substrate. Of all coatings, paint offers wood the greatest protection against weathering, but paint is *not* a preservative and cannot by itself prevent deterioration in wet wood. Nonporous paints retard moisture penetration, but no coating is 100-percent effective at preventing moisture from entering wood. In humid conditions, most paints offer rather poor protection against moisture.

The formulation of coatings is complicated and variable. Paints are broadly classified as water- or solvent-thinned. These are the basic components and functions of paint:

1. Pigment gives the mixture its color (color pigment) and influences other characteristics, such as hardness and flexibility (extender pigment). Pigment does not dissolve in the vehicle but rather is suspended in it. (Coloring agents that do dissolve are called dyes.)

2. Vehicle, the body of the paint, can contain three categories of ingredient: film-former, thinner, and additives.

   - Film-former, also called nonvolatile ingredients or resin, is the material that forms the structure of the dried coating.

   - Thinner contains either solvent or diluent, or both. A solvent dissolves the film-former; a diluent dilutes it. Thinner can be water or an organic solvent.

   - Additives are used for such purposes as controlling drying rate, increasing flexibility, and fighting mildew.

Paint components are usually listed on the label. The amount of each ingredient is given as a percentage by weight. This percentage can be a percentage of the whole paint or a percentage of the pigment or vehicle in the paint. Sometimes a range of percentages is given instead of an exact figure.

PAINT FILM QUALITIES

The qualities of a film depend on its job. These characteristics of a film are usually desired:

Hardness and durability—the resistance to abrasion and cutting—are influenced by the paint's molecular structure. Cross-linked polymers are harder than linear polymers. Linear polymers of high molecular weight are tougher than linear polymers with low molecular weight. (Hardness can also produce brittleness, which is rarely wanted.)

Adhesion is the ability to stick to the substrate. This quality obviously depends on the nature and condition of the substrate as well as the formulation of the paint.

Flexibility is the ability to expand and contract without cracking or peeling. Cross-links in cross-linked film must be located far enough apart or the paint will be too brittle. To prevent the same problem with linear polymer, smaller molecules are sometimes combined with the longer ones.

Resistance to weathering is the ability to avoid degradation by factors in the environment. Water, oxygen, other chemicals, and ultraviolet light can all attack polymers. Degradation occurs when a polymer loses its cohesiveness, and particles escape the chemical structure. (While paint helps increase resistance to weathering, it is not a preservative and cannot prevent fungus from growing in the substrate if conditions are ripe.)

Ease of repair and repainting are both important in the future, if not the present. Surfaces that may need cleaning must resist abrasion and chemicals in cleaning agents. Linear polymers can be repainted because solvent in the new paint can dissolve the old paint. Cross-linked polymers are insoluble in solvents. If they must be patched, the new paint may not adhere to the old.

Gloss is the ability to reflect a visual image. A mirror is an example of a very glossy surface. Gloss is reduced by the presence of pigment particles at the surface, so high-gloss paints have relatively little pigment, at least at the surface. Gloss is measured with a gloss meter.

Reflectance is the amount of light returned by a surface. A paint can have high gloss and low reflectance, or vice versa. White paints have a reflectance roughly between 70 and 90 percent, even though they need not be glossy.

Hiding is the ability to conceal whatever is beneath it. The amount of hiding power depends on pigmentation, color, the texture and absorption of the substrate, the application technique, and the dry film thickness. White and light colors have good hiding because they use opaque bases. Dark paint generally hides poorly because it is formulated with a clear tint base, and only the added pigments help the hiding.

Dry film thickness (DFT) is the thickness after drying; it indicates how well a particular coating will perform. DFT can be measured with a paint thickness gauge. It can also be calculated if you know the volume solids percentage (not weight solids) and the actual coverage per gallon.

Volume solids (%)	Actual coverage in sq. ft.	Mil. thickness
100 (no thinner)	1,600	1
	800	2
	400	4
50	800	1
	400	2
	200	4

HOW PAINT DRIES

Paint can change from liquid to solid in either of two ways: a) evaporation of the thinner, or b) polymerization. Polymerization is a chemical reaction that links up short molecules into long chains (polymers). Polymerization can occur between the paint and the atmosphere, or between compounds in the paint. Polymerization can produce either a linear or a cross-linked molecular structure. Cross-linked polymer makes the hardest and most durable paint, but linear polymers are easier to store, dry, patch, and polish.

- Paints that dry solely by evaporation are essentially polymers in a can. The linear polymers are dissolved or suspended by liquid in the can. Lacquer is a common example of this type of coating.

- Drying by chemical reaction between the paint and the atmosphere is probably the most common type of paint. It is used on house paint, alkyd paint, and many other materials. Oxygen can react with drying oils to polymerize them into a cross-linked chain. Water can react with isocyanates to produce similar results. Because the paint can has little air, the reaction cannot start until the can is opened. Because the reaction continues long after the paint seems dry to the touch, it's a good idea to protect a new coating for hours or even days after it seems dry.

• Drying by chemical reaction between paint ingredients can take place in a) a two-part paint, such as two-part epoxy, b) a paint that reacts only at elevated temperatures or under certain radiation, or c) a paint in which the reactive ingredients are diluted enough to prevent drying in the can. Principles a) and b) are more common in industrial paints. Polyester wood finishes, such as polyurethane, dry by method c).

MOISTURE-PROOFING OF COATINGS

Many coatings are surprisingly poor at preventing airborne moisture from entering a substrate. This is especially true when they are applied to wood, which is hygroscopic (likely to take up moisture). Even if a good coating is applied to all surfaces of a wooden object, some moisture can get in, which is why preservatives and water-repellent sealers are an important part of a painting system for exterior wood. Wax dipping and epoxy paints are the best materials for truly moisture-proofing wood.

DETERIORATION OF PAINT

All paint eventually fails. Interior paint can be injured by dirt or abrasion, but exterior paint faces more serious challenges. A good exterior paint will erode slowly and steadily from the top coat down, leaving the lower layers bonded to the earlier layers or the substrate. Paint that degrades this way is usually easy to recoat.

In the type of degradation called chalking, the paint cleans itself as the surface washes. Chalking is not harmful in itself, although it can damage nearby surfaces. It is especially difficult to remove from masonry.

Ultraviolet radiation in sunlight damages the chemical structure of paint, particularly clear coatings. This damage can cause brittleness and cracking within a year of application. Cracks allow water to penetrate, causing expansion and contraction, and permitting mildew growth. Paint deteriorates more slowly than clear coatings because its pigments absorb UV radiation and reduce the damage. (Another fatal problem for a coating is degradation of the substrate, which is of course one reason to paint in the first place.)

Rust inhibitors in paint and primer can also degrade over the years. These "sacrificial" elements must occasionally be replaced to maintain the protection.

PAINT COMPONENTS

The major categories of paint components are pigment and vehicle. Each may be comprised of several chemicals, depending on the paint's application.

Figure B1 Paint components

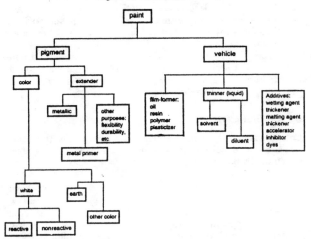

PIGMENT

Pigments have multiple functions in paint. Extender pigments impart brushability, strength, viscosity, adhesion, durability, resistance to mildew, and fire retardance, among other things. One of the most important categories of other pigments is the corrosion inhibitors. Color pigments lend color and opacity. Because color pigments reflect or absorb the ultraviolet rays that can deteriorate resin, paint has more exterior durability than varnish.

The greater the percentage of pigment, the lower the gloss, all other things being equal. This is because particles of pigment roughen the smooth surface that creates glossiness.

Lead has been used in pigments for thousands of years. However, it's become clear that millions of cases of lead poisoning have been caused by ingesting lead paint or paint dust. The ancient metal is now banned from interstate sales of household paint, and for many other paint uses. The banned pigments include white lead, lead chromates, red lead oxide, lead suboxide, blue lead, and many others. Even where lead is not prohibited, a painter should use caution because paints eventually are dispersed in the environment, due to weathering or demolition (if not to children biting painted door jambs).

Old paint is likely to contain lead. Due to its excellent rust inhibition, it was especially common in paint for ferrous metal. Sanding and burning are both dangerous for removing leaded paint because they liberate lead dust and fumes.

COLOR PIGMENTS

Color pigments are classified as white and other colors. (Pigments, which do not dissolve in the solvent, are distinguished from dyes, which do dissolve.)

White

White pigments can be "reactive" (able to neutralize the acids that form when oil-bearing films weather), or "nonreactive" (unable to neutralize these acids). Neutralization helps extend film life.

Reactive white pigments include zinc oxide, zinc silicates, aluminum silicates, leaded zinc oxide, basic silicate white lead, kaolin (a white clay), and calcium carbonate (limestone).

The most common nonreactive white pigment is rutile titanium dioxide, which is nonchalking and has great hiding power. The anatase form of titanium dioxide, and many other white pigments, do chalk. Chalking pigments should not be used in dark paint because they tend to streak.

Other color pigments

Nonwhite pigments absorb some wavelengths of incident light and reflect others. Earth pigments are color pigments extracted from the earth and used with little or no alteration. Earth pigments may be compounds of iron, magnesium, aluminum, and manganese. Elements like iron can make many colors.

Iron can produce red, black, or colors between yellow and brown. Raw sienna is a natural iron-bearing pigment that creates a clear, deep buff tone that can be shaded toward ivory. Burnt sienna is a heated version that makes a strong reddish-brown.

Raw umber is similar to raw sienna, but contains more manganese dioxide, and thus is more gray. With white pigments, it creates grays with slight brown or olive tones. Burnt umber is a richer, redder brown. French ochre is a yellow iron oxide mined in France.

Black pigments are used to a) create true black, or b) to darken (shade) other colors. Carbon black and lampblack are carbon compounds with tremendous hiding power. Carbon black is very fine and used primarily for true black. Lampblack is coarser and bluer, so it is used for grays. Lampblack added to orange paint may produce a green cast. If so, the paint can be grayed with additional red.

Pigment stability is an important factor in choosing exterior paints. Ultraviolet light can degrade susceptible pigments in just a few years if they are in sunny locations. It may be important to know how pigments will stand up before selecting a color of exterior paint. Paint stores or paint companies may have information on the topic.

EXTENDER PIGMENTS

Extender pigments may have little or no hiding or coloring power, but they impart many desirable qualities. Extender pigments should not be considered "inert ingredients" because they contribute in these ways:

- reduce glossiness

- improve flow and application properties

- increase adhesion and durability

- increase opacity

- reduce raw material costs

Metal primer

Most metal primer pigments are chosen for their ability to protect against corrosion. Red lead and blue lead were long the pigments of choice for ferrous metal because of their ability to resist rust. Now that lead has been banned for most uses, a variety of other metallic compounds, including zinc, zinc oxide, and zinc chromate, are used to inhibit corrosion in ferrous metal primer. Zinc powder may be packaged separately for mixing into paint just before application. Further environmental restrictions may continue changing the formulation of metal primers.

Metallic

Many metals are used in pigments. Lead, zinc, and iron have already been described.

- Aluminum is used in leafing and nonleafing forms. Leafing, the gathering of aluminum flakes in layers at the surface, forms almost a solid film of aluminum. Nonleafing aluminum pigment makes a metallic-gray surface. Due to its high reflectivity, aluminum paint is used to coat storage tanks, smoke stacks, and fire walls. It can also be used as sealer under or over primer on wide-grained, knotty, or creosoted wood.

- Gold is used primarily in the leaf form, for signs and decorative work.

- Bronze pigment is used for an imitation gold finish. It does not hide as well as aluminum.

VEHICLE

Vehicle, the liquid portion of paint, is composed of film-former, thinner, and additives.

THINNER

Thinner (liquid) disperses the paint's solids and can have some or all of these functions:

• To dissolve and/or dilute the film former

• To reduce the solution to proper viscosity for application

• To control the rate of evaporation

A "diluent," or diluting agent, is a thinner that holds solids in suspension. A "solvent" is a liquid that chemically dissolves the solids. Solvents are used in lacquer and shellac. The matter is confusing because thinner is often called "solvent" even though it is usually a diluent. However, diluent *and* solvent may be used in a single paint.

The nature of the diluent influences such important properties as drying rate. If both diluent and solvent are present, the diluent should evaporate before the solvent.

Solvent and diluent use are restricted in some areas because of concern that volatile organic compounds (VOCs) pollute the air. Evaporated VOCs can be converted into ozone, a potent pollutant in the lower atmosphere that causes chest pain and heart attacks. So-called "low VOC" materials may be substituted in these areas.

Paint manufacturers specify the proper thinner on the label. A good test for compatibility of thinner and paint is to pour a few drops of thinner into a capful of paint. If the thinner immediately disperses, it is probably compatible. Try another chemical if the thinner shows any of these signs:

• disperses slowly or not at all

• produces something that looks like cottage cheese

• causes the paint to separate

Many paint thinners are chemically called solvents. *Hydrocarbon* solvents are distilled from crude oil. The two categories of hydrocarbon solvents are aliphatic and aromatic. Aromatic hydrocarbons (benzene, toluene, and xylene), contain a benzene ring and are stronger and more toxic than aliphatic solvents. Consequently, aromatic solvents are more commonly used in industrial coatings than in maintenance and architectural painting. (At least one aromatic solvent, benzene, is a potent cause of cancer that should be avoided.)

Aliphatic hydrocarbons (hexane, heptane, and odorless mineral spirits) are safer than the aromatics but still hazardous.

Toluene (toluol) is used to dissolve the nitrocellulose, which is the resin in lacquer.

Xylene (xylol) is used in synthetic resin finishes, such as epoxy.

Mineral spirits distill between 300°F and 400°F. They are the modern substitute for gum turpentine as a solvent and thinner. Use relatively volatile mineral spirits in cold weather and less volatile types in warm weather. Mineral spirits will not thin all varnishes and enamels.

V.M. and P. naptha (varnish makers' and painters' naptha) is a fast-drying solvent sometimes used to speed drying. Naptha reduces setting time and leveling time, so it should be used carefully. (Naptha is sometimes called "benzine," a misleading term that can be mistaken for a different solvent, benzene.)

Acetone is a simple member of the ketone family that evaporates quickly and is used in paint and paint removers.

Denatured alcohol is used to thin and clean up after alcohol-based primer sealer.

Terpenes, made from pine products, include turpentine, dipentene, and pine oil. Gum spirits of turpentine is tapped from the live tree; wood turpentine is distilled from pine stumps. Due to the cost and odor of turpentine, mineral spirits is usually substituted for it.

FILM-FORMER

Film-former is the component that dries into the final coating. Film-former may include oil or resin (chemicals that solidify into films), and plasticizers, which control the flexibility, or plasticity, of the final film. Oils and resins have similar roles in the film-former.

Oil

Oil can have these functions:

- increases durability in exterior paint
- lends flexibility
- improves gloss
- increases resistance to water, soap, and other chemicals
- prevents wrinkling
- improves leveling and penetration

These oils are commonly used in paint:

Linseed oil is a standard component of oil paint, but it has low resistance to alkali and acid. Linseed oil will yellow on interior surfaces, so it is rarely used in light-colored interior paint. There are five kinds of linseed oil:

Raw linseed oil is a greenish-brown oil that is extracted from flax seed. Raw linseed oil is one of the best components of rusty metal primers due to its ability to wet the substrate and displace water. It is used primarily in industry.

Boiled linseed oil has been heated to about 200°F (not to the point of evaporation) and blown with air. The oil contains driers (metallic compounds) to speed drying.

Heated bodied linseed oil is an alkali-refined oil.

Oxidized linseed oil is blown with air to increase viscosity.

Refined linseed oil is refined with alkali or acid to remove color bodies and other impurities.

Tung oil (chinawood oil) comes from the nut of the tung tree, which grows in China. The oil must be heated during manufacture; otherwise it will dry to a soft, opaque film. Tung oil dries rapidly and is used in quick-drying paints and varnishes. Tung oil can be compounded into a highly water-and-weather-resistant varnish suitable for interior or exterior use.

Soybean oil (soya) is replacing linseed oil, especially in alkyd resins. The oil is pressed from the edible soybean plant. Soybean oil is a color-retaining, semi-drying oil which must be treated to allow full drying.

Tall oil is actually a combination of fatty acids without glycerol, but with rosin. Tall oil is produced when Southern pine wood is pulped for paper. Tall oil is more or less interchangeable with soybean oil.

Natural resin

Resins may be of natural or synthetic origin. The natural resins include rosin and shellac.

Rosin is a natural resin derived from tree sap. It can be treated with lime or glycerin to produce a film that is tough, hard, glossy, and fast-drying. Rosin has poor resistance to alkali and water, and is not good at retaining color. It may be used in floor paint, barn paint, and utility varnishes.

Shellac is a natural resin that is soluble in alcohol, not in mineral spirits or turpentine. See Shellac, page 92.

Synthetic resin

Modern paints depend on the excellent qualities of the synthetic resins.

Alkyd resins are named for their composition: *al*-cohol and ac-*id*. Alkyds dry by reacting with oxygen in the air. Alkyd resins are probably the most important resins in modern paint because they dry quickly into flexible and durable films. Gloss and color retention are also good, and the resin makes an excellent white paint. Although alkyd paints have replaced oil paints, they are often erroneously called "oil paints."

Due to their all-around qualities, alkyds are used in exterior, interior, and marine paints. However, they do not have the best chemical or corrosion resistance, so are not suited for immersed or high-corrosion applications.

The amount of oil can be varied to change the character of alkyd paint:

"Long-oil" or "medium-oil" alkyds have a high percentage of drying oils. These formulations are more flexible and weather-resistant when dried, but are less chemical resistant and dry more slowly.

"Short-oil" or "nondrying" alkyds have a low percentage of oil, or have a nondrying oil. These formulations dry faster and are used in industrial paints, baking finishes, and lacquers.

"Thixotropic" alkyds have a consistency like jelly when undisturbed, to prevent separation in storage. When stirred or brushed, these paints flow more or less like normal paint. Thixotropic paints are excellent for ceilings or walls, and can be applied in relatively thick coats.

Pure *phenolic resins* are synthetics with many good qualities: resistance to water, alcohol, and many chemicals. All phenolic resins tend to yellow. Solvent-type phenolics must be cured with heat and are used primarily in industrial coatings and tank linings. Oil-type phenolics are used in general paints and spar and marine varnishes. Modified phenolic resins have less resistance and durability. They are used extensively in varnishes, sealers, and paints for floors, porches, and decks.

Epoxy resins are excellent for surfaces exposed to salt or other severe corrosion inducers. Epoxy resins do not resist weathering as well as alkyds. Synthetic epoxy resin is a two-part paint with great durability, hardness, and chemical resistance. Epoxy adheres well to difficult surfaces and can be formulated for air- or heat-drying.

Rubber-based resins are based on synthetic rubber and have high resistance to water, chemicals, and alkalies, and have good flexibility. These resins can be used on stucco and concrete floors.

Acrylic resins are glossy, color-retaining synthetics commonly used in water-based paints and other applications. Acrylic resins can be formulated with other resin types for better wetting and adhesion.

Several types of *urethanes* are used in paint and varnish due to their excellent water resistance and hardness. Polyurethane varnish and paint are both excellent uses of synthetic urethane resin. The finish is so hard that adhesion between coats can be a problem. Recoat polyurethane varnish before too much hardening has taken place, or abrade the first coat lightly before recoating.

ADDITIVES

Additives are used in small quantities to impart certain properties to paint. Not all the following additives are needed for a single paint:

Antisettling agents are used to prevent pigment and vehicle from separating in the can.

Antiskinning agents prevent oxidation and drying in the can.

Antifloating agents prevent pigments from separating during storage and application.

Driers are added to speed polymerization, oxidation, or both. Driers can be liquids or metallic soaps of cobalt, lead, manganese, calcium, or other metals.

Loss-of-dry inhibitors increase shelf life by replacing driers that break down in the can.

Freeze-thaw stabilizers work like antifreeze in an automobile radiator; they prevent damage to water-based paint caused by freezing in the can.

Anti-foaming agents prevent foam during manufacture, storage, or application. Foaming is more problematic in water-based than solvent-based paint.

Preservatives are needed for shelf life and stability on the wall. Mildewicides prevent mildew from growing on damp paint. (Note that paint, with or without mildewicide, does not prevent fungus from growing in the substrate.) Mercury mildewicides are being phased out in favor of other chemicals.

Bodying and puffing agents increase paint's viscosity for proper application and drying.

Leveling agents are used to reduce brush or roller marks.

Antisagging agents prevent curtains, runs, or sags in wet paint. These goals may also be met by antisettling agents.

Glossing and flatting agents change the sheen of the paint.

Coalescing agents soften latex particles to help them flow into a continuous film.

COATING SYSTEMS

Coatings are getting more and more complicated, and that means they must be understood, chosen, and applied as systems of harmonious elements. The best source of advice here is paint manufacturers. With so many coatings now available, only the manufacturers can keep track of what is compatible with what. Failing to follow manufacturer's directions is just asking for trouble.

A coating system may include preparing the surface; pretreatment; selecting and applying first, second, and other coats; and protecting the coating while it dries.

For a detailed description of the suitability and durability of exterior wood coatings, see Part D, ABCs.

In choosing paint, it's important to remember that material cost is a small fraction, perhaps as little as 10 percent, of the system cost. The greater the scaffolding, surface preparation, and application expense, the smaller this percentage becomes. Therefore, the use of superior, expensive coatings should be encouraged to ensure longer, more satisfactory service at little increase in cost.

The effectiveness of a protective coating depends in large degree on its thickness. Thus even though applying overly thinned material may save effort, it usually costs durability. The dry film thickness of a protective coating for steel should range between 3 1/2 and 5 mils (about the thickness of newsprint), depending on the severity of the exposure. While each coat of paint should be as thick as practical, several coats are usually needed to build up adequate thickness. Applying several coats helps prevent sagging, increases the drying speed, and helps ensure coverage of holidays (gaps) in previous coats.

PREPARATORY COATS

Several types of coats are used to support the topcoat. One preparatory material can accomplish several tasks—for example, primer-sealer seals the surface and prepares it for topcoat.

Filler has a high solids content to fill holes and irregularities in the surface. Wood filler can be used on porous wood such as oak. Block filler is used to smooth rough masonry before coating.

Surfacers are highly pigmented materials that level irregularities and ensure adhesion between primer and topcoat.

Primers are an important category of material that promote adhesion of the upper coats to the substrate. Corrosion-inhibitive primers also protect metal from corrosion. Primers may also fill small cracks and voids in the substrate, and solve compatibility problems between existing and new coatings.

Sealers: a) reduce suction to inhibit penetration of the finish coat; b) stop stains from reaching the topcoat; and c) prevent anything else from migrating between layers. Sealer and size serve similar functions. Sealer for plaster is usually a chemical-resistant varnish, sometimes with a slight amount of pigment. Sealer for drywall and other porous surfaces contains more pigment.

Wall sizes are chemicals used to prepare walls for wallcovering. See Part F, Wallcovering.

PRIMER

Primer or primer-sealer is needed because most topcoats have too little penetrating power because they: a) have too much pigment; b) are designed to resist deterioration from external attack; and/or c) are formulated for appearance instead of penetration.

The choice of primer is usually dictated by the topcoat manufacturer. Make sure to specify exterior material for outdoor usage.

Primer is not needed for a "self-priming" coating placed on a sound substrate, or for many surfaces with a sound coating. Always check the label when choosing whether to prime and which primer to use. A surface with a broken coating, such as a house exterior, may need either spot priming or a complete coat of primer. As a rule, if the surface is 50 percent degraded, it's best to remove the entire coating and apply a complete coat of primer.

Artists painting from the fifteenth century onward have obeyed this rule in matching primer with topcoat: work from lean to fat. The primer should dry to a hard surface, and the topcoat should have a higher concentration of oil so it is more flexible and durable. If you ignore this rule, you risk problems like alligatoring, the breakup of the surface that results when a rigid topcoat rests on a soft primer.

Sizing, which was often used as a short-cut replacement for primer, is rarely used today because it peels off if moisture is present. Some water-based primers are compatible with alkyd and water-based paints. Latex primers are poor for covering glossy surfaces (you may be able to dull an enamel to prepare it for a latex coat). Dulling or deglossing a surface is virtually always a good idea before coating.

Masonry should be allowed to cure for several weeks before priming. Use an alkaliresistant primer, especially with new masonry, which contains a great deal of alkali. Latex primer and alkali-resistant primer are all good for masonry. Portland cement paints are self-priming and not subject to alkali degradation (but they are not primers). Epoxy paint can be used for a heavy-duty, chemical-resistant coating on new or painted masonry. Avoid painting cinder blocks containing iron with latex primer, because water in the paint is likely to corrode the iron particles.

Unpainted plaster should be allowed to cure for at least thirty days in 60°F or warmer temperature. The exact curing time will depend on temperature, humidity, and ventilation at the job site. The two possible problems with painting plaster are excess moisture and excess alkali. Moisture can allow soluble salts in the plaster to migrate to the surface. Test the plaster with a moisture meter in accordance with the coating manufacturer's suggestion. Test for alkali with red litmus paper. If the paper turns blue, the surface is excessively alkaline and should be treated with zinc sulfate solution before coating.

Prime plaster with alkyd-based or latex primer-sealer. The primer can be tinted to reduce the number of topcoats needed. If chalk is present, alkyd-based primer-sealers will wet the surface better than latex primer-sealers. It's still best to remove as much chalk as possible first.

Prime *unpainted drywall* with latex, acrylic latex, or vinyl latex primer. Some manufacturers recommend applying a "skim coat" of thinned drywall compound to the surface before priming. The skim coat smooths the surface but does not seal the drywall. Alkyd- or oil-based primers will raise the nap on drywall paper and should be avoided.

Metal primers work by inhibiting rust and/or sealing the metal against moisture and oxygen. Materials like zinc chromate inhibit rust by neutralizing acid. Due to their low permeability, lacquer and bituminous coatings are best for sealing metal. Apply several coats to difficult areas like corners and welds.

"Wetting" is the ability to reach solid substrate through rust on the surface. Wetting is vital because the attractive forces between molecules of substrate and primer operate only at extremely close range. Primer's ability to wet steel depends on the condition of the steel. Clean, pickled, or white-blasted steel can be painted with excellent results using synthetic resin paints, but these paints cannot wet a surface with mill scale or rust. Raw linseed oil is considered the best for priming slightly rusty steel. The best rule is to prepare the substrate as well as time and money will allow, and then to choose a primer that can adequately wet the substrate.

Galvanized steel should be allowed to weather for six months before painting to remove oils and etch the material slightly. Certain recommended pretreatments for galvanized steel, including acetic acid and copper sulfate, have not been found to be effective, and may be harmful. However, it is a good idea to wash the surface with solvent to remove any grease or oil. Primer pigmented with zinc dust is a good choice for intact galvanized steel. Rusty areas should be primed with a material suitable for rusty steel.

PRIMER VARIETIES

Alcohol-based primer-sealer is used to seal surfaces with resin or stains (such as from permanent markers). This material forms a strong vapor barrier, dries quickly, and is inexpensive. It can be thinned with denatured alcohol.

Alkali-resistant primer is designed for masonry and concrete; two coats may be needed.

Alkyd primer has replaced oil-based primers because it is harder and dries faster. It has good resistance to bleeding and is not likely to dissolve stains, which could then bleed through the topcoat. Alkyd primer may cause peeling problems on masonry.

Alkyd-based metal primer dries faster than traditional oil-based primers. Zinc-bearing primer is especially good at inhibiting corrosion.

Latex metal primer is made in white and is quick drying.

Latex, acrylic latex, or vinyl primer is commonly used on drywall or wood.

Oil primer offers controlled penetration into wood, but is slow-drying.

Oil-based metal primer is particularly suitable for galvanized steel. A high zinc content is desirable.

Phenolic-resin primer-sealer can be used under spar varnish, enamel, or house paint on wood with pronounced soft spring and hard summer growth, such as fir plywood.

Stain-blocking primer is used over stained or oily substrate: B-I-N (based on white pigmented alcohol-shellac), polyvinyl acetate latex primer, or latex primer plus a stain sealer, can be used before latex, alkyd, or oil paint.

Several other materials can be used for priming. Exterior aluminum paint or shellac will coat resinous areas. Aluminum paint is especially valuable for wide-grain wood. Paint sealer and thinned varnish can be used in some circumstances.

TOPCOATS

Because exterior paints must resist sunlight, dirt, and pollution, the easy-to-clean medium- and high-gloss paints are preferred. Interior paints need not resist these conditions but should be washable and stain resistant. Interior wall and ceiling paints are commonly matte, egg-shell, or semi-gloss. Interior paint for kitchens, bathrooms, and laboratories, which may need to resist staining and chemical assault, should be high gloss and washable. (The terms "paint" and "topcoat" are used to describe most types of topcoating materials here, both opaque and transparent.)

Enamel is a type of topcoat that is usually formulated to produce a semi- or full-gloss, although flat enamel is available. Enamel pigments are finely ground and mixed with a vehicle, usually alkyd resin. An enamel should rest on a sealing primer so it can remain on the surface. For information on lacquer, see "Transparent coatings," below.

The degree of gloss is determined by the amount of pigment on the surface. A high percentage of pigment roughens the surface of a matte paint, causing it to reflect diffused light. Semi-gloss enamel has a higher percentage of pigment than high-gloss enamel. The formulation of the film-former also helps determine glossiness.

Paints are classified by composition in the following description of the major nonindustrial types of paint.

LATEX (EMULSION)

Latex, or emulsion, paint is a suspension of very fine particles of resins or oil in water. When the water evaporates or absorbs into the substrate, the particles become enmeshed in a solid-resin matrix. It is this matrix that holds the pigment and forms the film.

Latex paints have many advantages:

- Eliminate cost and environmental problem of solvent thinning.
- Fast drying; two coats can be applied from a single setup of the scaffold. (Environmental conditions will affect the drying rate; never repaint until the previous coat is dry.)
- Soap-and-water cleanup of tools (water alone may be sufficient).
- Fewer moisture problems. The porous film can breathe, decreasing blistering. This is especially valuable over masonry, which is difficult to paint with non-porous paint.
- Low odor and reduced toxicity (rooms should be ventilated after any painting—there have been reports of mercury toxicity from the mildewicide used in some latex paint).

The porosity of latex paints does make them subject to staining from rust or knots. Observe minimum application temperature—about 45°F to 50°F. Emulsion paints adhere poorly to glossy or chalky surfaces. Latex paint can turn sour if it is stored too long—check for the unmistakably foul odor of spoiled latex paint.

ACRYLIC

Acrylic-based paints, made of polymers of certain esters, are usually waterborne. They produce a washable film with excellent color and gloss retention. Acrylic resins may be blended with other resins. Interior acrylic paint can be used over the same primers as latex paint. Some of these paints, such as acrylic lacquer, must be thinned with the solvent specified by the manufacturer.

ALKYD

Alkyd paint has replaced oil paint for most interior and exterior work, due to its faster drying, good hiding power, low price, and greater durability. Alkyd dries more slowly than latex but forms a tougher surface. Alkyd paint may be formulated as one-coat material or dripless ceiling paint. Thin with mineral spirits or turpentine.

Contrary to myth, alkyd paint can be applied over latex, and latex can be applied over alkyd. The confusion probably stems from the fact that latex should not be applied over old-fashioned oil paint, and because alkyd is sometimes mistakenly called "oil paint."

OIL-BASED PAINT

The oldest and perhaps the simplest paints are oil-based coatings. These materials can be used for interior and exterior applications, with sheens ranging from flat to gloss.

True oil paint is an antique material mainly used to duplicate existing paint in restoration jobs. Oil paint dries slowly, has a strong odor, and, once dry, is hard to paint over. Oil paint has been used for trim, barn paint, roofs, shingles and shakes, floors and decks. It can be made to be highly water-resistant, flexible, colorfast, washable, and resistant to chemical attack. Exterior oil paint is designed to self-clean by chalking. Thin with mineral spirits or turpentine.

Oil paint has been largely replaced by alkyd paint, which is faster-drying, cheaper, and more durable.

EPOXY

Epoxy paint is a one- or two-part system that adheres well to nonporous substrates and resists most chemical attack. It is suited to relatively high temperatures and makes an extremely hard surface. The material is self-priming and suitable for counters, appliances, heavy-use areas, and coating over glossy enamel.

Epoxy may have these disadvantages:

- will not work over every existing finish
- hard to apply because application time is limited
- must be cleaned up with specific solvents before setting
- makes toxic fumes

TABLE B1
Primer and paint selection
Interior

Surface	Primer material	Topcoat
Acoustical, fiberboard	Alkyd wall paint or latex wall paint	Same
Drywall	Latex, acrylic latex, or vinyl latex	(2) Latex or alkyd wall paint. (2) Epoxy paint for heavy duty
Plaster	Alkyd or latex primer	(2) Latex or alkyd wall paint or enamel
Masonry: concrete, concrete block, unglazed brick, cement board	Latex wall primer, epoxy primer	(2) alkyd enamel, (2) latex wall paint or enamel, (2) epoxy
Concrete or masonry floors	a) Concrete sealer b) Epoxy	a) (2) Industrial enamel b) (2) Epoxy
Aluminum	Zinc chromate	(2) Latex or alkyd wall paint or enamel, or (2) aluminum paint
Galvanized steel	Acrylic metal primer or as specified by manufacturer	(2) Latex or alkyd wall paint or enamel
Structural steel and ornamental iron	Lead-free alkyd metal primer with rust inhibitors	(2) Latex or alkyd wall paint or enamel

TABLE B1 (continued)

Surface	Primer material	Topcoat
Wood walls, ceilings, trim, cabinet work, hardboard, etc.	Alkyd undercoater	(2) Latex or alkyd wall paint or enamel
Painted wood floors	Industrial enamel or epoxy	Same as primer
Stained wood floors	Stain followed by thinned oil, polyurethane varnish, or floor wax	Same varnish full strength (renew wax occasionally, do not varnish)

Exterior

Masonry: asbestos siding, transite, shingle, stucco, common brick, concrete walls	Self-priming latex house paint	Same as primer
Masonry: concrete and cinder block	Block filler followed by self-priming latex house paint	Same as primer
Concrete floors, patios, steps, platforms	a) Concrete sealer b) Epoxy paint	a) (2) Industrial alkyd enamel b) Epoxy paint
Aluminum	a) Zinc chromate b) Self-priming house and trim acrylic or latex	a) (2) Alkyd enamel, industrial alkyd enamel, or oleoresinous aluminum paint b) Same as primer
Galvanized steel	a) Bonding agent	a) Per instructions of bonding agent manufacturer

Surface	Primer material	Topcoat
Galvanized steel (cont.)	b) Alkyd metal primer	b) (2) Medium- or long-oil alkyd enamel, alkyd house and trim paint
Ornamental and structural steel	Rust-inhibiting alkyd primer	(2) Aluminum paint, medium- or long-oil alkyd
Pre-finished metal siding and panels	Latex or alkyd house paint	Same as primer
Wood floors and platforms	Self-priming medium oil industrial enamel	Same as primer
Plywood	a) Semitransparent preservative stain, or opaque exterior stain b) Pigmented acrylic emulsion	a) Same as primer b) (2) Latex exterior solid color stain, or (2) latex house and trim
Shingles, shakes, rough-sawn lumber	a) Alkyd exterior primer b) Semitransparent preservative stain, or opaque stain	a) (2) Latex or alkyd house paint b) Same as primer
Siding, trim, doors, hardboard (bare or primed)	a) Alkyd exterior primer b) Semitransparent preservative stain, opaque stain; c) Exterior varnish	a) (2) Alkyd or latex house and trim, or alkyd house paint; or (2) latex exterior solid color stain b) Same as primer c) (2) Exterior varnish

If more than one coat is required, the number of coats is shown in parentheses.

Always consult the label and follow manufacturer's instructions carefully. Changes in formulation over time and problems with terminology impair the accuracy of any paint selection table.

Aluminum paint is excellent for priming wide-grain wood and plywood. A paintable, water-repellent preservative is recommended before priming many types of exterior wood.

Most two-part epoxies must be job-mixed and applied rather quickly. Consult manufacturer's data on temperature and humidity required for curing. There may be a time limit on recoating. Consult the label for thinning and clean-up information. Use extreme caution, especially if methyl ethyl ketone is the solvent.

High-build epoxies, with up to 90 percent solids by volume, can leave a 6-mil coating in a single application. Coal tar two-part epoxies contain black coal tar as a pigment and have about 75 percent solids. Coal-tar epoxies are used to protect steel, aluminum, and concrete because they have excellent resistance to salt water and many chemicals. Brush the first coat into all crevices. The first coat can be thinned, but the topcoat should be sprayed full strength.

CHLORINATED RUBBER

Chlorinated (solvent-thinned) rubber paints are heavy-duty moisture- and abrasion-resistant paints for masonry, steel, and aluminum. They are suited to immersion and commonly used for concrete floors and swimming pools. These paints are a good substitute for latex in places where the water in the base can cause rust stains. Examples include masonry containing iron, such as slag- or cinderblocks. Chemical resistance of these paints however, is not as good as that of epoxy paints.

PORTLAND CEMENT

Portland cement paint contains portland cement, lime, and pigments, with the possible addition of sand, additives, and binders. The material has excellent durability on masonry, forming a hard surface that resists liquid water. Because portland cement paint is permeable to water vapor, trapped moisture cannot cause blistering or peeling. The paint becomes an integral part of the masonry and cannot peel after correct application. The color changes if the surface gets wet, but it returns to normal after drying.

A heavy coating of portland cement paint will repair small cracks in masonry. The paint can also prepare a masonry surface for a clear waterproofing treatment.

Portland cement paint can be applied to fresh concrete or masonry, but four weeks of curing is preferable. Do not apply over existing coatings. Moisten the wall first, and apply with a short-bristled brush. Because the goal is to coat the entire rough surface, use a scrubbing, not a painting motion. Apply first to the mortar joints and then return to coat the entire wall. On a smooth surface, a trowel can be used for the second coat. Allow twelve hours and recoat. Cure for forty-eight hours with adequate moisture and temperature. Portland cement paints containing latex need no moist curing.

PAINT FOR METAL

Like other materials, metal can be painted for protection and/or decoration. Because almost all ferrous metals (iron and steel) must be coated for protection against corrosion, the primer and paint must be able to inhibit or prevent corrosion for a reasonable lifetime. Paint for metal must adhere tightly and should inhibit penetration of oxygen and water.

Surface preparation for metal uses physical and/or chemical techniques to remove as much rust and other contaminants as possible. Select a rust-inhibitive primer that is compatible with the topcoat. Remember, "rust never sleeps." If you paint over rust, it will continue eating away the substrate. Several topcoats are a good idea for the best protection.

High-performance paints for metal include various types of epoxy, chlorinated rubber, and aluminum paint. For residential and commercial applications, many types of enamel or house and trim paint may be applied over the correct primer.

TEXTURE PAINT

Texture paint is a thick vehicle used to create texture and/or hide surface defects. Texture paint can mimic some plastered or sprayed textures on walls and ceilings. For best results, cover with a top coat.

Texture paint is usually water-based, but it can be oil- or acrylic-based. A heavy grade of texture paint can be used to create a pebbly texture or a stucco finish. Due to its thickness, texture paint covers only about 50 to 150 square feet per gallon. A sand-finish texture paint can be used to match sand-finish plaster (or add sand to the primer and/or finish). Texture can also be created with a plaster or drywall finish coat (see Texture Finishes, page 113).

TRANSPARENT COATINGS AND FILLERS

Clear finishes usually contain solvent, vehicle, and additives. Some extender pigment may be added to achieve a flatting effect. Because they lack pigment, clear finishes are less durable than paint for exterior use.

LACQUER

Lacquer dries quickly to a hard, sandable, and durable surface. The material can be clear or colored, and glossiness can range from flat to high gloss. Some lacquer finishes can be sprayed to simulate a hand-rubbed look. Lacquer is more common in industrial than architectural painting. Thin and clean up with the type of lacquer thinner specified on the label.

Lacquer dries by evaporation of the solvent, not polymerization. It generally contains three components:

- Cellulosic, the film-forming material, usually contains nitrocellulose or another form of cellulose.
- Plasticizer is used to decrease brittleness of the film and perhaps to increase thickness.
- Resin increases adhesion, thickness, and gloss, while reducing shrinkage.

The solvent in lacquers can soften or blister an existing finish. Always apply a sample on the previous finish before lacquering a whole surface. Lacquer can even soften previous coats of lacquer, so it's good to brush out runs or sags almost immediately.

VARNISH

Varnish, a film-former without color pigment, is a transparent material used to protect wood grain without obscuring it. Old varnish formulations are degraded and yellowed by sunlight. New, polyurethane varnish is resistant to yellowing, water, alcohol, grease, and dirt, and is hard, resistant to yellowing, and easy to apply. This varnish excels on counters, tables, floors, and stairs. Polyurethane is an exception to the rule that open-grained woods should be filled before finishing. The material is self-priming and available in flat, semi-gloss, and gloss varieties, in two-part formulations, and in interior and exterior formulations.

Drying rates of polyurethane varnishes vary. Check the label for the thinner. Check compatibility of polyurethanes with other elements of the coating system. Polyurethanes are not compatible with stearates, and will peel if placed on top of them.

Be sure to observe timing limitations with polyurethane. If the first coat becomes too hard, you must roughen it before applying the second coat. Polyurethane is difficult to patch invisibly. (See Part D, Repairing Floor Finish.)

Exterior, or "spar" varnish, is a tough, flexible grade of varnish designed to resist degradation by ultraviolet light and water.

SHELLAC

Shellac is an old-fashioned sealing and finishing material with a number of virtues. It is very hard, dries and sands well, and enhances wood grain. Normal shellac has a warm, orange hue; a whitened variety is available. A coat of shellac is thinner than a coat of varnish, so more coats are needed for the same effect. Shellac spots if water lingers on it, so it should not be the topcoat in areas that can get wet. Shellac may crack if exposed to intense sunlight.

To seal wood before staining (to prevent excess or uneven penetration), use about 5 parts high-quality denatured alcohol to 1 part shellac. Low-grade alcohol may contain water or other impurities that could damage the finish.

Shellac is described by how many pounds of solid shellac are dissolved in each gallon of denatured alcohol. "3 lb. cut shellac" is 3 pounds of shellac per gallon.

Shellac is dated on the can; it should be used before expiration. Before using shellac, it is a good idea to check that it will dry quickly enough. If it dries too slowly, add alcohol and retest. If the shellac still does not dry adequately, discard it.

Shellac can be applied with a brush or airless sprayer in much the same manner as other clear finishes. Even though shellac is glossy, repairs and refinishing are easier than other clear finishes because solvents in the new coat should soften the existing coat. Although it is not absolutely necessary to roughen an old coat for adhesion, it's probably a good idea. Damaged areas or drips can be repaired by rubbing with a rag moistened in solvent. Then feather in the new material.

LINSEED OIL AND TURPENTINE

Boiled linseed oil and turpentine can be combined into an interior furniture coating that shows off the patina of the wood. The mix is excellent for building up a high finish on things like gun stocks. Mix equal parts boiled linseed oil and turpentine, then rub the solution onto clean wood with a rag. Wait about thirty minutes, remove the excess finish, and repeat once or twice. Renew the finish occasionally.

WOOD SEALER

Wood sealer is used to eliminate suction, inhibit penetration of topcoats, improve adhesion, and seal stains that could be softened by the topcoat. Sealer is fast drying, can be somewhat brittle, and may contain some filler. It can be top-coated relatively quickly.

The three materials that are thinned and used as sealer are lacquer, shellac, and varnish. Sanding sealer is a variety of sealer that is fast-drying and relatively easy to sand.

Use only as much sealer as necessary to prevent suction and improve adhesion. Many coats of sealer may be needed, depending on manufacturer's directions. Sealer should be used whenever you are preparing a surface for a clear topcoat. Make sure the sealer is compatible with the substrate and topcoat. Some sealers are universal; others are designed for a particular topcoat.

PASTE FILLER

Paste filler is a thick material that is rubbed across the grain to fill pores in open-grained wood like oak, mahogany, ash, and walnut. Filler is not necessary on close-grained wood. Paste filler is made of silex (a type of colorless silica), linseed oil, and drier. The filler can be prestained or tinted with colors-in-oils or dry pigment and can be thinned with turpentine. (Wood filler is different from wood putty, even though both are sometimes called "filler.")

Because of the difficulty of applying paste filler, it is hard to find and used only on premium jobs. If the filler sets on the surface too long, it will be extremely difficult to remove, but if removed too soon, it will pull out of the pores. As soon as the filler starts to lose its sheen, it's time to wipe it off. If the filler goes on top of a coat of stain, apply a thin shellac or sealer coat on top of the filler.

LIQUID FILLER

Liquid filler is essentially thickened varnish, with the possible addition of silica, clay, starch, zinc, whiting, or other pigments. Liquid filler is used to seal and fill in a single operation. The smaller the proportion of solvent (generally mineral spirits), the more effective the sealing will be. A liquid filler with a brushing consistency can be applied across the grain and rubbed with the grain.

CLEAR MASONRY SEALERS

Clear sealers made of silicon or other materials can be used to control dusting and increase water resistance on many types of masonry. Several coats may be needed, and the treatment should be renewed regularly. Because these materials can prevent moisture from escaping a wall, they should not be used on walls with a source of water behind them. The coating is usually flooded onto the surface so it can run down about half a foot.

PENETRATING WOOD FINISHES

Penetrating finishes seep into the wood to "protect the surface from below" without building up a film. These materials have three essential functions: to improve appearance, repel water, and/ or to kill microorganisms that can destroy wood. Because penetrating finishes do not create a film, they should be renewed more frequently than paint—sometimes as often as once a year, depending on wind, rain, and sun exposure.

WATER REPELLENT

Water repellent can be used as a natural wood finish or the first coat in a paint system. The first application may only protect for one to two years, but successive applications should last two to four years. Paint will increase the longevity of the repellent treatment. Make sure the repellent is paintable—if it has a high wax content, paint will not adhere. A paintable, water-repellent preservative covered with paint is one of the best solutions for preparing wood (see below).

The benefits of using water repellent to protect wood from moisture include:

- Fungus usually cannot live in dry wood
- Less expansion and contraction (which helps destroy coatings and pulls out fasteners)
- Reduced warping
- Less water staining at end grain

PRESERVATIVES

Preservatives protect against fungus; they can be applied by brush, roller, rag, or immersion. Usually, the most effective application method is pressure-treatment. Preservative may be combined with a water-repellent.

The three categories of wood preservatives are:

- Preservative oils, primarily coal-tar creosote, a toxic material that is rarely used except in industry
- Organic solvent preservative, primarily pentachlorophenol (penta), a toxic material that is no longer on the market
- Waterborne salts, which are popular due to their relatively low toxicity and ability to show the grain. Wood treated with water-based preservatives is stable and rot-resistant. Water-based pressure treatments are designated as follows:
  CCA   Chromated copper arsenate
  ACA   Ammoniacal copper arsenate
  ACC   Acid copper chromate
  TZX   Chromated zinc chloride

All preservatives prevent decay, but not all protect the surface from degradation by ultraviolet light, erosion, and insects. Preservatives containing chromium protect against UV light. A surface coating is rarely required for practical reasons on preserved wood if it is protected from UV. Oil-base, semitransparent penetrating stain can be used on preserved wood after one to two years of exposure. CCA-treated woods can be painted or stained without this exposure. Check with the manufacturer of the treated wood for details. (Wood that has been treated with a wax-based preservative, such as penta, usually cannot be painted or stained.)

The U.S. Forest Service's Forest Products Laboratory strongly recommends the use of *a paintable, water-repellent preservative* before priming new wood. The water-repellent preservative prevents rain or dew from penetrating the wood and decreases swelling and shrinking. Fungicide inhibits decay beneath the coating. On repaint jobs, apply the preservative after scraping as much failed paint as possible. Pay particular attention to butt joints and corners, which soak up the most water.

STAIN

Stains are used to alter wood's color, enhance the grain, or obscure the grain completely. Several tints are usually available for stain products. To match an existing surface, bring a sample of the wood to the paint store. (Use the back of molding if nothing else is available.) Wipe on some stain and allow it to sink in. Swab with a rag and compare to the existing finish (in daylight if possible). Stains may be colored with universal colors or colors-in-oil, or by mixing several cans.

Penetrating stain (also called impregnating paint, architectural stain, or exterior stain) is a pigmented wood finish. Penetrating stain is essentially a water-repellent preservative with the addition of pigment and possibly fungicide. Because the color pigment protects against some ultraviolet light, this material is more durable than clear water repellent or clear finish.

Penetrating stain seeps into the grain at a controlled rate, is self-priming, and can be used over new or stained wood. Some penetrating stain works over existing paint. It should not be used indoors.

Penetrating stain can have either a solvent or latex base. Latex stain, however, does not penetrate the wood, and is thus not truly a penetrating stain. Latex stain is probably less durable than solvent-based penetrating stain. Solvent-based stain also gives more working time.

Penetrating stain is sold in "semitransparent" and "opaque" varieties. Semitransparent stain is mainly designed for stained or unpainted wood—it does not have enough pigment to hide opaque stain or paint. Stains called "heavy-bodied," "solid color," or "opaque" are more like paint than stain in terms of protection, because they form a film on the surface. These materials are a good choice for hardboard material and textured surfaces. A special stain is sold for treating pressure-treated lumber.

Penetrating stain toughens the grain, increasing its resistance to water. It does not blister or peel, which is a vital advantage in architectural work, and may be cheaper than paint in terms of original and maintenance costs.

Penetrating stain is often considered the coating of choice for rough-sawn, weathered, or textured wood. The rough surface allows more penetration, increasing the protection. Penetrating stain is also good on flat-sawn lumber and dense species, both of which are typically poor at holding paint, and on decking, trim, fences, and other exterior applications.

If a good deal of end grain is present, seal the surface first. Wiping off the stain stops the penetrating action, so you can control the shade by timing when you do the wiping. If more than one coat of penetrating stain is needed, recoat before the first coat has hardened. Otherwise the second coat may not penetrate.

Wiping stain (pigmented stain) is similar to thinned paint. Wiping stain clouds the grain and may be used on poor wood or wherever you want to obscure the surface. With the proper tooling, a heavy application can be used to create artificial grain. Because wiping stain does not penetrate, it can be used to lighten or darken a surface.

Heavy pigmented stains are not suited to open-grained wood, as the pigment tends to build up in the pores, leaving a cloudy or gummy look. A sealer of thinned shellac may be used before applying wiping stain; this is especially helpful with end grain. It's best to test the application before covering large areas.

Water-based stain (sometimes called acid stain) is packaged in dye packets that are dissolved in boiling water. Water stain penetrates deep into the wood, does not hide the grain, and is capable of bright color. Dampen the wood and sand the grain before applying (water in the stain will raise the grain unless you take this step). This material will darken earlywood more than latewood and reverse the natural color pattern. (Pigmented oil stain does not have this problem, so it is more appropriate for softwood that is not sealed.) If you wish to seal the wood first to control penetration and color, use an *extremely* thin coat of shellac.

Water-based stain is difficult to apply and is probably best sprayed. Keep a wet edge during application or the color will be inconsistent. One technique is to apply with a good brush until the entire surface is wet, then keep brushing until the stain is entirely absorbed, or wipe all at once. Thin the stain with water before applying to end grain; otherwise the increased absorption can leave a very dark result. Water stain is almost impossible to touch up without leaving dark spots or lap marks.

After staining and before sanding, it may help to apply a very thin coat of shellac to protect the dye coat, which is right on the surface.

Non-grain-raising (NGR) stain is formulated with special solvents, such as acetone or ketones, to restrict penetration and raising of the grain. NGR stain works well on oak, maple, and walnut. The stains are fast-drying, harder to apply than penetrating oil stain, and suited to spray application. Brushing and wiping may also work. Apply with a full wet coat.

Spirit stain is made from aniline dye dissolved in a solvent such as acetone or alcohol. This stain is very fast-drying and difficult to work with, so spraying is the best application technique. Spirit stain can be used for touch-up because it is fast-drying and can penetrate other finishes. Add some shellac to an alcohol-based spirit stain to increase brushability and drying time.

CHEMICAL AND ACID TREATMENTS

Several chemical reactions can be used to change the natural color of wood. These methods are usually used in industry, but knowing about them can be helpful for matching purposes.

- Potassium chromate produces red and brown.

- Potassium chloride produces green.

- Hydrochloric acid is used for artificial aging.

- Fuming is a manufacturing technique used to darken wood with ammonia; it is usually used with oak.

PAINT DISPOSAL

Dispose of all paint, coatings, solvents and contaminated clothing carefully. Make a habit of reading the label and material data safety sheets to determine the properties of material with which you are working.

Solvent-based paints are generally more hazardous than latex, but even latex paint should not be thrown in the trash, because it can leach out of a landfill and pollute groundwater. Extra paint should never be dumped on the ground or down a sewer or drain. Follow these guidelines for disposing of paint:

- Give it to the customer for future touch-up. To ensure that the customer knows the properties of the material, make sure the label is legible.

- Donate it to worthy causes, such as charities. Again, make sure the paint is in its original container with a legible label.

- Allow water-based paint to dry with the lid off, in the can. Keep the paint in a safe place, away from children and animals. When the paint is fully dry, it is legal for disposal in most municipalities. Keep the lid off so the sanitation workers can see that the paint is dry.

- Solvent-based paint must be disposed in a manner consistent with its hazardous nature. Homeowners may be able to dispose of this paint at a household hazardous waste disposal day. Facilities designed to handle hazardous waste are becoming more common as municipalities try to prevent more water supplies from being poisoned by leaking landfills.

• Paint thinner must be disposed with care because it is flammable and toxic. Thinner used for brush cleaning can be reused. Let the paint particles settle out and then pour off and reuse the liquid on top. Absorb the sludge and dispose as a hazardous material. Try to avoid letting thinner evaporate, as it contributes to ozone smog and air pollution.

PAINT AND VARNISH STRIPPERS

Paint and varnish removers are chemical mixtures that soften old finishes so they can be removed with a putty knife, steel wool, or scraper. Special removers may be needed for certain paints. Flammable removers should only be used when the extra danger is justified by increased efficacy.

In *wax-type* removers, a film of wax builds up over the wet remover to slow evaporation of the remover and extend its working life. Because the wax can interfere with adhesion of the finish, the stripper should be removed with alcohol. Be careful because solvents can dissolve the wax and carry it into pores in the wood, further interfering with the bond. Wash with trisodium phosphate to remove traces of wax, rinse twice with water, and allow to dry.

Wax-free removers work more slowly, but leave no wax to clean up. Many wax-free strippers can be removed with water and detergent. Some removers, made for special purposes like auto refinishing, are strong enough to darken wood. You may need to bleach a wood like elm that has been darkened by paint remover.

ABRASIVES

Abrasives, commonly sandpaper, are used for surface preparation and smoothing between coats. An abrasive should be able to resist "loading," a filling with dust that decreases effectiveness. Various materials are gauged differently, as can be seen from Table B2. The numbers listed for silicon carbide, aluminum oxide, and garnet are seen most commonly.

- Flint is a grayish-white abrasive with a short working life and low price. It loads up quickly and is intended for a single use.

- Garnet is harder than flint paper and more common.

- Silicon carbide crystals are hard, brittle, and black. They are used for auto body work and cutting glass, plastic, and ceramics.

- Emery is used mainly for removing corrosion. It is soft and seldom used on wood.

- Aluminum oxide is a sharp and extremely hard paper that resists loading. It is used for abrasive wheels and paper for cutting hardwoods.

Waterproof papers may be needed to reduce loading and/or dusting. Water lets the cuttings float out and speeds cutting, but it can also raise wood grain. Because wet sanding controls dust, it is a good procedure for old paint that may contain lead. (If you suspect that the paint contains lead, it's better to call a lead-paint removal contractor.) Drywall joint compound can also be wet-sanded to reduce dusting.

Paper with thin backing is useful for complex surfaces; heavy backing is best for flat surfaces. "Open coat" paper is designed to prevent loading. Whack sandpaper against something solid occasionally to release the cuttings, and try to distribute the wear all over the sheet.

Steel wool is used to: a) remove corrosion from metal, b) remove bubbles and dust from basecoats, and c) finish and polish various surfaces. Grade No. 4 is the coarsest; 0000 (No. 4/0) is the finest.

TABLE B2
Abrasive grain sizes

Silicon carbide, aluminum oxide, garnet	flint	emery	equivalent in symbol series
600	Fine		12/0
500			11/0
400			10/0
360			
320			9/0
280			8/0
240			7/0
220	4/0		6/0
	3/0		
180		3/0	5/0
150	2/0	2/0	4/0
120		1/0	3/0
100	1/2	1/2	2/0
80	1	1	1/0
60		1 1/2	1/2
50	1 1/2	2	1
40	2	2 1/2	1 1/2
36	2 1/2	3	2
30	3		2 1/2
24			3
20			3 1/2
16			4
12	Coarse		4 1/2

TABLE B3
Steel wool use

Gauge	Grade	Uses
0000	Super fine	Smooth shellac, lacquer, varnish before final topcoat. Buff furniture wax, dull high-gloss paint.
000	Extra fine	Clean and polish stainless steel, prepare surfaces between coats of varnish.
00	Very fine	Restore original appearance to aluminum windows, clean up old brass and copper, repair varnished surfaces.
0	Fine	Clean grouting between tiles, clean roofs before soldering.
1	Medium	Prepare wall surfaces before painting, remove rust from stoves and cast iron (using turpentine).
2	Medium coarse	Remove paint from moldings and awkward corners, remove scratches and burrs from copper and brass, remove old varnish from antiques (using varnish remover), clean wire screens and porcelain.
3	Coarse	Remove lacquer and varnish, remove paint from glass and tile, remove paint and varnish from floors, restore exterior woodwork.
4 (4/0)	Extra coarse	Remove rust from metal and tile (using turpentine), heavy-duty stripping.

COURTESY RHODES AMERICAN

MASKING TAPE

Masking tape is formulated to hold temporarily and release easily. It is available in widths ranging from 1/2 to about 2 inches. When masking large areas, minimize the use of masking tape by placing a sheet of newspaper or a strip of masking paper under the edge of the tape.

It's best to remove masking tape from windows before the paint is fully set, or the bond between the paint and glass may be impaired. And if you wait too long, the tape can get too sticky, making removal difficult, especially in warm or sunny conditions. But do not pull up the tape before the paint makes its mechanical bond, because this could pull up the paint.

Wet newspaper makes a cheap masking for windows, but make sure the sash stays dry.

CAULKING

Caulks are used to fill voids between adjacent building materials for two reasons: to increase weather resistance and to improve appearance. Caulk should be stored in a cool, nonfreezing location. A good caulk must:

- adhere tightly to the substrate
- form a tough skin and remain flexible in the interior through its service temperature range
- stretch and compress when building elements move
- have very low volatility
- resist weathering
- resist mildew (especially in damp climates or wet locations, such as near the ground)
- permit tooling to an attractive appearance
- take paint after setting (desirable but not always essential)
- wash up with water

Caulkings are constantly being improved. For standard construction use (sealing around windows, doors, and trim), latex, acrylic latex, or silicone sealants are most common. Latex caulk can generally be coated with latex-based paint within an hour of installation; it is often available only in white. Latex is not recommended for damp locations, but it is great for patching small cracks between walls and woodwork before interior painting. Acrylic latex caulk has greater durability and is available in many colors. It is not recommended for gutters or skylights.

TABLE B4 Caulking Selector

General Applications

● Excellent ◗ Better ◔ Good ○ NR—Not Recommended

Match the Product to the Job.

	DOW CORNING General Purpose Silicone Sealant	DOW CORNING PERFORMANCE PLUS Silicone Sealant	DAP "230" Sealant	DAP Acrylic Latex Caulk with Silicone	RELY-ON Acrylic Latex Caulk	RELY-ON Latex Caulk
Product Characteristics:						
Life Expectancy (a)	100+ Yrs.	100+ Yrs.	50+ Yrs.	25+ Yrs.	10+ Yrs.	5+ Yrs.
Water Cleanup	NO	YES	YES	YES	YES	YES
Paintable	NO (b)	YES	YES	YES	YES	YES
Temperature Service Range	-60°F to 450°F	-40°F to 270°F	-30°F to 180°F	-30°F to 180°F	-30°F to 180°F	-20°F to 180°F
Resistance to Cleansers, Soaps	●	●	◗	◗	○	○
Industrial Specifications	TT-S-00230C		TT-S-00230C (c)	ASTM C-834-76(d)		
Surface Adhesion:						
Glass, Ceramic Tile, Porcelain	●	●	●	●	◗	◔
Brick	●	◗	●	●	◗	◔
Wood	◗	◗	●	●	◗	◔
Metal	◔(e)	●	●	●	○	○
Concrete	◔(f)	●(f)	●	●	◔	◔
Suggested Uses:						
Window & Door Frames, Siding Corner Joints	●	●	●	●	◗	◔
Baseboards, Trim, Splashboards, Eaves	●	●	●	●	◗	◔
Air Conditioners, Vents, Ducts, Pipes	●	●	●	●	◗	◔
Thresholds	●	●	○	○	NR	NR
Gutters, Downspouts	●(f)	●(f)	◔	◔	○	○
Foundations	●(g)	●	●	●	NR	NR
Skylights	●	●	○	○	NR	NR
Showers, Tubs, Sinks	●	●	●	●	NR	NR
Marina RV (h)	●(h)	●	○	●	NR	NR

(a) Estimated using laboratory tests and product data. (b) Dow Corning Paintable Silicone Sealant recommended. (c) Meets performance requirements TT-S-00230C, Type II, Class A. (d) Class does not meet this spec. (e) Discolors copper and brass. (f) Refer to Dow Corning Silicone Concrete Crack Sealant. (g) Rating refers to Dow Corning Silicone Bathtub Caulk. (h) Above water line.

Courtesy of USG Corporation

Silicone caulks are the most durable and flexible caulks available, and some are even guaranteed for the lifetime of the homeowner. Some silicone caulks clean up with water, and some are paintable. Most silicone caulks should be applied with good ventilation.

Insert a foam backing material into deep cracks before caulking. The foam allows the caulk to be forced against the edges of the crack.

Concrete and mortar patch is supplied in a gun-grade for use on small patch areas. The degree of matching will depend on the color of the masonry. These caulks are not good at matching the texture of mortar. (See Part D, Caulking Procedure.)

Most caulks are available in 10.3 fl. oz. (.304 liter) tubes. One tube will cover approximately 50 feet of an 1/8 × 1/4 inch bead. This is roughly enough to caulk the exterior of five windows.

TABLE B5
Linear coverage of caulking

Joint width	1/16"	1/8"	1/4"	1/2"
Joint depth				
1/16"	423'	211'	105'	52'
1/8"	211'	105'	52'	26'
1/4"	105'	52'	26'	13'
3/8"	70'	35'	17'	9'

Section 2:
Patching Material

Many materials are used for repairing, patching, and spackling. Familiarity with these materials will speed up work and increase the chance of matching the substrate in terms of texture, stability, and appearance.

Patching materials are sold either dry or premixed. In general, dry materials are better suited to large and deep repairs, as premixed materials have more tendency to shrink, and are usually more expensive.

Gypsum and lime are two of the basic substances used to repair plaster, drywall, and masonry. A third important material, portland cement, combines gypsum, lime, and other substances.

Gypsum achieves its hardness by combining chemically with mixing water in a process called hydration. Most materials based on gypsum should not be "retempered" by the addition of water; this only weakens the batch. If the material becomes too stiff to work, discard it. Materials based on portland cement can be retempered within reason. The package should explain how much retempering is allowed.

Repair materials like joint compound and spackling do not set by hydration, and some can be retempered or thinned during application.

Many patching problems are caused by failing to control the amount of moisture in the patch and substrate. Products made of portland cement, gypsum, or lime will not set properly if they dry out too quickly due to absorption or evaporation. The patch may also get too stiff before you have a chance to level and smooth it. For these reasons, it's often a good idea to moisten the margins of the patch with water from a sponge, rag, or brush. Moisten absorbent substrates several times, especially in hot, dry weather and/or when the patch is thin or narrow.

A second problem with many plaster and portland cement patching products is that they shrink slightly during setting and leave cracks around the patch. You can avoid this problem by using nonshrink crack-filling material or by using techniques to minimize shrinkage. Apply the patching in thin layers, allow some drying and shrinkage, and force the patch against the edges of the substrate to make it bond.

WOOD PUTTY AND HOLE FILLER

Wood putty is a stiff material used to fill nail heads, cracks, and other voids in wood that will be painted or stained. Wood putty may be based on solvent or water. Putty that is excessively soft can be stiffened with the addition of a little cornstarch.

A good emergency putty can be made with the old carpenter's trick of mixing sawdust from the wood that will be repaired with liquid wood glue.

Wood hole filler, sold under brand names like "Plastic Wood," is a handy filler. Wood hole filler is solvent-thinned and available in various colors. The filler can present problems when used before staining because the filler seals itself and the adjacent wood, preventing the stain from penetrating and leaving the patch lighter than the surroundings.

Solvent-based wood filler can dry out quite rapidly if the can is left open. Close the cover after removing material, and make sure to pound down the cover firmly when you finish. Do not buy more than you will use in a year or so, as it's likely to go bad before you use it.

Water putty is a dry material that is mixed with water just before use. Because it generally does not absorb stain, water putty should be pre-tinted or painted. Water putty is immune to the problem of drying out in the can.

Swedish putty is a homemade blend of whiting, spackle, or plaster of paris with linseed oil (sometimes thinned with solvent). Swedish putty can be colored for interior use. Driers can be added for exterior use.

Exterior putty can be homemade by blending spackling compound with exterior paint.

Hole-filling materials can also be purchased in pre-colored stick form. These pencils are based on lacquer or shellac and are suitable for small, fast repairs. Some of these pencils must be heated with a candle or gas flame before application.

GYPSUM

Gypsum, a soft grayish-white rock, is the basic material in plaster and drywall. Gypsum, or calcium sulfate ($CaSO_4$), has about 20 percent water in its crystal structure. When gypsum is crushed and heated in "calcining," the water of crystallization is removed. Partly calcined gypsum is called plaster of Paris. Further calcining and grinding are used to make other gypsum products. The water of crystallization is replaced when calcined gypsum is mixed to make drywall or plaster. This water reenters the crystal structure, recreating the original gypsum rock. Gypsum products can retard the spread of fire because heating one molecule of gypsum releases two molecules of water.

Gauging plaster is gypsum powder that is mixed with a "putty" of slaked lime to make lime-gauging finish plaster. Gauging plaster brings early set and hardness to the material and prevents shrinkage cracks. Lime-gauging finish plaster must be applied over a gypsum basecoat. Various setting times are available; aggregate may be incorporated in the finish coat for application over lightweight-aggregate basecoats.

Keene cement is a strong white plaster that is mixed with lime putty to make a durable, crack-resistant finish for areas with heavy wear. Keene cement can produce a sand-float or trowel finish. Because it can be retempered, a large batch of Keene cement can be tinted for a whole job. The material is available in regular and fast-setting varieties.

Additives are used with gypsum products to adjust the setting rate. *Accelerators* are useful for small areas or dry locations to make sure the material sets before it dries. Accelerators are also used in cold conditions, where plaster could rot before setting. Accelerator is commonly blended into patching material. A cheap and effective accelerator is already set gypsum plaster (make sure to screen out the chunks).

Retarder slows the set of plaster to ensure enough application time and prevent the need to retemper. Many gypsum plasters contain retarder, but you can add more for covering large areas or working in hot conditions. Use retarder carefully—it can cause plaster to dry abnormally slowly, delay the application of finish coats or decoration, or even cause the plaster to rot before setting.

Bonding agents are chemicals that increase adhesion to a substrate. A resin emulsion or synthetic latex may be used to bond gypsum, lime, or portland cement mortar to any clean, sound surface. Bonding agents can be blended into the mixing water or brushed, rolled, or sprayed on the substrate.

LIME

Lime is an alkaline mineral component of finish coats and masonry cement. Lime is obtained from limestone, shells, or other natural sources. The raw material is heated to 2,500°F to remove moisture and some gases. This process of "burning" lime produces quicklime (CaO), which is extremely caustic, and difficult to handle because it reacts violently with water. Quicklime is slaked (hydrated) to produce hydrated lime, or hydrated calcium oxide ($Ca(OH)_2$). Hydrated lime hardens slowly through a process of "recarbonation," in which it absorbs carbon dioxide (CO_2) from the air to form calcium carbonate ($CaCO_3$).

Sand and lime have been used since antiquity to make mortar and plaster. Lime putty is a blend of hydrated lime and water that makes a finish-coat material. Because lime putty can take several months to harden, gauging plaster (see above) is often added to speed the set and increase hardness. Pre-mixed finish coat plasters that require only the addition of water are available. Lime-gauging plaster products need no painting if the color is acceptable.

PORTLAND CEMENT

Portland cement can be used in mortar, plaster, patching material, or paint (see Coating Systems, Topcoats, page 83). Portland cement is a mix of lime and clay that is ground and then calcined at about 2,700°F. Gypsum and other materials are added to the mix. Portland cement is sold in bags containing one cubic foot of material. The weight per bag depends on the type of portland cement.

Portland cement is especially valued for its ability to resist moisture. White portland cement produces a relatively white surface, depending on the aggregate used.

Because portland cement sets by hydration—the addition of water to the crystal structure—the cement must set before it dries. It is often necessary to protect a portland cement product from drying before setting, which can take several days. Repeated fogging may be required.

BASECOAT PLASTER

Plaster is a mix of gypsum, aggregate, and additives. Sand is the traditional aggregate, but lightweight aggregates are popular due to their ease of application. The lightweight aggregates include perlite, an expanded type of volcanic rock; pumice, a ground-up volcanic material; and vermiculite, a "popped" ore similar to mica. Each aggregate imparts its peculiar texture, so you must choose the aggregate carefully in patching if the basecoat will be visible.

Basecoat plaster is either job- or mill-blended with aggregate to make the first (scratch) and second (brown) coat. Some basecoat varieties are suited only to hand application, others to machine application. Wood fiber can be added to basecoat plaster to increase adhesion to metal lath.

Three plaster coats are necessary on metal lath and desirable on gypsum lath. Two coats are acceptable on well-supported gypsum lath, and on rough concrete block, clay tile, and porous brick. (On exterior applications, furring over the masonry will protect the plaster from condensation that could ruin it.)

SPACKLE AND PATCHING PLASTER

Spackling compound is used to repair cracks and small voids in plaster and drywall. Joint compound or quick-setting compound can be substituted.

Plaster of paris (calcium sulfate) is a quick-setting, fine-grained material for patching drywall and plaster and for repairing molded (ornamental) plaster. You can slow the hardening somewhat by adding a little vinegar or a weak glue size. A similar product, *patching plaster*, sets more slowly.

QUICK-SETTING COMPOUND

Quick-setting compound, like the proprietary Durabond, is excellent for patching deep holes in plaster, drywall, and concrete. Unlike joint compound, the material does not sag or shrink in deep repairs. Quick-setting compound is especially useful for preparing drywall for taping. It can fill gaps between sheets, around windows and doors—wherever a large dollop of joint compound would cause bulging, sagging, or ridging.

Quick-setting compound has these advantages:

- quick-setting (rate varies with the formulation)
- can decorate the day after application
- low or no shrinkage
- extremely hard
- unaffected by humidity during drying
- can be used on interiors or exteriors

Quick-setting material is sold in several "speeds." A number in the name indicates how many minutes are required for setting. Be aware that the compound accelerates itself and can set very quickly. Keep tools clean, and mix only as much as you can apply within the setting time. Do not retemper Durabond—throw it out if it begins setting before you can apply it. Seal the compound against moisture, which can cause cracking.

Quick-setting compound can be substituted for joint compound in finishing drywall, but it is usually very hard to sand. A softer material, like joint compound, is much easier to use as a surface treatment. Do not use quick-setting compound in a taping machine.

FINISH COAT MATERIAL

Hydrated (regular) lime can be soaked overnight and used as a trowel-finish or float-finish. Sand is usually added, especially for a float finish.

Autoclaved lime is double-hydrated by the manufacturer, so it needs no soaking on the job.

Fibered lime is autoclaved lime with fibers; it can be used in lime-cement mixes to make all types of stucco and plaster.

The following recipes can be used for finish coats:

Plaster finish coats—parts dry weight		
Lime	Gauging plaster	Sand
2	1	0
2	1	8
Lime	Keene cement	Sand
2	1	8
1	2	0
1	2	8

Portland cement–lime plaster is used for exterior stucco, and for plastering moist interiors or areas subject to extreme wear. Do not use Keene cement–lime putty as a finish coat on portland cement–lime plaster. Use these proportions:

Portland cement–lime plaster			
Coat	Mason's lime (50 lb. bags)	Portland cement (94 lb. bags)	Sand (cu. ft.)
Scratch	3/4 to 1	1	5 to 6
Brown	1	1	6 to 7
Finish	2	1	7 to 10

Do not apply portland cement–lime plaster to gypsum or smooth, dense substrates. To assure adhesion to questionable surfaces: a) apply the coating to self-furring lath, b) add a bonding agent to the mixing water, or c) apply a bonding agent to the substrate. Control joints are recommended to regulate cracking during drying.

TEXTURE FINISH

Various texture finishes are available for creating surface textures and/or hiding surface imperfections. Most textures are applied by spray, although brush, roller, or trowel can also be used.

Texture finishes should be painted to improve cleanability or protect against abrasion. Primer may be needed, depending on the texture finish and paint characteristics. In general, walls should be painted after texturing; ceilings need not be painted if the coating is thick and the color is acceptable. Acoustical finish is a particularly rough surface intended to break up echoes and silence a room. Painting some acoustical surfaces will impair their ability to control noise.

JOINT COMPOUND

Joint compound is a water-based vinyl material used for thin applications, primarily for embedding and covering drywall tape, and for covering nails in drywall. It is also used to fill shallow depressions and narrow gaps in plaster and drywall.

Joint compound sets by drying. Several coats should be applied to deep areas, but it's better to fill deep holes with a quick-setting compound, and save joint compound for the thin coats.

Most joint compound is only for interior use. Three joint compound materials are available. *Taping compound* is a strong and crack-resistant material used to embed tape. *Topping compound* is used to cover tape and nails because it has better sanding characteristics, less shrinkage, and leaves a smoother surface. *All-purpose compound* is a compromise material for embedding and covering tape.

All three types of joint compound are available ready-mixed or dry. Powder is cheaper but harder to use. Standard joint compound can be used in a taping machine.

Store ready-mixed compound above freezing temperatures. If the material freezes, thaw slowly at room temperature and mix thoroughly before use.

To create textures to match existing surfaces, apply joint compound with roller, brush, or trowel. Make sure each layer is fully dry before applying the next. Prime joint compound before painting, generally with latex or vinyl latex primer.

Table B6 Joint compound characteristics

Conditions or requirements	Product				
	Easy Sand	Sheetrock setting-type joint compound (powder)	Sheetrock joint compounds (powder)	Sheetrock ready-mixed joint compounds	Plus 3
Hot, dry weather	Good	Good	Good	Ex.	VG
Cold, wet weather	VG	Ex.	Fair	Good	Good
Filling concrete surfaces	Ex.	Ex.	NR	NR	NR
Patching fine cracks	VG	VG	Good	VG	Ex.
Large fills	Ex.	Ex.	Good	Good	VG
Lowest applied cost	VG	Good	Good	VG	Ex.
Easiest sanding	VG	NR	Good	VG	Ex.
One-day finishing	Ex.	VG	NR	NR	NR
Machine application	NR	NR	Good	Ex.	Good
Texturing	Good	Good	VG	Ex.	Good
Strength	Good	Ex.	Good	VG	Good
Bond	Good	Ex.	Good	Good	VG
Resistance to shrinkage	Ex.	Ex.	Good	Good	VG
Slip	VG	Good	VG	Ex.	Ex.
Mixed life	NR	NR	Good	Ex.	Ex.
Container life	Good	Good	Good	Ex.	Ex.
Resistance to cratering	Good	Good	Good	Good	Good
Hardening or drying time	Ex.	Ex.	Good	Good	Good
Edge crack resistance	Good	Good	Good	Ex.	Ex.
Check crack resistance	Ex.	Ex.	Good	Good	VG
Paint base	Good	Fair	Good	Ex.	Good

NR = not recommended; Ex = Excellent; VG = Very good
Courtesy USG Corp.

METAL LATH

Metal lath is expanded metal used to back up interior and exterior plaster and stucco. Metal lath is protected from corrosion with black asphaltum or galvanizing. The sheets are 27 × 96 inches.

Metal lath is a useful patching material because it can be fastened to dense or deteriorated masonry and concrete to secure a plaster basecoat. This saves the time and expense of preparing the surface. Use furring on an exterior surface to prevent condensation from damaging the plaster. "Self-furring" metal lath has dimples to lift itself off the substrate. Paper-backed metal lath reduces the waste caused by plaster dropping through the metal lath. Flexible sheets of metal lath can be fastened to irregular surfaces. Rigid sheets are designed for flat surfaces.

Figure B2 Metal lath

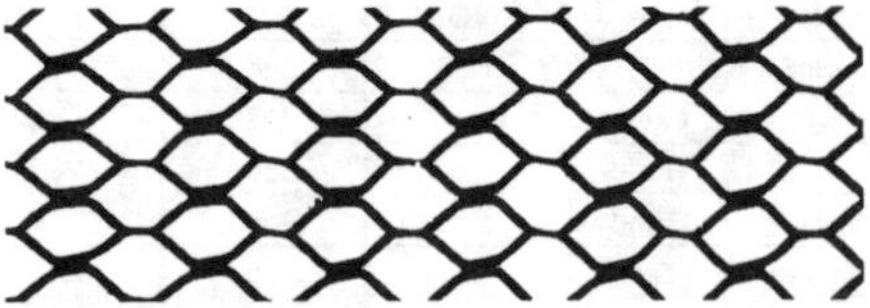

Junior Diamond Mesh Lath

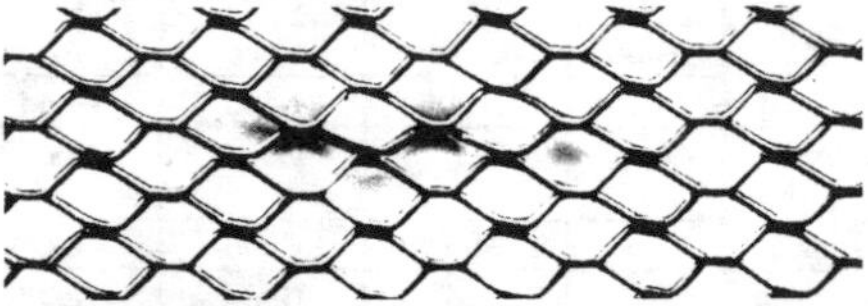

Self-Furring Diamond Mesh Lath

⅜" Riblath

Courtesy of USG Corporation

MORTAR

Mortar is used to lay brick, block, glass block, and stone, and to patch masonry, stucco, and concrete. Mortar contains portland cement, lime, sand, and water in various proportions. Mortar sets by hydration and must be kept moist until setting. Mortar is much better at holding things apart (compressive strength) than at holding them together (tensile strength).

Masonry cement—a blend of lime and portland cement—is sold in bags containing one cubic foot. Several types of masonry cement are available, with various degrees of strength. In general, the more workable the mortar, the weaker it is. Type S mortar is adequate for most above-grade, exterior or interior masonry, whether reinforced or not. Type S combines a strong tensile bond with good compressive strength and contains 1 part portland cement, 1/2 part lime, and 4 1/2 parts sand.

Sand for strong, durable mortar must be washed free of silt, salt, and organic matter. To test cleanliness, place a couple of inches of sand in a quart jar, fill with water, and shake. Wait an hour—if scum appears on top, the sand is dirty and should not be used.

Sand usually contains a certain amount of moisture—often 4 to 8 percent. This amount of water does not cause problems. Nearly saturated sand makes a slushy mortar even if no mixing water is added. If rain is forecast, protect sand with plastic.

Use only clean water for mortar. In general, if water is fit to drink, it is suitable. For mixes that specify water content by pounds, figure 8.33 pounds per gallon.

Retempering is permitted to remove water lost to evaporation, as long as not more than two hours have passed since mixing. While retempering may reduce compressive strength somewhat, failing to retemper will greatly cut tensile strength. In hot weather, reduce

Mortar recipes (parts by volume)

Purpose	mason's cement	sand
All-purpose and stone	1	3
Brick	1	2 1/2 to 3
Block	1	2 1/4

the need to retemper by shading the mortar and mixing small batches.

THIN MORTAR COATS

When working with mortar, remember that suction can absorb so much moisture that hydration cannot take place. You may have to moisten particularly dry surfaces as many as four times before applying patching material. Make sure not to saturate the surface, or the mortar will not adhere.

Thin mortar coats used for patching, plaster, or stucco can present bonding problems. A bonding agent can increase adhesion and reduce cracking. Bonding agents are particularly valuable for: a) highly absorbent substrate, b) shiny substrate, c) surface subject to heavy wear, and d) thin coating. The bonding agent may: a) replace part of the mixing water, or b) be blended into the mixing water before it is added to the cement and sand. Some bonding agents are applied directly to the substrate—consult the label.

Another technique for increasing adhesion to a masonry substrate is to prepare a paste of masonry or portland cement and water. Moisten the surface if it's very absorbent. Brush on the paste, not too thick, then apply the mortar before the paste begins to dry.

TUCKPOINTING AND GROUTING MORTARS

One of the most demanding uses for mortar is tuckpointing. The drying forces are intense, and any shrinkage will pull the mortar away from the substrate.

Waterproof, nonstaining, and nonshrinking tuckpointing mortar is sold in dry form. To make a low-shrinkage tuckpointing mortar from standard masonry cement, prehydrate it with this technique:

1. Mix sand and masonry cement dry.

2. Add just enough water to make a doughlike ball and mix.

3. Wait one or two hours, and add enough water to make the mortar workable. Then use the mortar.

COLORED MORTAR

A common mistake in patching masonry is failing to match the color of the existing mortar. A good patch should be visible only under close inspection. A gray patch will look positively amateurish on masonry that was laid in the old, white mortar made of lime and sand. It's best to repair such masonry with white masonry cement and sand. For an extremely white mortar, use white silica sand as the aggregate.

For buff, brown, red, or black mortar, you can: a) use pre-mixed, colored masonry cement, or b) add pigments to gray or white masonry cement. Excessive pigment reduces mortar strength. Use no more than 10 to 15 percent pigment, compared to the weight of the cement. When using carbon black, limit the pigment to 2 to 3 percent of the cement weight. Avoid retempering colored mortar, because it tends to fade the color.

Use this procedure to color mortar with pigments:

1. Premix the pigment with the mixing water, or mix it with the sand and cement.

2. Mix until the color is uniform.

3. Test that the pigment is fully incorporated by flattening some mortar under a trowel. If you see streaks, continue mixing.

4. Test whether the mortar is the correct color—colors can be deceptive in wet mortar. Allow some mortar to set on the actual surface to be repaired. A quicker method is to let some mortar dry on the blade of a trowel in the sun.

CONCRETE PATCHING

Concrete can be patched with mortar, concrete, or proprietary patching materials. You can save the time needed to track down gravel and sand by using dry, ready-mixed concrete for small jobs, but this material costs a lot more than job- or ready-mixed concrete. (Ready-mix can be expensive for patching due to the minimum-order requirements of ready-mix plants.)

A good concrete patching material will not shrink and pull away from the edges of the hole. If the patching seems likely to shrink, use the suggestions in Part E, Patching, to leave the patch flush with the surface.

Acrylic resin–base materials provide a strong, flexible, and durable patch for concrete. The material is sold dry, requiring only the addition of water. See also Hydraulic Cement, below.

HYDRAULIC CEMENT

Hydraulic cement is a portland cement compound with three useful properties: it expands as it sets, it sets under water, and it adheres to metal. The cement is sold dry and is mixed with water immediately before use. One pound will fill about 15 cubic inches of holes (a crack $3/4 \times 3/4 \times 28$ inches).

Hydraulic cement can be used to:

- waterproof cracks in below-grade structures, even if water is running through them

- repair blisters, honeycombs, and other construction faults in concrete

- set posts, bolts, railings, and other metal elements in concrete

- seal around pipes and other fittings protruding from masonry or concrete

- repair holes in foundations left by tie wires or spreaders

Section 3:
Wallcovering Material

Though it's commonly called wallpaper, modern wallcoverings can be made of cloth, felt, vinyl, cork, or other materials, sometimes coated and sometimes plain. The backing is usually a wood-pulp paper. The rollers used for printing wallcovering are usually 5 1/2-inch diameter, so the pattern repeats itself at 18-inch intervals.

Higher quality paper is printed with the rotogravure technique. The etched copper cylinder is capable of great depth of color. Screen printing uses silkscreening (a form of accurate stencil) to impart a design. Silkscreening is used primarily on expensive, handprinted wallcovering.

Paper goes through the printing press with about 1 inch of selvage on the edge. The selvage may carry registration marks or be unprinted. Selvage is removed at the factory from pretrimmed paper.

The paste on prepasted paper is applied at the factory and activated by a brief immersion in water.

Strippable wallpaper has enough structural integrity to be removed from the wall in large sheets, vastly simplifying the removal chore.

TYPES OF COVERINGS

LINING PAPER

Lining paper (liner or backing) is off-white paper used to improve the wall surface before facing paper is applied. Lining paper also absorbs moisture from the paste on the finish paper, which speeds up the adhesion and reduces the chance of staining. Lining paper is typically used under expensive coverings and for resurfacing block, wood panel, or damaged walls.

COMMON PAPER

Common paper is sold in untreated, vinyl-coated, and cloth-backed versions. Vinyl-coated paper is more resistant to staining than conventional paper, but it's not as durable as solid vinyl. Common paper is available in single, double, and triple rolls in widths ranging from 18 to 27 inches.

Common paper can be stained by grease and ink, so it's suited to areas with moderate wear, such as adult bedrooms, living rooms, and dining rooms. Wheat paste or stainless cellulose paste can be used for application. Some of these papers are strippable; they are commonly sold trimmed and prepasted.

You may be able to protect common paper against abrasion or soiling with a coat of clothing starch. The starch will give the paper a somewhat flatter sheen. Test first—do not use if the ink is water soluble.

HAND-PRINTED PAPER

Hand-printed wallpaper is an expensive material that is usually printed with silk-screening. Hand-printed paper can be fragile and likely to absorb moisture or wrinkle. Hand-printed paper may have a protective film or be printed on calendared stock to increase strength and simplify handling. Lining paper is usually needed to improve appearance. Do not roll seams very hard because it could leave an impression.

PREPASTED

Prepasted paper has a dry adhesive, usually cellulose and/or starch, on the back. This covering is designed as a convenience for do-it-yourselfers.

To prepare prepasted paper, roll up the hang with the pattern to the inside, dip it in a tray containing lukewarm water, pull the hang out from one end so it unrolls, and book for the proper relaxing period. Do not dip the paper too long, as the paste can wash away. Make sure to moisten the entire roll, as dry areas will not stick. Make sure the edges stay wet during relaxing.

Many professional installers supplement the adhesive so they can be sure prepasted paper stays stuck. To do this, wet the back of the paper with a sponge, and apply liquid adhesive (diluted about 50 percent) to it. Dilution prevents the adhesive from getting too thick, which would lengthen the drying time and perhaps allow seams to pull apart. And since no pools of thick paste will be present, it will be easier to locate and eliminate air pockets.

VINYL

Many varieties of vinyl covering are available. Vinyl can be laminated to paper or lightweight woven or nonwoven cloth. In addition, paper can be laminated to lightweight woven cloth that is then coated with vinyl. In general, the vinyls offer better wear and resistance to stains, making them suitable to kitchens, bathrooms, and children's rooms. Most vinyls are strippable. Solid vinyls are the most durable type of modern wallcovering. Due to their strength, vinyls are about the easiest to apply.

Vinyl-to-vinyl adhesive must be used wherever vinyl overlaps other vinyl (unless the overlap is double-cut). Vinyl's impermeability to water requires the use of mildew-resistant adhesive. The wall must be dry before application. Use a moisture tester if you're in doubt.

Vinyls are sold in the same roll size as common paper, with two or three rolls per bolt. Heavyweight vinyl is available in widths ranging to 54 inches for commercial applications. The standard bolt for these materials is 30 linear yards, or 45 square yards. The material can be purchased from the bolt in square-yard quantities.

The three weights of vinyl are:

weight	backing cloth	weight (oz. per sq. yd.)	thickness (mils)
light	cotton	3	6.5
medium	osnaburg cloth	16	13
heavy	broken twill fabric	22	15

The temperature should be at least 60° for hanging vinyl. Do not make wire or overlapped seams with heavy vinyl; double-cut instead. Paste is easily removed from the face of smooth vinyl; sponge it off as soon as possible after a strip is smoothed.

Smooth heavy-weight vinyls with a 10-inch broad knife or a stiff, short-bristled smoothing brush. Lighter weights can be smoothed with an 8-inch knife. Pierce blisters with a needle and smooth them down while the paste is still wet.

FOILS

Foils are made of metal foil or mylar (a plastic that resembles foil). Bolt sizes are the same as common papers. Foils are commonly used for accents in small locations. Due to their visual power, foils should be used with care. They can reflect an obnoxious amount of sunlight, and may be overbearing.

Foils are difficult to hang and will accentuate every wall defect. Use excellent surface preparation and/or lining paper to minimize wall defects. Foils do not allow the wall to breathe, so use mildew-resistant adhesive. Do not hang over existing covering, as moisture trapped in the wall can loosen the old paste. True metallic foils conduct electricity, so shut the power off before working near outlets, switches, or fixtures.

FLOCKS

Flock wallcovering is made by gluing fiber to a backing. The result is a textured material with great warmth for the right situation. Use special care to keep adhesive off the surface. Do not use a seam roller; it will leave marks. Brush or sponge down the seams instead.

If necessary, raise the nap on flock with a travel-type steam iron (no hot plate, just steam). Do not touch the iron to the material; apply the steam briefly and check the results.

MURALS

Murals are large images broken down into strips for application to the wall. Murals can be backed with paper, foil, or vinyl. Lining paper can be used to improve the wall before application. Due to their visual power, murals must be chosen and hung with extreme care.

CLOTH

Various types of designer fabrics can be adapted to wallcovering, including wool, silk, cotton, linen, and burlap. Liner paper is helpful for light cloth. Wide yardage can be difficult to apply. Standard wheat paste may be used. Some wallcovering or fabric dealers can spray waterproofing on yardage to help it resist dirt and stains.

OTHER MATERIALS

Cork veneer, leather, grasscloth, felt, burlap, and linen are available at a price for the right situation. Cork veneer is an extremely thin material that is laminated to paper and suitable for informal areas. Grasscloth is made in a variety of colors from synthetic or real grass. Because of inevitable color variations between strips, it may pay to cut all the strips and arrange them by eye on the floor. This will prevent jarring colors from ending up next to each other. Manufacturers often suggest that you avoid booking grasscloth and other natural materials laminated to paper, as they might separate from the backing.

Keep water off the surface of felt and be sure to brush the whole surface in the same direction. Reverse every other sheet to conceal slight variations in felt's random pattern.

PACKING AND DYE LOTS

The industry uses some rather confusing methods of packaging wallcoverings. The basic element is called the roll, but an "American" roll has a different length, width, and area than a "metric" roll.

To further confuse matters, rolls are commonly sold in bolts containing the equivalent of two or three rolls. Because bolts use material much more efficiently, they are preferable to single rolls. Nevertheless, wallcovering is commonly priced by the single roll.

Wallcovering is labeled with both pattern numbers and dye lot numbers. The pattern number designates the style of paper. The dye lot number indicates the setup at the factory; it changes each time something changes in the manufacturing. These alterations can affect the consistency of the coating, the ink, and the quality of embossing. The installer must ensure that all rolls on a job bear the same dye lot number.

Covering is usually packed according to the "right-hand rule"— the top of the pattern is at the outside of the roll.

TABLE B7

Wallcovering roll dimensions

System	width	length	actual sq. ft.	usable sq. ft.
American	18" to 36"	12' to 24'	34 to 36	approx. 30
metric	20 1/2" to 28"	13 1/2" to 16 1/2'	27 to 30	22 1/2

Roll dimensions and yield (36 sq. ft. roll)

Width	length per roll (feet)			hangs per double roll + scrap	
	Single	Double	Triple	Length: 8' 3"	Length: 10' 4"
18"	24'	48'	72'	5 + 6'9" scrap	4 + 6'8" scrap
20 1/2"	21'	42'	63'	5 + 9" scrap	4 + 8" scrap
24"	18'	36'	54'	4 + 3' scrap	3 + 5' scrap
27"	16'	32'	48'	3 + 7'3" scrap	3 + 1' scrap
36"	12'	24'	36'	2 + 7'6" scrap	2 + 3'4" scrap

INSPECTING

You can only get credit or exchange for poor-quality wallcovering if you show the problem to the dealer before you cut the material. Some flaws are minor, and the customer may approve the paper anyway. The best rule, whether the covering is going on your wall or somebody else's, is to examine first, install second.

Inspect wallcovering for these problems:

- missing patterns
- patterns printed on the bias (out-of-square)
- incorrect registration of the pattern (in any color)
- ink blotched or adhering poorly
- inconsistent or damaged coating, especially near the edges

The best way to inspect is to reroll the material in the opposite direction to the way it was packaged. Rerolling helps reverse the "window shade effect" left by time in the package. You can increase the straightening action by sliding the new roll back and forth after rerolling.

To ensure that the pattern repeat is consistent, unroll the length of one hang from each of two rolls on a flat surface (not a carpet). Place a weight on the bottom of each strip, align the patterns at the top, and check that the repeat is consistent between the strips. Errors of 1/16 inch or so are no problem. In some cases, you may be able to "fudge" larger inconsistencies by aligning the patterns on the prominent part of the wall, and placing mismatches elsewhere.

SIZING

Sizing refers to both a coating that is a foundation for wallpaper and the process of preparing a wall for covering. The major effect of sizing is to give a wall uniform porosity. Walls with too much porosity suck water from the adhesive too quickly, leaving too little time to adjust and smooth the covering. Walls with too little porosity prevent the adhesive from dissipating (setting up) quickly enough.

Sizing also regulates the adhesion. With too little adhesion, the paper can fall off; with too much adhesion, it cannot be pulled from the wall when it's time to redecorate.

Either primer-sealer or sizing can be used to prepare a wall. Sometimes both are needed, depending on the manufacturer's instructions.

Many types of sizing are available. The components may include glue, casein, varnish, starch, and shellac. The best choices are manufactured sizing (in powder or paste form) or a thinned-down application of the adhesive used for the wallcovering. Some sizes contain an indicator that turns pink if the surface is excessively alkaline.

PRIMER-SEALER

Primer-sealers prime and seal walls before application of wallcovering. The material may be able to compensate to some degree for a poor coat of paint.

Several types of *acrylic* primer-sealers can be used. Regular acrylic primer-sealer is clear (has no hiding power) for use on existing wallpaper. Acrylic primer-sealer can be so good at promoting adhesion that the paper cannot be removed from the wall without a great deal of damage.

A *stain-killing* primer-sealer should be used only for sealing stains that could destroy the wallcovering. Remove stains such as lipstick, crayon, grease, and food traces as thoroughly as possible with detergent before applying the stain-killing primer-sealer. This material will seal the surface, so you must take measures to prevent mildew if you will apply a nonbreatheable covering on top. A liner paper or a clay-based adhesive may help in this regard.

Pigmented acrylic primer-sealer should be used when the new covering is not opaque enough to cover the existing surface. Pigmented sealer is useful on poor latex, glossy surfaces, and existing wallpaper. This material is expensive, and should be used only when needed.

ADHESIVE

Wallcovering adhesive (paste) is based on wheat, cellulose, or vinyl. Wheat paste, the traditional material, is adequate for many situations, but vinyl is stronger and should be used for heavy material. Condensed liquids may be added to certain pastes to increase their effectiveness. Paste should have a mildewicide, especially when used with nonporous covering.

Wheat paste usually must be mixed on the job and allowed to mature for at least a half hour before use. Figure that a pound of dry paste will paste about six rolls of paper. If the mix is on the thick side, the covering will be easier to manipulate.

Cellulose paste has excellent mildew and stain resistance.

Vinyl paste, often used with vinyl covering, is usually sold premixed. A gallon of adhesive is sufficient for three or four rolls. A stronger version of vinyl paste is used with commercial, heavyweight vinyl. Vinyl adhesive is sometimes used to augment the adhesion of prepasted papers. Thin the premixed adhesive with about an equal amount of water.

Table B8
Comparing wallcovering adhesives

Type	Early tack	Slip	Bond	Mildew resistance	Nonstaining	Economy	Low-moisture[1]	Dries without air
Wheat paste	weak	best	good	weak	good	best	weak	weak
Cellulose paste	weak	fair	weak	best	best	good	good	fair
Powdered vinyl adhesive	best	good	good	best	best	good	good	fair
Premixed vinyl adhesive	best	fair	best	good	good	weak	best	best
Wheat paste vinyl adhesive	weak	good	good	fair	good	best	weak	fair
Vinyl-to-vinyl adhesive	good	weak	best	best	good	weak	good	best

[1]Useful for the rare coverings printed with water-soluble ink.

Vinyl-to-vinyl adhesive is required for pasting vinyl over existing vinyl coverings and for making overlapped seams on vinyl. This adhesive is usually sold in small tubes.

The amount and viscosity of the paste are both vital to achieving good results. An excessively thick application is likely to grab too slowly, and may cause excess shrinkage and pulling away of seams.

PART C

COLOR

Color is the product of three factors: a source of light, a modification of that light, and the brain's response to the radiation reaching the eye. Understanding the fundamentals of light and color will help painters deal with color—and customers—more effectively.

Visible light is a form of electromagnetic radiation, which also includes heat (infrared), radio, and X-rays. The eye can detect radiation (called visible light) in a narrow band of the electromagnetic spectrum—wavelengths between .4 and .7 microns (millionth of a meter).

Paint and all other reflective objects produce color by absorbing some wavelengths and reflecting others. The eye only sees the reflected wavelengths. Filters and lenses, on the other hand, absorb certain colors and allow others to pass through. Those that pass are what we see when looking through a filter.

The "visible spectrum" is produced when white light is broken down upon passing through a prism. The colors of the visible spectrum are also visible in a rainbow: red, orange, yellow, green, blue, indigo, and violet. This works in reverse as well: the three primary colors that can be combined in the "additive process" to produce white are red, green, and blue. The additive principle governs the interaction of light beams.

A second principle, subtraction, is more important to painters because it governs the interaction of pigments. The primary colors in the subtractive process are red, blue, and yellow. Unlike the additive process, these colors cannot be added in the subtractive process to produce white.

White surfaces reflect practically all wavelengths of visible light. Black reflects essentially no incoming (incident) light. Other colors absorb some colors and reflect others. For example, green paint reflects green and absorbs the violet and red portions of white light. In coatings, this selective absorption can take place at the surface, in the coating, or at the substrate.

Light Sources and Color

The color of reflected light is also influenced by the color of the incident light. Thus, a building in the trees may be under greenish light, and it could appear green even if it were painted white. Surfaces that do not reflect a certain color will seem black if lighted by that color. For example, blue-green surfaces absorb red light, so if you place a blue-green surface under red light, it will appear black.

These principles can cause problems for surfaces illuminated by artificial light. Incandescent lights are stronger in the orange and yellow parts of the spectrum, so they tend to accentuate surfaces that are already red, orange, or yellow. At the same time, incandescent lights tend to dull out blues and greens.

The picture is more complicated for fluorescent light, because each type produces a characteristic flavor of light:

- Cool white bulbs emit yellowish-green light, accentuating yellow, blue, and green, and making warm colors duller.

- Soft white fluorescent lights give a warmer light, similar to incandescent light.

- Daylight fluorescent bulbs are close to daylight in coloration.

The need for artificial light can be decreased by using light-colored paint and floorcoverings and installing reflective surfaces, such as mirrors. Rooms with a good deal of natural light can be decorated in monochrome or analogous color schemes to make them seem bigger. Cool tints and neutrals will reduce the glaring effect of desert light.

The angle of the incoming light and the roughness of the surface both influence how we perceive a surface. Dull, flat paint reflects and scatters light beams. Glossy paint reflects purer beams. Extremely glossy paint acts like a mirror.

Figure C1 Reflection

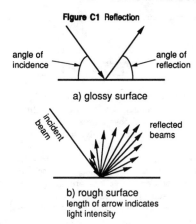

a) glossy surface

b) rough surface
length of arrow indicates
light intensity

Reflection from a glossy surface obeys a law stating that the angle of incidence equals the angle of reflection. The higher the angle of incidence, the greater the amount of light that will be reflected.

Painters should know about color for two major reasons: to help customers choose colors, and to mix paint. You can never substitute your taste for your customer's taste, but you can give unbiased advice about how colors will affect the appearance of a room or building. Remember, when offering advice, the customer must make the final decision.

Paint chips can be misleading if the light in the store is different from the light in the building where the paint will be used. This problem can be overcome by examining paint chips in the actual room light. If there is any question about the suitability of a color, it's a good idea to apply a quart to a surface before deciding. In extreme cases, apply wall and trim paint next to each other to see how they interact. Mistakes are much cheaper to correct at this stage than after a job is half finished!

Knowing about color will also help you mix paint. Once you realize that rose is a tint of red, it becomes obvious that you will get a rose color by mixing white into red paint. To get olive, a shade of green-yellow, you would mix green and yellow paints, then shade with black.

Terminology

Additive coloring describes how several beams of light interact. Each beam adds a certain frequency to the mix of light.

Complementary colors are located opposite each other on the color wheel. In the additive process only, two complementary colors combine to produce white.

Hues are the twelve colors on the color wheel. Red is a hue.

Intermediate colors combine a primary and a secondary color. The six intermediate colors are yellow-orange, yellow-green, blue-green, blue-violet, red-violet, and red-orange.

Midtones are hues that have been toned with equal amounts of black and white.

Neutrals are subtle colors such as white, gray, brown, black, and the important decorator colors off-white, beige, and light gray. These colors are restful and compatible with many others. (But if a beige contains too much red or yellow, it loses some compatibility.)

Pastels are colors with high values.

Primary colors are any three colors that can be combined to produce all colors of the spectrum. Primaries for the additive process are red, blue, and green. Primaries for the subtractive (pigmentary) process are red, blue, and yellow.

Saturation is the degree of brightness of a color.

Secondary colors are produced by combining equal parts of two primary colors.

Shades are hues with black added; they produce a color that is duller than the original hue. Brown is a shade of orange. In general, rich shades are based on cool colors.

Subtractive process is the rule used to combine pigments—each pigment subtracts some wavelengths from incoming light.

Tertiary colors are mixtures of two secondary colors.

Tints are hues with white added. Rose is a tint of red. Tinting tends to make colors colder.

Tones are colors that have received both white and black in a process called "graying." See "midtones."

Value is the degree of lightness or darkness of a color. Colors of equal value are said to be equally bright.

The Color Wheels

A color wheel arranges the major colors to show some relationships between them. The "additive color wheel" explains the behavior of light beams (which use the additive process). Only the "pigmentary color wheel"—using the subtractive process—concerns painters.

The primaries on the pigmentary wheel are red, blue, and yellow. Then the secondary colors are added: green (blue and yellow), orange (yellow and red), and purple (red and blue). From these the wheel is extended to the six tertiary hues (red and purple give red-purple; blue and green give blue-green, etc). The pigmentary color wheel has twelve colors.

Relationships on the color wheel can help select colors that harmonize with each other to make a color scheme. You can observe these relationships in many products: plaid shirts, autos, and wallpaper, for example. The simplest relationships are based on the idea of complementarity. Hues opposite each other (purple and yellow, or green and red) are called complements. When using the following relationships, it's important to remember that the chosen hues can be shaded or tinted to prevent a garish or boring color scheme.

Monochromatic harmony uses shades and tints of a single hue. This technique can be used to make a room feel more spacious or to hide unpleasant or overbearing features. For example, various shades and tints of blue can be used to good effect.

The *analogous combination* uses colors that are adjacent on the wheel. These "analogous" colors are similar and unlikely to jolt the observer.

The *true complement* is simply two colors opposite each other on the wheel. Because you can shade or tint the colors, you need not

Figure C2 Pigmentary color wheel

a) true complements

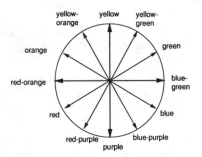

b) split complement

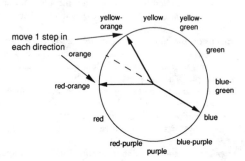

choose bright orange and bright blue. Bright orange and shaded blue are also true complements.

The *split complement* uses three colors. Instead of orange and blue, the scheme would be blue and the colors adjacent to the complement: red-orange and yellow-orange.

The *triad* is a Y-shaped configuration with equal angles between the legs. A triad might produce red, yellow, and blue. For example,

Figure C2 (continued)

c) triad

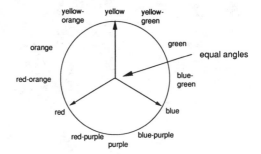

d) mutual complement

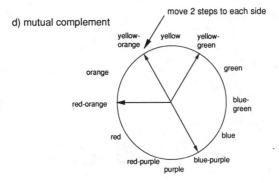

red could be shaded to the woodwork color, yellow tinted or muted to make light beige or off-white, and a tone of blue used for an accent.

The *mutual complement* uses one set of complements (such as yellow-orange and blue-purple) and two colors (such as yellow-green and red-orange) that are each two steps away from one complement. This system offers both the contrast of the complements and the similarity of the colors near one complement.

Figure C2 (continued)

e) double complement

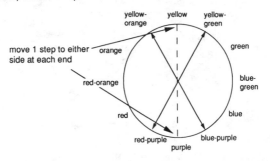

move 1 step to either side at each end

f) split mutual complement
split on one end, 5 adjacent colors on other side

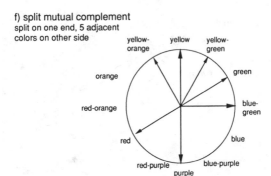

The *double complement* uses two pairs of complements. Find the colors by drawing a diameter across the color wheel, then moving one color to each side at each end. An example would be yellow-orange, yellow-green, red-purple, and blue-purple.

The *split mutual complement* uses two pairs of complements, such as red and green, and purple and yellow, plus three adjacent colors on one side of the wheel.

Perceptual Effects

Colors can have definite psychological and perceptual effects. Some of these effects are fairly uniform, while others vary with the person and could be called "taste." Colors are rarely used alone, and the presence of nearby colors influences our perceptions. For example, white and black both tend to raise the intensity of nearby colors.

Colors are said to "advance" or "retreat." Red, orange, and yellow tend to advance to the viewer. Due to their similarity to the sun and fire, they are considered "warm" colors. Blue and green tend to retreat; they are called "cool" colors because they resemble snow, ice, and water.

Warm and cool colors can be used to manipulate the feelings of building occupants. You can visually cool a hot room by painting it a cool color. This is especially useful in south and southwest exposures. You can warm a cold room by painting it a hot color, which could be useful for north- and northeast-facing rooms.

Hot colors tend to shrink rooms, while cool colors tend to expand them. Take the size of a room into account. For example, you would want more light in a large room like a kitchen than in a small room like a bathroom.

Red is an active color, associated with blood, aggression, and action. Red increases heart rate and blood pressure. Darker reds, such as burgundy and maroon, are associated with wealth and power. Red is good for accents but difficult to use in large areas.

Blue is the color of tranquility. It's associated with sky and water and is likely to calm the viewer. Navy blue has a trustworthy connotation.

Green is a tranquil color that reminds us of the outdoors. It is suitable for both sunny and shady locations.

Yellow is an energetic, warm, and cheerful color that is good for northern exposures. Yellow also tends to increase anxiety and anger. Because it can make complexions look sallow, it's a poor choice near a mirror.

Gray is a neutral that is influenced by its surroundings. Too much gray can be boring, and it can be depressing in the long and dark winters of northern climates. A warm gray contains umber, red, or yellow; a cool gray contains blue, green, or violet.

Brown is considered good around food. Beiges are a common neutral brown with many applications.

Purple is dramatic, regal, and romantic. It's good for accents, but can be overbearing on large areas.

These principles will help you avoid common mistakes and use colors to maximum advantage:

• If you use contrasting colors, do not use them on equal areas.

• Use bright colors for accents. The brightness of a color increases with its area.

• Dark colors can be depressing in large areas.

• Balance the amount of pattern and plain areas in a room. Plain colors or textures can be boring; intense patterns and rough textures can be overwhelming.

USING COLOR TO ALTER A ROOM

The following material is reprinted with permission from The Personality of Color, *published by Pratt & Lambert Paints, Inc.*

By following simple color rules, you can perform visual "magic." You can reshape rooms, change their "temperature," disguise their defects, create emotionally exciting environments, or make a room feel serene . . . all with the use of color trickery.

To visually expand space:

• Use light, cool values and limit the number of colors. Monochromatic color schemes (using various values from just one color family) are particularly successful. Paint all the surfaces in a room the same color and cover bulky furniture with fabric that matches that color. Camouflage moldings, ugly architectural features or awkward windows by painting them the wall color.

• To raise a low ceiling, paint it white or a light tint or the same color as the walls if that color is a light value. Also keep the floor color light.

- Shiny, reflective walls, floors, and ceilings will make a room look larger and increase the amount of light. Mirrors at right angles to a window will provide maximum light reflectance and visually double the space. Use clear or openwork furniture.
- Use plenty of light to expand space. Wash the walls with artificial light to soften hard edges and make space seemingly expand!
- Dark prints or patterns with a white background will make a room look larger; or use the same small scale print, on a light background, everywhere!
- Use vertical patterns or floor-to-ceiling cupboards or bookcases, emphasizing the verticals with paint color to "raise" the ceiling.
- Paint contrasting diagonals on the floor to stretch the width of a room, or on a wall from ceiling to floor to visually create more height.
- Create a three-dimensional perspective design (one that appears to recede in depth) with declining values of a color; paint a scenic mural on one wall or a "fake" window with an outdoor view!
- Diagonals on the floor will visually widen a room.
- Emphasize the verticals in a room to make a ceiling seem higher.

To visually shrink space:

- Paint walls and ceiling with warm, dark colors. Select furniture that is large in scale and also furniture made of warm-colored woods.
- Use many different patterns and textures to "fill" space visually.
- Paint multiple-color bands to divide space on walls. Make two or more lines under the ceiling line. Continue down the corners and around doors and windows. Or divide the flat

wall surfaces into rectangular "panels" with molding, and
paint the molding and the area within it different colors from
the rest of the wall.

- Divide walls horizontally with a "wainscoating" effect (paint
  the top half of the wall, wood panel and color stain the bottom half; or divide the wall with two different paint colors
  and add a molding between them). To "lower" a ceiling, use
  a dark value paint and drop the ceiling color line 6 inches or
  more on to the walls.

- Divide the wall surfaces in different ways to visually diminish
  the size of a room.

- Light side walls and dark end walls will visually "square" a
  narrow room or hallway.

To visually alter the dimensions of a room or to add character:

- To "square" a long, narrow room or hallway, use a warm,
  dark color on the shorter, end walls and a cool, light tint or
  off-white on the long side walls.

- To make a wide room look narrower, use a warm, dark value
  color on the side walls and a cool light neutral tint or off-
  white on the shorter wall.

- To add interest to a square room without a focal point (like a
  fireplace), paint one wall a rich accent color and add a painted texture using two or three paint colors.

- To camouflage ugly ceiling textures, defects, ducts or pipes,
  paint everything, including the ceiling, black or a very dark
  color.

- Remember these simple color facts to visually alter space:

  Dark colors absorb light.
  Light colors reflect light.
  Warm colors absorb light.
  Light colors reflect light.
  Warm colors "fill" space.
  Cool colors recede and are more expansive.

SELECTING A COLOR SCHEME

The following material is reprinted with permission from The Personality of Color, *published by Pratt & Lambert Paints, Inc.*

Selecting a color scheme for any part of your home should not be a haphazard guessing game. Changing the color in your home can make the most difference for the least cost than anything else you can do in decorating.

Here is a handy checklist of all the things you should give thought to before selecting colors:

- How will the room or area be used and by whom? Will it be a hide-away for a single person, a family living area, or a place for entertaining friends? If it's primarily a place for one individual, then only that person's tastes need be considered. If, however, you are decorating an area to be enjoyed by many in the family, then poll your family members to get some idea of their collective color preferences.

- Take a look at your entire home and especially those rooms that are immediately adjacent to and in view of the one you will be decorating. Color schemes should relate from one room to the next.

- Based on the usage of the room, and the "style" of your home in general, what decorating style do you want the room to be, i.e., casual or formal; a specific period or decorating style?

- Will the room be used primarily in the daytime or at night? This is extremely important since natural light exposures and the type of artificial light you will be using will greatly affect the colors in a room.

- Do the dimensions of your room need to be visually altered? Is it too narrow or is the ceiling too high, for example?

- Note any particular architectural details, and any wood finishes in the room that will stay. Varnish color will also affect color selection, or you may opt to change that, too.

- What pieces of furniture and elements of the decor will be staying? Draperies? Rug? Also consider any paintings or other accessories you will keep.

- What is your lifestyle? Are you looking for easy care solutions or doesn't that matter? Is your home important for business entertaining?

- What type of ambience would you like? Calm and relaxing? Sophisticated? Warm and casual?

- In what kind of climate do you live?

- How much color area will be involved? How many walls? Are you considering changing the ceiling and floor, too?

Color Schedule

A color schedule is a list of which color is to be applied to each surface on a job. A complete schedule should list the paint type and everything else you need to do a job. When you receive a color schedule, check its completeness while walking through the building. Make sure you understand the names of each room, and which surfaces are described in the schedule. If a schedule is incomplete or confusing, you can lose a lot of time figuring out which color goes where.

The Munsell System

Paint manufacturers all have elaborate schemes for creating thousands of colors. But to describe a particular color without using a manufacturer's scheme, you can use a technique like the Munsell system. The Munsell system, which allows the use of letter and numerical designation for any color, shade, tint, etc., is used in government and institutional color specifications. If a contract specifies a Munsell color, a paint company should be able to match it. The system relies on three principles:

Colors are classified into five *hues:* red, yellow, green, blue, and purple, and five intermediate hues: yellow-red, green-yellow, blue-green, purple-blue, and red-purple. Every color is found within one of these ten hue families. Hue is indicated by a capitalized initial: R for red, GY for green-yellow, and so on. As can be

Figure C3 Munsell system

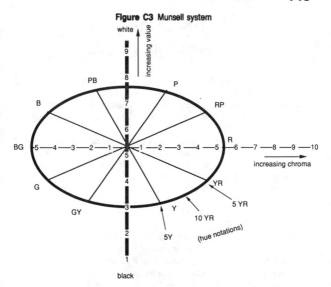

seen from Figure C3, 5Y is pure yellow, 5YR is pure yellow-red, and 10YR is midway between yellow-red and yellow. This breakdown establishes 100 hues, each designated by a number and one or two letters.

The lightness or darkness of a color is indicated by its *value*. 0 indicates pure black; 10 indicates pure white. In reality, paint can create values between 1 and 9.5. Value is followed by a "/." Neutral value is listed on the Munsell designation as 5/.

The intensity of a color—its saturation—is called *chroma*. Neutral gray has a chroma of 0. A very saturated color, such as chartreuse, can have a chroma as high as 12 or 14.

These terms are joined into a notation: Hue Value/Chroma. A rose, listed as 5R 5/4, would be a full red, with an intermediate value and relatively low saturation. The grays, ranging from white to black, are considered neutrals. Neutral gray is written NV/. Black is N 1/ and white is N 9.5/.

Colors-in-oil and Universal Colors

Colors-in-oil are oil-based materials used to change the color of solvent-based paint. Universal colors are a newer product which can disperse in either solvent- or water-based paint. Universal colors are also compatible with certain clear coatings—consult the coating manufacturer.

Colors-in-oil and universal colors can be used to alter incorrect color matches or to color paint for touch-up work. Observe manufacturer's limitations on the amount of colorant to add—generally not more than 8 to 12 ounces total colorant per gallon.

Use this procedure to mix colorant into paint:

1. Test a small sample of paint with some colorant to make sure you are going in the right direction.

2. When satisfied, start adding colorant to the full amount of paint you will need. (It's very difficult to achieve the same color in a second batch, but it may be a good idea to count the number of drops or ounces of each colorant just in case you must color more paint. See Mixing Two Colors of Paint, below.)

3. Mix the paint container thoroughly. Check the color and add slowly when you approach the desired color.

4. For a final check, let the paint dry and examine it under the actual lighting conditions. Wet paint can be deceptive—it is usually brighter and lighter than dried paint.

Mixing Two Colors of Paint

You may need to mix two colors of paint to achieve a certain color. Never mix different brands or types of paint. The usual practice is to add a little of the darker paint to the lighter paint. Test the paint often on a surface similar to the one you will coat. When you think you are close, allow the sample to dry. Then inspect it in the actual room with the correct light. Keep a record of the proportions but try to mix enough for the whole job in one batch, so you do not need to repeat the mixing process. Remember to look for subtleties: off-white shaded with blue is different from off-white shaded with black.

If you must hand-mix a second batch of paint, it's good practice to: a) begin mixing the two batches together before the first runs out, or b) start the second batch at a corner or other discontinuity (even if you must waste some of the first batch).

THE ABCs
OF PAINTING

Estimating

Estimates are a fact of life for a painting contractor. Making accurate, profitable estimates is a skill that can only be learned through experience. A good estimate does at least three things: tells you what to charge for a job; provides a reasonable amount of profit; and gives you a chance at getting the job.

Low estimates can result in unprofitable work; high estimates can lose you work that might be profitable. On occasions, you may want to bid low to keep up the volume of work or to get or retain customers. Or you may choose to bid high to control the workload or ensure that a tough job will go to someone else. In general, making a large number of estimates will increase your chances of getting relatively high bids accepted. You may want to bid some complicated jobs on the basis of time and materials, but this leads some customers to suspect that you are looking for a free ride at their expense. A firm price is usually preferred by both sides.

One key to accurate estimating is accounting for every material, surface, and task. Even if you misestimate the time needed to strip a door or stain a window, the estimate will still be more accurate than one that does not account for all tasks.

A second key to good estimating is recording what previous jobs have cost in time and materials. It's a good practice to review how well each job has met your projections of time and material costs.

The estimating process starts with a conversation with the customer. Take into account what the customer wants—this is the benchmark by which you will be judged in the end. The customer's comments on the existing paint job will help you evaluate how picky he or she is, and what you will have to do to please him or her.

Walk through the job, or go over the blueprints, asking plenty of questions. Take your time, and ask to look the job over again if necessary. Write details on the estimating form, making sure you understand which room is which.

Spend plenty of time inspecting surfaces, windows, and doors. How clean are they? Are any windows painted shut? Will you have to sand glossy surfaces? Run your fingers along walls, feeling for hairline cracks. Is the plaster sound and the paint securely adhered? Is the exterior extensively chalked? Each of these conditions will require additional preparation, and that should be reflected in the bid. Will the job require many colors? Then allot extra time to clean equipment. Make sure to include "common materials"—items like rags and sandpaper.

Write down what type of surface prep the estimate covers, and specify the hourly cost of additional work. Agree on who will do preparation work like moving furniture and covering shrubs. The customer should always move artwork and other fragile or valuable items.

Cases of extreme deterioration are hard to estimate, so you may want to present these choices to the customer:

• to work for time and materials

• to work for a set price

• to find another firm to do the preparation before you paint

• to paint over the deteriorated surface after obtaining the customer's written understanding that you do not guarantee the job

If you can, complete the estimate and deliver it at the first meeting. If the customer is rushed, phone in the total when you figure it, then follow up by mailing a written estimate. But if you are in doubt about how much to charge, take your time rather than risk "shooting from the hip" with a bogus estimate.

One way to simplify estimating is to set prices per square foot for production work. These figures would apply to new residential

TABLE D1 Estimate form

Date due: _____ Date estimate written: _____

Customer: _____ Person requesting (if different): _____

Address: _____

Phone: _____ Type of project: _____

Date of blueprints: _____

Total square footage: _____ Total price: _____

Exterior

Item and surface prep:	Surface material	Sq.ft. or:	Primer type	Primer quan.	Topcoat type & #	Topcoat quantity	Price
Walls							$
Overhang							
Doors		(no.)					
Windows		(no.)					
Garage							
Garage door							
Shutters		(no.)					
Other trim (specify)							
Soffit							
Fascia							
Siding							
Gutters and downspouts		(lin. ft.)					
Flashing		(lin. ft.)					
Railings		(lin. ft.)					
Fences		(lin. ft.)					
Wrought iron		(sq. ft.)					
						Total:	$

TABLE D1 Estimate form (continued)

Interior

Item and surface prep:	Surface material	Sq.ft. or:	Primer type	Primer quan.	Topcoat type & #	Topcoat quantity	Price
Walls							$
Ceilings							
Doors		(no.)					
Windows		(no.)					
Kitchen cabinets							
Other cabinets							
Railings		(lin. ft.)					
Shutters							
Trim (specify)							
						Total:	$

TABLE D2 Common materials form

Item	Type	Quantity	Cost
Sandpaper			$
Sandpaper			
Spackle			
Patching compound			
Putty			
Caulking		(tubes)	
Paint thinner			
Lacquer thinner			
Rags		(lbs)	
Roller			
Roller			
Masking tape		(rolls)	
Dropcloths			
		Total:	$

construction, where conditions allow quick, uniform application. Painting walls before the trim is fastened can save a great deal of time and effort—which can be reflected in the price. Likewise, trim is easier to stain before it's fastened. Per-square-foot prices can be a trap on repaint jobs, especially for old or complicated structures.

Estimates must reflect not only per-job costs, like materials and labor, but also overhead (office expenses, insurance, etc.) and profit. The Painting and Decorating Contractors Association of America offers courses on estimating, and makes an estimating guide available to members.

Apprenticeship

Apprenticeship is one of the oldest forms of trade education, and still one of the best. This unique format allows a person to learn hands-on skills at the jobsite and theoretical knowledge in the classroom, all the while getting paid for the effort. Few other programs offer the convenience and in-depth training of apprenticeship. Due to the scope of today's painting and decorating industry, it is difficult to gain such a wide education in any other way.

The advantages of apprenticeship include:

- provides a life-long skill

- enhances economic security—graduates are wanted for their in-depth knowledge of the trade

- offers variety—the range of skills and knowledge allow journeymen to work in many specialties of the trade

- gives journeymen a good background for starting a business.

Apprenticeship is a legal contract, or indenture, that confers benefits to the trainee in return for an obligation to work in the industry for a certain period. The indenture specifies the duration of training, wages and raises, school attendance, and skills the apprentice will learn.

Apprentices must pass through a four- or five-year program that includes about 8,000 to 10,000 hours of on-the-job training and at least 576 hours of classroom instruction. All work is supervised by journeymen. Apprentices are paid a percentage of the journeymen's pay; this pay increases with experience. After finishing the program, an apprentice receives a certificate of completion of apprenticeship and becomes a fully trained and qualified journeyman.

The topics covered in a painting and decorating apprenticeship include:

- wood finishing
- wallcovering
- special decorative finishes
- special coatings
- spray painting
- scaffold and rigging
- color theory, color mixing and matching
- drywall taping and finishing
- abrasive and water blasting
- paint failures and remedies
- blueprint reading
- health and safety
- estimating

Apprenticeship programs are administered by Joint Apprenticeship and Training Committees, which have representatives from contractors and the union local. The Committee may cooperate with vocational schools or other educational institutions.

Information on apprenticeship is available from the Bureau of Apprenticeship and Training in the U.S. Department of Labor. Many states have agencies dealing with apprenticeship. Vocational colleges or the following national organizations can also provide information:

International Brotherhood of Painters and Allied Trades
1750 New York Avenue NW
Washington, D.C. 20006
(202) 637-0720

National Joint Painting, Decorating, and Drywall Apprenticeship
  and Training Committee
1750 New York Avenue NW
Washington, D.C. 20006
(202) 783-7770

Surface Preparation

Even a bumbling painter can tell you that surface preparation is the
key to a good job. According to Sherwin-Williams Co., "as high as
80 percent of all coatings failures can be directly attributed to inadequate surface preparation that affects coating adhesion." Without
adequate preparation, there is no way for the new paint to grab the
substrate, and that's a guarantee of failure. The amount and type of
preparation needed depends on the coating, the nature of the substrate, and the environment in which the coating must function.

  Preparation can take as long as or longer than the application
itself. Details for specific surfaces are found starting on page 186,
Preparing and Painting Common Surfaces. Follow these guidelines:

• Check the requirements of the new coating system.

• Clean off all possible foreign material from the surface: dirt,
  mildew, moisture, rust, mill scale, oil, grease, wax, stains,
  pitch, and degraded coatings. Use the most effective means
  available, but do not clean more than is required for the system. (For complete removal of paint or varnish, see Stripping
  paint, below.)

• Some surface preparation may be needed between coats—to ensure adhesion or to smooth off dust or bubbles in the previous
  coat.

• Use power equipment when needed for cleaning and preparation.

• Roughen the substrate to increase adhesion with abrasive blasting or sandpapering.

- Check with the paint manufacturer about using chemicals to soften the existing finish to ensure adhesion of the first coat.

- When recoating, figure out why the previous paint failed (see Paint failure, page 229).

HAND CLEANING TECHNIQUES

Hand cleaning with water, detergent, and solvents can remove dirt and stains that dissolve in the cleaning agent. Hand cleaning is less effective than power cleaning, but can be used where abrasive dust would cause problems, or where the size of the job does not warrant using power equipment. Buckets, rubber gloves, and a stiff brush or sponge are the major equipment requirements; a garden hose can help rinse off afterward.

POWER CLEANING

Power cleaners usually use electricity or pneumatic force to speed the cleaning action, and to reduce the operator's effort. Power-cleaning tools include water and steam blasters, wire brushes, disk sanders, scalers, and scrapers.

Keep a *wire brush* moving to prevent polishing a metal substrate. Excessive brushing creates a glassy surface that reduces adhesion. Because wire brushing can spread oil and grease, it's important to clean the surface before coating.

Water blasting, generally with a detergent, is commonly used to prepare houses for painting. Water blasting can remove some peeling paint. Hold the spray wand at a sharp angle to the surface so the water can get under peeling paint. Make sure the building has enough time to dry before painting.

Steam cleaning can be done with or without detergent. Again, wait until the surface dries before painting.

Flame cleaning uses an oxy-acetylene torch to heat steel quickly enough so the surface rust pops off and oil or grease burn off. Flame cleaning is not effective against heavy mill scale. Follow up immediately with wire brushing and the primer coat, because warm, dry metal is quite receptive to paint.

CHEMICAL CLEANING

Chemicals may be used in hand- and power-cleaning techniques. Mineral spirits will remove many surface contaminants, but it must be washed off with another solvent before painting. Solvents are dangerous and unhealthy, and should not be used if another cleaning system will do the job.

One of the simplest ways to clean and abrade a glossy surface in a single operation is to thoroughly scrub with an abrasive kitchen cleanser, then allow to dry.

Trisodium phosphate (TSP) is a popular cleaner because it emulsifies greasy dirt. TSP must be rinsed off with water because it interferes with paint adhesion. Other alkali cleaners include caustic sodas and silicated alkali. Commercial cleaners may contain mildewicides. Heating the cleaning solution to 150 to 200°F will greatly speed the action. Do not use alkali cleaners on aluminum or stainless steel.

A clear rinse after applying the alkali cleaner is essential. Use pH paper to check that the surface is neutral before painting.

Acid cleaning can be used on steel and masonry. Pickling with phosphoric acid is a good way to remove rust from steel and etch the metal at the same time. Spray, wipe, or rinse 5 to 7 percent acid by weight onto the surface. A dry, grayish-white powder should remain on the surface afterward. If you see a sticky residue, the acid was too strong.

Muriatic acid, a generic name for hydrochloric acid, is used to clean scrap mortar from masonry.

Paint remover can be used to strip a thick paint buildup that could otherwise cause alligatoring (see Stripping Paint, below).

ABRASIVE BLASTING

Abrasive blasters propel small particles of abrasives against a substrate. The process takes more equipment and labor than most cleaning systems, but it's far and away the best cleaning technique for surfaces like rusty steel. Abrasive blasting is also highly effective for removing dirt and paint from masonry. Use blasting cautiously because it creates dangerous dust, can penetrate rusted steel, and will accelerate the weathering of masonry.

Choose the abrasive according to the job. Sharp particles cut better; round particles are better for polishing. Cutting is preferred for paint preparation because it removes material faster and increases the tooth.

The four degrees of abrasive blasting for steel are:

- white metal—removes all coating and corrosion
- near-white metal—removes about 95 percent of coating and corrosion
- commercial blast—removes about 2/3 of visible contamination
- brush-off blast—removes loose contamination, mill scale, and coating

STRIPPING PAINT

Paint stripping is an adventure in an unknown amount of work and misery, and that's a good reason to leave the job to dip strippers if possible. Otherwise, try to bid these jobs on the basis of time and materials, as you can never tell how hard they will be. (See Paint and Varnish Strippers, page 100.)

The objective in stripping paint is to minimize effort, use of toxic chemicals, and damage to the substrate. The job will vary with the existing coating, substrate, and remover. Multiple coats of paint can be a real nightmare, especially on an intricate surface. You may need several coats of stripper, and even then paint can cling in the grooves, only to become glaringly obvious when stain is applied.

Prepare to strip by removing all hardware, covering the floor, and scraping off any flaking paint. Try to strip an entire surface at one time. For intricate work, find knives, scrapers, or anything else with the contour of the wood. On fine work, make sure the paint is soft enough so you can strip with minimal scraping—otherwise you can gouge the wood.

Make provisions for good ventilation, then use this procedure:

1. Apply the stripper with an old brush, and give it time to work. Do not spread it around more than necessary.

2. After a few minutes, scrape the surface with the grain, using a putty knife or steel wool.

3. Use repeated applications on heavy buildups, and scrape after each one.

4. Scrub off with steel wool and water, adding a nonfoaming detergent. Then scrub the surface with clear water and steel wool. Remove all traces of stripper while the wood is wet, and keep the entire surface wet until you are finished.

5. Use wood bleach if needed to lighten the wood.

Warning: Removers can burn your skin, clothing, and adjacent surfaces. Use rubber gloves, respirator, goggles, and caution. Read the label and take it seriously. Use special caution with flammable removers. Take care with surrounding objects—some paint removers can etch glass. Do not use stripper containing the extremely toxic chemical methylene chloride.

Paint can also be removed with heat from an electric gun or propane torch. Use care—the goal is not to burn the paint but to soften it for removal with a scraper. A propane torch can cause a fire or scorch the wood. Remove paint some other way if you plan to use a clear finish on the wood. Keep a hose or fire extinguisher handy, and do not direct the flame toward paint remover, which is flammable. Keep the flame moving, and when the paint starts to blister, immediately attack it with the scraper.

STRIPPING WALLPAPER

The method for stripping wallpaper depends on the nature of the paper. The paste on many plain wallpapers can be softened by applying water with a wide brush, sponge, or spray hose. Steam may be used to liquify adhesives, but steamers are heavy and can take some time to work. Enzyme strippers attack wheat paste, but not all modern adhesives. Test first. Once the paste is liquefied by water, steam, or enzyme, it is a relatively simple matter to remove the paper. Be sure to clean the wall with TSP and rinse before priming.

If some old paper refuses to be removed, you may be able to feather its edges with fine sandpaper. An alternative is to smooth off the wall with joint compound after stripping. But it's best to remove all the old paper.

Strippable paper can be pulled down in large sheets.

Composite plastic-fabric and other papers may also be pulled from the wall in whole sheets.

To remove *standard wallpaper* (the type without a washable surface), use a steamer or enzyme stripper.

Washable wallpaper (paper coated with acrylic or vinyl) is difficult to remove because water and steam cannot penetrate through the coating to reach the glue. To solve this problem, score the surface with a knife, a tool called a "paper tiger," or coarse sandpaper. It's possible that denatured alcohol will remove enough of the coating to allow steam to penetrate. Experiment for the best method before devoting too much effort to one.

Painted wallpaper can be treated like washable paper.

Paper-backed vinyl can be attacked by peeling off the vinyl and wetting or steaming the remaining paper layer.

If you encounter several layers, use the above suggestions on the various layers as you reach them.

Caulking Procedure

Caulking is a part of most residential painting jobs. It can also be used indoors as a quick and dirty means of patching cracks between walls and trim. Use a paintable latex caulk for this purpose.

1. Remove old caulk, dirt, dust, and all other foreign matter. Clean with a whisk broom or compressed air. Fill wide cracks with caulking backer.

2. Cut the tube tip at 45°—slightly smaller than the gap you are caulking. Pierce the seal inside the tube with a long nail.

3. Hold the gun at 45° to the surface and engage the handle. Move along the joint at a speed that fills the joint without spilling too much.

4. Tool the joint with a putty knife, moistened finger (for water-cleanup material), or a rag dampened in the correct solvent.

5. Clean spillage before it sets with a rag moistened in water or solvent.

6. After curing, cut away excess with a utility knife or scraper.

Paint Application

One key to a profitable painting business is knowing how to allocate time, personnel, materials, and equipment in the most efficient manner. When planning the application, take into account whether the area is occupied and/or contains furniture, finish flooring, and other fragile items that may slow you down. Also figure in the amount of surface preparation needed for each area, the type of coating material, the number of coats, and the quality of job required. For exterior work, you must take the weather into account. Trees and shrubs may need pruning or protection.

Although paints in general dry faster than they used to, drying time remains a key consideration in planning a paint job. Try to schedule so one coat is drying while another area is being applied.

Talk to other contractors so you can have the building to yourself; this prevents dust and confusion.

WEATHER CONDITIONS

The conditions during application and drying must be within the range described on the paint can. Ideal drying conditions are a light breeze, 70°F, and low humidity. Do not paint when relative humidity exceeds 85 percent.

At high temperatures, paint becomes less viscous, and tends to apply too thinly. Avoid painting in strong summer sunlight because solvent can evaporate too fast and cause bubbles; move around the building to stay in the shade. Gloss may be reduced by moisture and extreme temperatures during curing. To paint with latex in hot, sunny conditions, spray the surface a few minutes before painting to cool it. (Latex paint is an exception to the rule that damp surfaces should never be painted.)

At cool temperatures, paint is likely to run due to increased viscosity and slow drying. Do not paint if freezing conditions are likely before the paint dries. Latex paints cannot react chemically to create a film below 50°F. A good rule of thumb is not to apply latex below 55°F and solvent-based paint below 50°F—but consult the label to be sure.

High humidity has two important effects. It slows drying of many types of paint, and increases the chance of surface moisture. Metal below 40°F is likely to have condensation, even if it appears dry. Use a heated structure, an infra-red heater, or a flame dehydrater to prepare cold metal for painting. Never paint a moist surface (except with latex paint). Never paint an icy surface.

Strong drafts during drying may affect the luster of interior paint. Wind can blow insects or dust into exterior paint. Wind can also interfere with spray painting, particularly air-atomization. The main problem may be increased overspray, which can damage nearby surfaces and/or reduce adhesion.

PREPARING THE SHOP AND JOB

It's a good idea to prepare a shop area at the job for pouring and mixing paint, and cleaning tools. Find an isolated area, away from children and animals. Remove anything paint could damage. Cover the floor with plastic (to prevent bleed-through) and a cloth drop cloth (to prevent tracking paint into the premises). Weight the corners of the tarp.

Try to keep the shop area neat, so you can find tools easily and avoid spills and mistakes. Cover the shop when the day is done to avoid attracting children and vandals. Keep handy a good supply of rags and cleaning solvent for spills and drips.

In preparing the area to be painted, the goal is to make enough room so you can work without worrying about spills or spatters. Use the following procedure:

1. Remove anything portable that needs protection. Move remaining furniture to the center, and cover with a clean plastic dropcloth, preferably fresh from the package. Cover the plastic with a cloth drop, to hold the plastic in place and absorb wet paint.

2. Mask the baseboards or carpet (if the baseboards will be painted). If you are painting the ceiling and walls, lay drop cloths on everything in the room. To paint walls alone, get a long, narrow drop cloth (a "runner").

3. Remove wall plates and lighting fixtures. Put masking tape over the exposed parts of electric outlets. Mask a ceiling fixture by shutting off the power and loosening the screws holding the base plate to the ceiling. Treat the fixture gingerly—insulation on old wiring can break and cause a short circuit. Mask the base plate and cover the rest of the fixture with lightweight plastic sheeting. (Never use a light that's shrouded this way, as it can quickly overheat.)

4. With a broom and putty knife, examine the room for accumulations of dirt, cracks, protruding nails, peeling paint, rotted

plaster, or anything else that will interfere with adhesion of the new paint or the appearance of the job.

5. Sweep off all horizontal surfaces, such as head jambs and baseboards. Look for cobwebs and remove them.

6. Wash all old surfaces with TSP or the equivalent and rinse.

7. Patch cracks in plaster and drywall (see Part E). Caulk small cracks between the trim and walls with white latex caulk, which dries quickly, needs no primer, and can be painted in half an hour or so.

8. If you have found peeling, alligatored, or otherwise damaged paint, it's time to deal with that. First scrape with paint scraper, power sander, or wire brush or water blaster (for exterior paint). Whatever method you use, make sure the paint is fully removed.

9. Look for glossy surfaces, and dull with fine sandpaper or "liquid sandpaper."

10. Use the other preparation suggestions in Preparing and Painting Common Surfaces, starting on page 186.

MIXING

Some paint, including many latexes, needs little or no mixing. Other paint must be mixed to blend all components and to ensure even coloration. Paint with heavy pigment may need considerable mixing.

Mix paint manually or by machine. Manual mixing is effective for containers up to 5 gallons. A paint mixer may be fastened to an electric drill. Paint stores have shakers that are real timesavers. Do not shake certain materials, including polyurethane varnish, because too many bubbles are created. When using several cans of the same color, it's best to "box" them to blend out slight color variations.

Use this procedure to mix badly settled paint:

1. Pry up the cover and probe the bottom with a stirrer to determine the condition of the paint. If there is a skin on top, cut it away from the edges and carefully lift it out.

2. If a great deal of pigment has settled, pour off most of the liquid into another container so you can stir vigorously.

3. Stir up the pigment, making sure to scrape the entire bottom. Press lumps against the wall to crumble them.

4. Gradually return some liquid and continue stirring. Pour the liquid back into the other container and check the sediment.

5. When all pigment is liquified, pour from one container to the other to ensure full mixing.

6. Strain the paint if lumps are visible.

A good trick for keeping the can rim clean is to punch a few holes in the rim with a medium-size nail. The holes allow paint to drip out before it gets tacky. Occasionally swipe out the rim with the brush if you are painting from the can. A clean rim prevents drips, which can hide the label and prevent a seal when the can is closed. When capping a can for overnight or longer, clean the rim again with the brush and rap the lid with a hammer in several places.

THINNING

There are endless debates about whether and when to thin paint. Many painters swear that paint is often sold too thick for good application (and overly thick paint can leave brush marks and sags; it can also wear out the hand). Enamel that is too thick will grab the end of a brush like a glob of glue. However, experts counter that over-thinning is a key cause of early paint failure. Overly thin paint leaves a thin coat, which offers inadequate hiding and protection. It also drips and runs from the brush and surface.

Job conditions help determine the amount of thinner needed. On hot, windy days, it's almost inevitable that you will need to thin the paint, because thinner in the paint evaporates quickly in those conditions. It's a good idea to hold some paint aside when thinning, so if you pour in excess thinner, you can add back some paint to thicken the batch.

PRIMING AND SEALING

Do not take the first coats for granted or skip any necessary steps in applying them. Primer and sealer have important roles in most paint systems: to establish a sound footing for the topcoats, to prevent stains from bleeding through, and to prevent too much topcoat from seeping into the substrate.

Primer on wood and rough steel should be brushed if possible, as this guarantees the best coverage. Spraying is adequate for clean steel. Otherwise, application procedures are no different than for topcoats.

You can improve hiding by tinting the first coat close to the topcoat. If the coats are not identical in color, holidays will be visible, but the primer will increase the color coverage. This may eliminate the need for a second topcoat.

BRUSHING

The brushing technique must fit the substrate, the coating, the brush itself, and the painter's preference and experience. (See Part A, Brush, for brush care.) These tips may help speed the work:

- Don't use the brush to stir paint.
- Hold the brush almost perpendicular to the work surface, but slightly slanted toward the direction you are travelling.
- Hold the brush comfortably. Strive for a relaxed grip, using no more effort than necessary. Change grips occasionally to reduce strain. Paint with wrist and arm motions.

Figure D1 Brushing techniques

a) loading the brush

b) cutting in

c) painting into a corner

- Dip the brush in the can no more than half the length of the bristles. Dipping deeper will cause splatters and allow paint to build up in the heel, and possibly drip down your hand.

- Pat the brush against the inner wall of the can to remove excess paint. Dragging the brush against the rim will remove too much paint and cut your efficiency.

- Deliver the new brushful a few inches into a dry area. It may help to dab the brush lightly on a couple of locations. Then expand the new area to both sides and back to the previously painted area.

- Keep the leading edge wet, work small areas, and return to them quickly to prevent lap marks. This is especially important with glossy paint.

- Don't press too hard—it's tiring and pushes paint to the heel.

- If paint is building up in the heel, occasionally rub it against a dry part of the surface.

- Wiggle the bristles gently into corners, especially intricate ones. Do not jab the brush crudely into corners—this injures the bristles.

- When finishing a section, "lay it off" by brushing across large areas. Laying off catches drips and produces a glossy enamel, but do this before the paint skins over. Take special care in intersections, including window muntins, and on complicated hardware, where drips are especially likely.

- Paint wood with the grain.

- On vertical surfaces, work from the top down.

- Flow varnish on with even strokes, taking care not to cause bubbles. Use the fewest possible strokes, and observe label directions.

- Glossy paint shows more brush marks than flat paint. Use care to keep the edge wet and to lay off regularly.

- Fast-drying paints, especially those containing synthetic solvent, cannot be brushed much. The best you can do is quickly dab the brush in a few spots and smooth the paint before drying starts.

• Protect the brush and paint from drying in hot weather. For a short break, soak a rag in solvent and lay it across the can, with the brush laid across the rim. For breaks longer than a half hour, soak the brush in solvent and cap the can.

CUTTING-IN

Cutting-in is the practice of brushing corners and edges before rolling wall surfaces. A 2- or 2 1/2-inch brush is good for this purpose. The technique can be learned fairly easily—for best results, look at where you are going rather than at the brush itself. Learn to keep an even fill on the brush so the brushing action is predictable.

With some paint colors, particularly dark ones, the cut-in area will not match the rolled area. This problem can be solved by rolling before the cutting-in dries. Take the roller as close as possible to the corners. Or use a corner roller or pencil roller to get into corners.

Before cutting in next to a sprayed acoustic ceiling, you must remove some of the "popcorn." Run your putty knife around the ceiling break to remove the popcorn and make a slight groove, which will become the color joint. Cut in about 4 inches of paint all the way around the room before rolling.

COLOR JOINT

A color joint is simply an intersection of two colors. Two methods can be used to make a color joint: masking tape and a groove in the wall. Start either method by painting the first color slighly beyond the color joint and allowing to dry.

Masking tape works best on nonporous surfaces because paint can bleed through tape on a porous surface. When the first color is dry, draw the line carefully, using a string or straightedge. Apply masking tape to protect the first color, and burnish slightly to seal the tape to the surface. Paint the second color, taking care not to go beyond the masking tape.

To make a slight groove, hold a straightedge along the color joint and scribe with a screwdriver or putty knife. Apply the second color, bringing the brush just to the depression. The paint should be drawn into the groove, but not across it.

ROLLING

Rollers are a fast way of spreading paint, especially for interior walls. However, the technique leaves a "stippled" effect that may be undesired, and it can create considerable spatter.

A roller pan should have a grid so the roller will rotate when you wet it. Dip the roller in the pan, roll it out a bit, and remove it when it has an even coating. An alternative is to place a roller grid in a five-gallon pail. The procedure is the same: dip the roller in the paint, then roll it out on the grid. Five-gallon pails have a couple of advantages over roller pans: they hold much more paint and are a lot harder to step in.

Roll out the paint in an "M" pattern, making the first stroke upward to avoid spillage that can be caused by downward pressure on a loaded roller. Apply in one direction and lay off at an angle, or perpendicular, to the first stroke. The size of the pattern depends on surface porosity and how much paint can be carried in the roller. When the application starts to thin, return across the pattern to even up the coating. Keep the pressure constant. Finally, lightly go over the area to soak up lap marks and other heavy spots. Roll as close to obstructions or adjacent walls as possible without touching them.

If lap marks are a problem (most will disappear with drying, at least on flat paint), dry out the roller ends by applying from the ends after removing the roller from the pan, then continue rolling as usual.

SPRAYING

Spray painting presents unusual challenges to painters in terms of preparation, application, and cleanup. A large part of the work in spraying is not the application but the preparation.

Figure D2 Roller technique

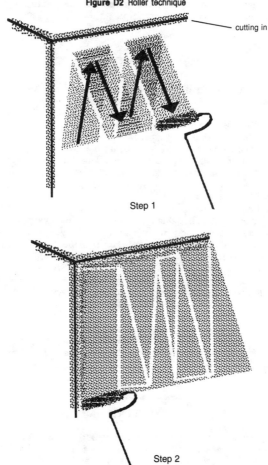

cutting in

Step 1

Step 2

PREPARING FOR A SPRAY JOB

1. Inspect the equipment before bringing it to the job to ensure it's in operating condition. Make sure you have all necessary personal protective equipment.

2. Plan the number of dropcloths, ladders, scaffolding, hoses, and respirators needed.

3. Determine the operating pressure and orifice you will need for the coating.

4. Place the equipment in a convenient location.

5. Take safety precautions for others working in area.

6. Provide ventilation for interior work.

7. Mix paint properly and strain it.

8. Test viscosity and adjust if needed.

Preparation for interior work:

9. Lay out dropcloths on all horizontal surfaces.

10. Place damp newspapers over window panes, but keep the wood dry.

11. Mask woodwork, base trim, light fixtures, switches, outlets, exhaust d fans, etc.

Preparation for exterior work:

9. Do not spray on windy days.

10. Cover shrubbery with dropcloth (do not use plastic on hot days).

11. Mask trim, windows, etc. Move any vehicles that could be painted with drift.

SIX ESSENTIALS OF SPRAY PAINTING

Control of the following factors will simplify both air-atomization and airless spray painting.

- Travel speed: move the gun smoothly (the rate depends on distance from the work, deposition rate for the equipment and material, and desired wet film thickness).

- Arm motion: move the gun evenly from your shoulder (or move your whole body). If you swing from just the elbow, the gun will arc and the deposit will be thicker at the center than the edges.

- The correct angle: keep the gun perpendicular to the surface. "Arcing" is holding the gun nonsquare to the surface, when seen from above. "Tilting" is failing to hold the gun so it sprays horizontally. Either problem will deposit an uneven coating.

- The correct distance from the work: the distance reflects travel speed, equipment type and setup, and coating material. Short distance increases deposition rate, encouraging sags and runs and requiring faster travel. Excess distance encourages dusting, a partial drying before the paint reaches the surface that increases bounce-back. The distance is usually greater for airless guns (10 to 15 inches) than air-atomization guns (6 to 8 inches). Once you establish the correct distance, maintain it for the whole project.

- The correct overlap: usually about 50 percent over the previous stroke. You can get this overlap by aiming the center of each stroke at the edge of the previous one.

- The correct timing: trigger the gun before it begins passing across the area to be painted, and release the trigger when the gun has passed beyond the work and is still moving.

SPRAYING TECHNIQUE

The principles of spray application must be adapted for various shapes. Start spraying a *panel* by "banding" its vertical edges. This will reduce waste at the beginning and end of each horizontal stroke.

Spray a *long panel* with vertical strokes. If you use horizontal strokes, overlap strokes from the left and right in an area about 4 inches wide.

Figure D3 Spray techniques

a) correct: hold gun
perpendicular to work

coating should be wet and
consistent on the surface

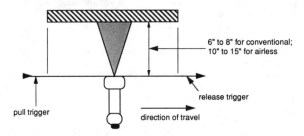

6" to 8" for conventional;
10" to 15" for airless

pull trigger

release trigger

direction of travel

b) incorrect--gun follows an arc
coating will be uneven

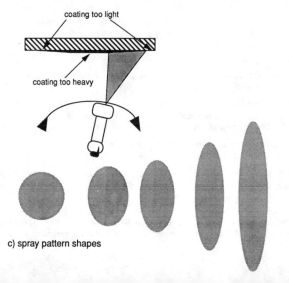

coating too light

coating too heavy

c) spray pattern shapes

To spray a three-dimensional object like a *box*, start by painting the corners head-on. Then spray each panel individually.

Vertical surfaces are easier to spray than horizontal ones. Tilt a horizontal surface as far as possible toward vertical. Otherwise, begin spraying from the closer side and work away from you. This procedure allows overspray to land on an uncoated area, rather than on new finish. Hold the gun as horizontally as possible. A siphon gun can clog if tilted too much, although special cups are available to remedy this problem.

To spray a cabinet, spray the insides first, next the back, and finally the face. Spraying directly into inside corners will leave an uneven coating. If you need a very even coating, spray perpendicular to each panel where it meets the inside corner. Low air pressure on an air-atomization system will reduce bounce-back from inside corners.

AIR-ATOMIZATION TECHNIQUE

The adjustment of air spray equipment depends on its type. In many cases, the orifice recommended in a chart may be inappropriate. If you are losing control because too much material is being deposited, select a smaller orifice. If the pattern is starved, select a larger orifice.

Adjust a *siphon system* with this procedure:

1. Set the atomization pressure at about 25 psi, and test-spray a small area.

2. If the material does not atomize sufficiently, increase the pressure about 10 psi and try again. To increase the atomization, reduce the fluid flow by slightly closing the fluid control knob.

3. When atomization is correct, adjust the fan width by using the fan width adjusting screw (if present).

If you cannot get the paint to atomize, it might need thinning. Excess pressure (above about 50 to 60 psi) wastes material and produces too much overspray.

Try to use minimum fluid and air pressure in a *pressure-feed system*. Excess pressure will increase bounce-back and drift. The fluid control should remain wide open. Adjust the fluid and air pressure,

Figure D4 Spraying shapes

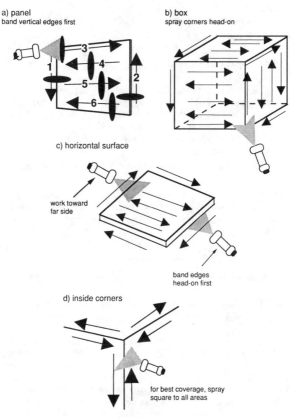

a) panel
band vertical edges first

b) box
spray corners head-on

c) horizontal surface

work toward far side

band edges head-on first

d) inside corners

for best coverage, spray square to all areas

and the fluid orifice, to control the pattern size and the degree of atomization.

Use this procedure to start up and adjust a pressure-feed system:

1. Choose the correct fluid nozzle according to manufacturer's directions or the tables in Part A.

2. Set the fluid pressure for your paint at its viscosity. To get a rough idea of correct fluid pressure, remove the air cap, leaving the fluid nozzle in place. Pull the trigger and increase the fluid pressure until a stream of paint shoots out straight for about 3 feet. If the stream runs straight farther than this, reduce the fluid pressure because the paint is probably flowing too fast for good atomization. When the pressure is adjusted, replace the air cap.

3. Set atomization pressure at about 25 psi, and test atomization by spraying against a piece of cardboard.

4. If the material does not atomize sufficiently, increase the air pressure about 10 psi and try again. You can reduce the fluid flow to increase atomization by slightly closing the fluid control knob.

5. When the atomization is sufficient, adjust the fan width by using the fan-width adjusting screw (if present).

6. Change the pattern orientation if necessary by rotating the nozzle.

A few practice runs on cardboard or newspaper will allow you to get the feel of the particular paint and equipment combination.

An *ideal spray pattern*, also called a fan, covers a long, narrow oval. The edges are finely feathered, and the oval is symmetrical. On an external-mix air cap, you can alter the pattern by screwing the side port (spreader) adjusting valve. This valve controls the air supply to the side port holes in the wings. Air from these holes compresses the fan, so opening the valve makes the oval longer and narrower. One disadvantage of the internal-mix air cap is that the fan shape is not adjustable because it has no side ports.

CLEANUP

Shutdown and cleanup are essential to maintaining air spray equipment. Follow these steps if manufacturer's literature is not available:

Siphon system

1. Shut off air pressure to the gun.

2. Empty and rinse the paint container.

3. Place the siphon tube in a container of solvent (water for water-based paint).

4. Start the sprayer, and operate the trigger repeatedly until the solvent sprays out clean. Go to step 7 below.

Pressure system

1. Depressurize the container by shutting off air to the pressure tank. Open the vent on the tank.

2. Loosen the air nozzle, and press a wad of cloth against it.

3. Pull the trigger to blow paint back in the paint line to the container.

4. Pour paint out of the container.

5. Rinse the container until clean, and fill with the proper solvent.

6. Repressurize the container, and spray (with fluid on and air off) into a closed container until the solvent runs clear. Trigger repeatedly to speed up the cleaning.

7. Remove the air nozzle, and clean in solvent. Clean the nozzle only with a brush made for the job. Clean the threads on the nozzle with a toothbrush or bottle brush. Blow out the nozzle with air.

TABLE D3 Air atomization troubleshooting

Condition	Cause	Correction
A. Heavy top or bottom pattern.	1. Material build-up on air cap, partially plugged horn holes, center hole or jets. Material build-up on fluid tip or partially plugged fluid tip.	1. Soak cap or tip in suitable solvent and wipe clean. To clean orifices use a broom straw or toothpick. Never use a wire or hard instrument. This damages holes and distorts spray pattern.
B. Heavy right or left side pattern.	NOTE: To determine where material build-up is, invert cap and test spray. If pattern shape stays in same position the condition is caused by material build-up on fluid tip. If pattern changes with cap movement, the condition is in the air cap.	
C. Heavy center pattern.	1. Too much material. 2. Material too thick.	1. Reduce fluid flow by turning fluid needle adjusting screw clockwise. Reduce fluid pressure or increase atomization pressure. 2. Thin.
D. Split spray pattern.	1. Not enough material or too high atomization pressure.	1. Reduce air pressure or increase fluid flow by turning fluid needle adjusting screw counterclockwise or increase fluid pressure on pressure feed container.
E. Jerky or fluttering spray.	*1. Loose fluid tip or damaged tip seat. 2. Gun (with cup) tipped at excessive angle. 3. Obstructed fluid passage or hose. 4. Loose or cracked fluid tube in cup or tank. 5. Insufficient fluid in cup or pressure tank. 6. Too heavy fluid for suction feed. 7. Dry or worn packing or loose packing nut. 8. Plugged lid vent on suction feed cup.	1. Tighten or repair. 2. Do not tip excessively or rotate fluid tube. 3. Clean. 4. Tighten or replace 5. Fill cup or tank. 6. Thin material or change to pressure feed. 7. Lubricate or replace. Tighten. 8. Clear vent hole in cup lid.
F. Improper spray pattern.	1. Gun improperly adjusted. 2. Dirty air cap. 3. Fluid tip obstructed. 4. Sluggish needle.	1. Readjust gun. Follow instructions carefully. 2. Clean air cap. 3. Clean. 4. Lubricate. See "Lubrication."
G. Unable to get round spray.	1. Fan adjustment screw not seating properly.	1. Clean or replace.

*Most common problem.

TABLE D3 (continued)

Condition	Cause	Correction
H. Will not spray.	1. No air pressure at gun.	1. Check air supply and air lines.
	2. Internal mix or pressure feed air cap used with suction feed.	2. Change to proper suction feed air cap.
	3. Fluid pressure too low with internal mix cap and pressure tank.	3. Increase fluid pressure at tank.
	4. Fluid needle adjusting screw not open enough.	4. Open fluid needle adjusting screw.
	5. Fluid too heavy for suction feed.	5. Thin material or change to pressure feed.
I. Fluid leakage from packing nut.	1. Packing nut loose.	1. Tighten, but not so tight as to grip needle.
	2. Packing worn or dry.	2. Replace packing or lubricate. See "Preventive Maintenance."
J. Dripping from fluid tip.	1. Dry packing.	1. Lubricate. See "Preventive Maintenance."
	2. Sluggish needle.	2. Lubricate. See "Preventive Maintenance."
	3. Tight packing nut.	3. Adjust.
	4. Sprayhead misaligned. (Only applies to MBC gun.)	4. Align sprayhead & replace gasket.
	5. Worn fluid tip or needle.	5. For pressure feed, replace with new tip and needle.
K. Runs and sags.	1. Too much material flow.	1. Adjust gun or reduce fluid pressure.
	2. Material too thin.	2. Mix properly or apply light coats.
	3. Gun tilted on an angle.	3. Hold gun at right angle to work and adapt to proper gun technique.
L. Excessive overspray.	1. Too much atomization air pressure.	1. Reduce air pressure.
	2. Gun too far from surface.	2. Check distance. (Normally 6"-8")
	3. Improper technique i.e. arching, and fanning the gun.	3. Move at moderate pace, parallel to work surface.
M. Thin, sandy coarse finish drying before it flows out.	1. Gun too far from surface.	1. Check distance. (Normally 6"-8")
	2. To much air pressure.	2. Reduce air pressure and check spray pattern.
	3. Improper thinner being used.	3. Follow paint manufacturer's mixing instructions.
N. Thick dimpled finish "orange peel." Too much material coarsely atomized.	1. Gun too close to surface.	1. Check distance. (Normally 6 "-8")
	2. Air pressure too low.	2. Increase air pressure or reduce fluid pressure.
	3. Improper thinner being used.	3. Follow paint manufacturer's mixing instructions.
	4. Material not properly mixed.	4. Follow paint manufacturer's mixing instructions.
	5. Surface rough, oily, dirty.	5. Properly clean and prepare.

COURTESY OF DEVILBISS CO.

8. Clean gun, container, and hose with solvent-dampened rag. Clean buildup from the wings. Do not immerse the gun in solvent; this can damage leather packings around valves and stems and cause leaks.

9. If you have been cleaning with water, prevent rust by putting a solvent like mineral spirits in the tank and running it through the system.

10. Blow solvent from gun, hose, and container. (Some manufacturers recommend that the system contain a slow-evaporating solvent for long-term storage. Make sure to remove this solvent before use.)

11. Lubricate the needle valve spring assembly with petroleum jelly.

12. Oil packings on the fluid needle, air valve, and side port controls with light machine oil (not oil containing silicon.) Oil the pivot points on the trigger.

13. Hang the gun up so it can drain, with the fluid tube pointing down.

COMPRESSOR MAINTENANCE

Daily:

1. Drain receiver and transformer.
2. Check oil level.
3. Check operation of safety relief valve.
4. Turn motor over by hand to check that it turns freely.
5. Inspect belt and flywheel.
6. Replace any worn parts.
7. Clean hoses, gun, and compressor.

Weekly:

1. Check air intake strainer or filter.
2. Inspect for wear and leaks at hoses, fittings, gaskets, and connections.

3. Change crankcase oil when recommended.

4. Check valves and regulators by pressurizing the system and verifying that they work.

5. Check fluid tips and air cap for breakage, damage, and stray particles. Check seating of the fluid needle.

AIRLESS TECHNIQUE

For an overview of application techniques, see Six Essentials of Spray Painting, page 171. The following general technique is applicable to most airless systems:

1. Check that all connections are tight. Make sure the nozzle guard is on and the trigger is locked.

2. Place the pump fluid section or siphon tube into the paint container.

3. Close the pressure relief valve, and adjust the pump pressure to low pressure.

4. Start the unit, and begin spraying on a test surface. The pattern will probably have "tails" at this point. Increase the pressure with the adjusting knob until the tails disappear, but not much higher than this. Excess pressure will only distort the pattern and wear out the equipment. Change the pattern angle by installing a nozzle with a different angle. Change the flow rate by installing a nozzle with a different orifice.

Cleaning

1. Place the pump fluid intake into a solvent container. *While cleaning, never place a rag or your hand over the nozzle—the pressure is extremely dangerous. Don't shoot toward your face.*

2. Release the pressure, and remove the nozzle and tip guard.

3. Start the pump, and let the solvent circulate for several minutes. Trigger on and off to flex the packings clean of paint. When the solvent runs clean, raise the pressure 10 psi and trigger again.

4. When the solvent runs clear, shut down the pump. Then pull the plug or stop the gasoline engine.

5. If you will not use the system for a long time, protect it from residual paint by circulating a half-and-half mixture of light oil and solvent through the system. This also keeps the packings moist.

Maintenance

1. Inspect the air regulator for damage. Make sure the filter and valve are clean.

2. Inspect the high-pressure hose for damage. Do not attempt to patch a hose—replace it instead.

3. Use only parts designed for high pressure.

4. Use a wood toothpick to clean out the nozzle. A metal tool can damage the orifice.

5. Check packings in the fluid section, and replace if needed.

6. If paint appears on the piston shaft of a siphon pump, shut down the pump on the upstroke and clean the shaft. Release pressure in the pump, and snug down the packing gland nut.

TIP PLUGGING

Airless systems can be plugged by dried paint, dirt, or residue. Because some particles can pass through strainers or filters, it's wise to strain the paint before working and to clean the equipment thoroughly afterwards.

Pigments in some thick paints are large enough to plug strainers and tips. A plugged strainer can be mistaken for a plugged tip. If you have trouble maintaining a pattern, check the strainer. Some heavy paints may need to be sprayed with a big tip and no strainer. Thinning may allow you to spray with a smaller tip, giving you greater control at lower pressure.

SPRAY-PAINT SAFETY

In addition to the following guidelines, see Part G, Health and Safety, and "Protective Equipment" in Part A. These guidelines are

TABLE D4 Troubleshooting airless system

Spray Pattern Problems
WARNING: NEVER PULL TRIGGER WITH FINGER IN FRONT OF TIP

	PROBLEM	CAUSE	REMEDY
	Tails	**a** Inadequate Fluid Delivery	**a** 1 Increase fluid pressure. 2 Change to larger tip orifice size. 3 Reduce fluid viscosity. 4 Clean gun and filter(s). 5 Reduce number of guns using pump. 6 Install sapphire insert.
		b Fluid not Atomizing	
	Hour Glass	**a** Inadequate Fluid Delivery	**a** Same as 1 through 5 above.
	Distorted	**b** Plugged or Worn Nozzle Tip	**b** Clean or replace nozzle tip.
	Pattern Expanding & Contracting (Surge)	**a** Pulsating Fluid Delivery	**a** 1 Change to a smaller tip orifice size. 2 Install pulsation chamber in system, or drain existing one. 3 Reduce number of guns using pump. 4 Increase air supply to air motor. 5 Remove restrictions in system, clean tip screen or filter if used.
		b Suction Leak	**b** Inspect for siphon hose leak.
	Round Pattern	**a** Worn Tip	**a** Replace tip.
		b Fluid too Heavy for Tip	**b** 1 Increase pressure. 2 Thin material. 3 Change nozzle tip.

TROUBLE SHOOTING

	TROUBLE	CAUSE	REMEDY
	Spitting	**a** Air in system.	**a** Inspect for siphon hose leak.
		b Dirty gun.	**b** Disassemble and clean gun.
		c Cartridge out of adjustment or damaged.	**c** Inspect cartridge. Contact Binks representative for adjustment.
	Gun will not shut off	**a** Worn parts. Cartridge out of adjustment.	**a** Inspect gun. Replace defective parts. Inspect cartridge. Contact Binks representative for adjustment.
		b Dirty gun.	**b** Disassemble and clean gun.
		c Packing gland too tight.	**c** Loosen gland, oil needle, adjust.
	Gun does not spray any fluid	**a** Loss of air pressure.	**a** Check for leaks and repair as required.
		b Suction leak.	**b** Inspect for siphon hose leak.
		c No paint.	**c** Check fluid supply.
		d Plugged pump foot valve.	**d** Remove, clean, inspect foot valve.
		e Plugged filters or tip.	**e** Clean filters or tip.
		f Ball check valve stuck open.	**f** Clean and inspect pump ball check valve.

a summary of spray-painting health and safety, for air-atomization and airless systems:

- Never store food near the spraying operation.
- Do not eat or smoke in the spray area.
- Prevent horseplay.
- Store paint and rags in proper containers.
- Read and obey labels and warning signs.
- Follow federal and state health, safety, and environmental regulations.
- Be sure all equipment is in top shape.
- Do not use equipment unless you have been trained on it.

Spraying flammable material poses *fire and explosion* hazards:

- Clean up spilled liquids immediately.
- Keep flammable liquids in containers of 1 gallon or smaller.
- Use good ventilation.
- Keep the proper type of fire extinguisher available.
- Read instructions on all materials, and observe temperature limitations.
- Mix materials in ventilated areas. Do not smoke while mixing paint.
- Do not use flammable liquids closer than 50 feet to an open flame (remember pilot lights!).
- Dispose of oily rags in approved containers. Be aware of spontaneous combustion, which is caused when oily rags ignite by themselves.

AIRLESS SAFETY

Airless sprayers can develop pressures as high as 3,000 to 4,000 psi. Never handle an airless gun carelessly or leave it where an irresponsible person can handle it. *Never point an airless gun at yourself or anyone else.*

- Inspect the setup before each use. Tighten all fluid connections.

- Replace damaged hoses and fittings with hoses and connections designed to withstand the extreme pressure of airless systems. Treat hoses with respect—do not kink or bend them.

- Do not remove the tip unless the paint pump is shut off and pressure has been relieved. Trigger the gun to release pressure before removing the tip.

- If you must remove a clogged tip, shut down the pump and release the pressure by opening the bypass valve. Then remove the tip with a wrench.

- Do not spray solvent through the tip during cleanup because the static electricity can cause an explosion. Remove the tip and clean it in a container of solvent, then spray solvent through the gun.

- Ground an airless system to prevent static electricity from building up and starting an explosion by arcing. The compressor power cord must be the grounded, three-wire type. Make sure a grounding wire is embedded in the paint hose (or use hose with a conductive jacket). Fluid pumps and other metal components of the spray system should also be grounded.

- Keep the safety lock engaged when the gun is not in use.

- Always use the lowest pressure capable of doing the job. Extra pressure only increases wear on the equipment.

- Seek medical attention immediately if you inject paint under your skin, whether the wound is bleeding or not.

PADS

Pad applicators can be dragged along a surface to distribute paint. Various widths are available for different surfaces, such as siding, trim, shakes, and shingles.

Most people fill the pad in a roller pan. If you use the special container made for filling pads, tip the upper grid and allow the sump to fill. Dip the pad in the coating, then wipe it across the grid to remove excess paint.

Apply from a pad by making a straight swipe across the surface. Try for some overlap of the wet edge. A pad is a good complement to a roller because it cuts a clean line but does not spatter, and can eliminate the need for masking (but watch spatter from the roller). Use a pad to cut in near trim and color joints, then use the roller for the rest of the walls.

TOUCHUP

Most jobs need some sort of touchup for painter's holidays, drips, and smudges. Plan to take time at the end of any job to make sure the customer is happy with your work. Otherwise, you can hardly expect these people to direct their friends and associates to you.

When the painting is done, make a final inspection. Ask the customer about spots needing touchup and take care of them without complaint (even if the customer delights in finding tiny flaws). Then announce that you are finished, and deliver the bill. The customer should already know your payment policy, and if it's payment upon completion, now is the time to pick up the check.

It's a good business practice to label leftover cans for the customer's convenience. Use the same naming system as on the color schedule. (See Part B, Paint Disposal.)

Preparing and Painting Common Surfaces

This section describes painting techniques for common materials, including metal, drywall and plaster, and wood. It also contains detailed instructions for special situations, such as windows and doors. Special techniques, including stippling, stenciling, and metal leafing, are briefly described.

METAL

Iron and steel pose some of the greatest challenges to the painter, and the reason can be explained in one word: corrosion. Preventing corrosion calls for extensive and expensive surface preparation; it also restricts the choice of coating. Other metals are in general easier to paint than ferrous metals (iron and steel).

Corrosion is the degradation of metal by oxidation. Corrosion weakens metal, damages its appearance, and decreases its ability to conduct electricity and heat. Unchecked corrosion can cause total failure, but even moderate amounts can cause great damage. Corrosion losses are estimated to cost the U.S. economy more than $15 billion annually.

Corrosion takes place in a "corrosion cell," which contains an anode (a positive terminal), a cathode (a negative terminal), and a solution (called an electrolyte) that allows charged particles to flow between the poles.

The rate of corrosion depends on the metal, the electrical and chemical environment, and the effectiveness of coatings. Corrosion is greatly accelerated by the presence of acids, bases, water, and salts. Certain metals are extremely prone to corrosion, notably iron and steel, which suffer the type of corrosion called rust. Metals like copper and aluminum corrode on the surface but are immediately protected because the oxide adheres to the base metal. Under some circumstances, such as acidic conditions, this "self-protection" does not work.

There are three general types of corrosion:

- General attack is a uniform attack of an entire surface.
- Pitting (localized attack) can perforate metal very quickly and is considered the most dangerous form of corrosion.
- Galvanic corrosion occurs when different metals touch and create electrical currents that degrade metal very effectively. Ferrous metals in contact with nonferrous metals, such as steel pipe connected to copper fittings, are subject to galvanic corrosion. In

general, the farther apart the two metals are on the galvanic corrosion table, the more intense the galvanic corrosion.

These measures reduce corrosion:

- Preventing contact between metals that are far apart on the galvanic corrosion table.
- Using effective coatings and keeping them in good condition.
- Preventing water and condensation from dripping onto a surface.

IRON AND STEEL

Paint for ferrous metals should have these properties: a) low permeability to corrosive agents, including water and oxygen; b) rust inhibition; c) ability to thoroughly "wet" the surface; and d) good adhesion.

Ferrous metal can only rust, or oxidize, if oxygen is present. A coating with low permeability keeps out oxygen and other contributing factors, like water and pollutants. While paint films are not impenetrable to these substances, "barrier coatings" are. The effectiveness of a barrier coating increases along with its thickness.

A rust-inhibiting coating has chemical properties to reduce the rate of rusting. "Sacrificial pigments" corrode before the substrate. The most common of these pigments is zinc dust, which protects steel much as galvanizing does. Zinc chromate, also called zinc yellow, is another good rust inhibitor because it resists "creeping oxidation" at the edge of repairs.

Wetting is the ability to adhere to the substrate. Clean steel (free of rust, mill scale, dirt, and oil) is "organophilic"—easily wetted by the organic vehicles in metal primer and paint. Rusted steel is "hydrophilic"—able to absorb or condense moisture from the air and speed up the corrosion. Paint for rusted surfaces must be able to displace water from pores in the metal. Raw linseed oil is one of the best vehicles for wetting rusty steel.

The coating must adhere to the surface. Otherwise, the edge will corrode, and the undercutting will continue spreading and destroying the metal. Adhesion is promoted by good wetting and a well-prepared surface.

CLEANING

Ideally, virtually everything should be removed from the surface of ferrous metal before painting. New iron or steel often has a factory-applied coating of oil or grease to prevent rust. This coating can be removed with appropriate solvents.

Power-cleaning techniques like wire brushing are effective for removing certain forms of rust, but abrasive blasting is widely considered the best preparation for iron and steel. Blasting before priming can extend the life of a coating by many years. Mill scale, a tough remnant of the shaping processes at the steel mill, should be blasted or pickled. (See Chemical Cleaning, page 156.)

Do not use water to clean ferrous metal, as it can quickly cause rusting. A good rule is to coat ferrous metals as soon as possible after cleaning, to prevent rust from returning.

The degree of surface preparation depends to some extent on the environment in which the coating must serve. In corrosive conditions, better preparation (and higher quality paint) are required. In such conditions, use a "white metal blast" technique (remove all surface contaminants). In less extreme environments, a less intense blasting should be sufficient.

Galvanized steel should be weathered at least six months before painting, then washed with solvent before priming.

ALUMINUM

A surface coating of aluminum oxide quickly forms on aluminum. Because this oxide is "self-protective," aluminum needs paint only for decoration. Aluminum needs minimal surface preparation. Use a wire brush or steel wool to remove heavy dirt or paint buildup, then use detergents to remove remaining dirt and grease. There is no need to brighten the aluminum by removing all oxide. Special primers are available for aluminum, but many exterior primers work acceptably. Latex and alkyd topcoats are both suitable.

BRASS, BRONZE, AND COPPER

There is no need to remove a light layer of self-protective oxide from these metals, unless you want to for decorative reasons. Remove any lacquer with lacquer thinner. Remove heavy oxide and dirt with steel wool and ammonia. Clear lacquer will provide good protection while allowing the metal to be seen. Otherwise, use a good metal primer and appropriate paint. Brass and bronze should be primed with a material free of zinc.

HARDWARE

It's best to remove all hardware before beginning furniture or building restoration. Lacquer can be used for a clear finish, especially for brass, bronze, and copper. It's rarely worthwhile to paint glass, plastic, or porcelain, as the coating is unlikely to adhere in the long run. Epoxy paint may be an exception to this rule.

Use this procedure to paint hardware:

1. Clean the hardware with paint stripper and/or steel wool until all paint and rust is removed. (You need not remove all corrosion from brass and bronze.)

2. Wipe off wax and grease with mineral spirits.

3. Mask any areas that will not be painted.

4. Spread out the parts on wax paper or hang them from strings or nails.

5. Spray or brush the parts, applying a little paint at a time. Spraying is easier, better at coating complex surfaces, and faster to dry. Spray from several directions to ensure an even coat on complex surfaces.

6. Do not try to coat everything at once, or you will leave runs. Give the paint plenty of time to harden before returning the hardware to use.

MASONRY

Most sound masonry does not need paint for protection, but paint can be used for decoration, for waterproofing, or to simplify cleaning. The major problem with painting masonry is the presence of alkali, which can injure many types of paint. Make sure the primer and paint are alkali-resistant. It's best to wait six to twelve weeks before painting any masonry or concrete so the alkali can abate somewhat. If you must paint sooner than this, use an acidic wash on the surface. Not all paints can be used over this treatment, and it will degrade the mortar.

The masonry surface must be clean and sound. Remove efflorescence, which results when water picks up soluble salts in the masonry and deposits them on the surface. Prevent further efflorescence by finding and correcting the source of moisture.

Shiny or extremely hard concrete, brick, or stone present an adhesion problem. Abrasive blasting or etching may be needed to give enough tooth to the new coat.

Spraying and rolling are the easiest ways of coating rough masonry, although brushing (especially for the first coat) is the best guarantee of complete coverage.

Latex, acrylic, and portland-cement paint can be applied to damp masonry. You can simplify the application of these materials to absorbent masonry by moistening with a fogging hose or wetting brush. Masonry should be dry before receiving nonwaterbased paint. Epoxy paint can be used on high-traffic areas, like steps and walkways. When painting masonry or concrete steps, add some sand to prevent slipping in icy weather.

Do not coat a basement wall with vapor-proof material; it can trap moisture and cause degradation of the masonry or paint.

Asbestos siding can be coated if not too shiny. Take care working around asbestos, and use adequate respiratory protection. Remove all dust and dirt, and treat with masonry conditioner before painting.

CONCRETE

Most coatings will adhere poorly to concrete if a good deal of moisture is present. Test by tightly taping an asphalt tile or other impermeable plate to the surface for forty-eight hours. If the back of the tile is wet, or the concrete has darkened after this time, find and correct the source of moisture before proceeding.

Remove form oil and other contaminants with a detergent applied by hand or power equipment. Remove laitance, a deposit of fine cement on the surface of concrete, with a wire brush. Any hardener, sealer, etc., used on the surface must be compatible with the coating system.

Test a heavily troweled concrete by placing a few drops of water on it. If the water remains on top, etch the surface with abrasive blasting or acid, and retest. Use 10- to 15-percent muriatic acid or 50-percent phosphoric acid, applied at one gallon per 75 square feet. Scrub with a stiff brush until bubbling stops, then rinse several times and allow to dry. After etching or blasting, the concrete should have a texture like medium sandpaper.

If the concrete has large pores, they should be opened and filled. Otherwise, the pores will eventually open and cause gaps in the coating. The best method for opening pores is abrasive blasting, but small areas can be attacked with a hammer and chisel, a masonry hammer, or a chipper. Once the pores are opened, moisten the surface and fill with a grout of portland cement and water. Add a little sand to fill large voids.

CONCRETE BLOCKS

Allow concrete blocks to cure for three months before painting, then remove dust, dirt, and grease with detergent. Flush with plenty of water, and allow to dry thoroughly (if using solvent-based paint).

Fill pores in blocks to conserve paint and give a smooth appearance. Use either: a) polyester, epoxy, or acrylic resin filler, applied per manufacturer's instructions; or b) a grout of one part portland cement and three or four parts sand. Moisten the surface, and trowel or rub the grout into the pores. Allow the grout to set and its alkali content to fall for several weeks, then paint.

BRICK

Allow the surface to weather for one year. Remove loose and excess mortar, dirt, etc., with wire brush. Dull high gloss with an abrasive treatment such as blasting. Treat with one coat of masonry conditioner.

OLD MASONRY

Old masonry can be acid-cleaned as preparation for painting, or to brighten the surface:

1. Wet the surface with clean water.

2. Apply a solution of 5 to 10 percent by weight of muriatic (hydrochloric) acid.

3. Allow the acid to work for about five minutes. When the foaming stops, the acid is spent.

4. Clean off with several rinses of clean water.

5. Allow to dry before painting.

A conditioner can be used to seal old masonry before painting. Let the conditioner seep into the surface; it should not build up a coat.

STUCCO

Stucco is a rough surface that can present several coating problems. According to Dave Matis and Jobe H. Toole, authors of an excellent description of the business of painting called *Paint Contractor's Manual*, one of the worst problems is an old type of paint called water-bonding cement paint (BCP). This paint was used on homes in the 1930s and 1940s. Because BCP becomes chalky and loses its adhesion, it makes a poor substrate for a new coating.

Matis and Toole suggest testing a chalky stucco surface by dragging a brass key across it. If the key digs in and leaves a black mark, the paint is probably not BCP. If it leaves no black mark, it probably is. Remove BCP thoroughly with wire brushing or sandblasting. Skip these steps, and you risk having the new paint peel all the way down to bare stucco.

Stucco must be patched and caulked before painting (Part E, Patching). Prime new stucco with latex after a week of good drying conditions.

PLASTER

New plaster should be allowed to dry out for at least four weeks in warm, ventilated conditions. The plastering contractor should touch up the surface as needed. Treat textures, swirls, and soft, powdery plaster with one pint of household vinegar per gallon of water. Repeat until the surface hardens, then rinse with water and allow to dry before priming.

Examine old plaster for defects in the substrate or paint, then wash with detergent or TSP. See Part E, Patching, for repair suggestions.

Alkyd primer is usually chosen for plaster. Examine the surface after the primer dries, looking for glossy spots. If you find them, apply a second coat of primer. Topcoat with a compatible material: latex, acrylic, alkyd, or epoxy paint.

DRYWALL

Inspect new drywall before priming. Nails must be properly covered with drywall compound. Prime rusty nails with rusty metal primer or else the rust could bleed through the paint. Examine seams and make sure they are correctly taped and smooth. Do not scuff drywall paper covering while sanding, as the scuffs will show through paint. Remove sanding dust before priming.

Drywall is sometimes "skim-coated" with thinned drywall compound before priming. Prime drywall with a water-based primer. Slow-drying, alkyd- or oil-based primer is likely to raise the nap.

ACOUSTIC SURFACES

Two types of acoustic surfaces are found in homes.

Popcorn, a fragile sprayed coating used primarily on ceilings, is best spray painted. If you must roll popcorn, use a 1 1/2-inch nap roller cover and thin the paint. Be prepared for plenty of splatter.

Acoustic *tiles* have thousands of small holes to prevent the reflection of sound waves. Make sure the customer understands that painting acoustic tiles can ruin the ability to deaden sound. Vacuum tiles before painting, but do not wash because water will damage them. (Tiles with a water-repellent coating may be an exception to this rule.) Rolling or spraying is suitable for tile ceilings.

WOOD

Wood is classified as hardwood or softwood. Hardwoods come from broad-leafed trees, such as walnut and oak; they are used primarily for floors, trim, and furniture. Softwoods come from needle-bearing trees, such as pine and fir, and are used for millwork, framing, siding, and manufactured products like plywood.

"Hardwood" and "softwood" do not necessarily describe how hard or soft a wood actually is. Softwoods generally have a more uniform fiber structure; hardwoods are usually harder, less resinous, and denser than softwoods.

Many factors determine how well wood will hold paint: the species, condition, and grain structure; the properties of the finish; the application method; and the severity of exposure.

The expansion and contraction of wood caused by changes in moisture content interfere with paint adhesion. Dense wood is more difficult to paint because it expands and contracts far more than light wood like white pine. Ideally, installed wood will have minimal expansion and contraction. Edge- (vertical) grained wood is more stable than flat-grained wood, especially in humid condi-

Figure D5 Grain of wood

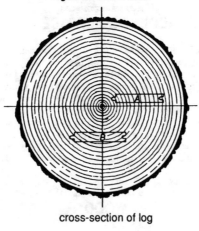

cross-section of log

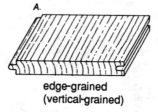

A.

edge-grained
(vertical-grained)

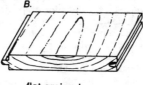

B.

flat-grained
(plain-sawed)

tions. Vertical-grained heartwoods of western red cedar and red-wood are excellent substrates for painting.

Wood with flat grain structure, like plywood or oriented strandboard, has a great deal of expansion and contraction. When coated with resin-impregnated paper, these materials are an excellent substrate for paint.

Many coating systems have been developed for wood. They range from film-formers like paint and lacquer to penetrating materials like stain and preservative. Several materials can be combined. For example, stain and varnish can be used to enhance grain and protect wood.

FINISHING ORDER

The general order for applying wood-finishing products is as follows (not every step is needed for every application):

Product	Purpose	Comment
1. sealer (thinned varnish, lacquer, or shellac)	Controls penetration of following coats	Use on very absorbent wood to prevent blotchy appearance
2. stain (oil or water)	Colors wood and shows off grain	May be the final coating
3. filler (sanding sealer or paste filler)	Fills pores and controls penetration	Apply across grain, force into pores, rub off, sand when dry
4. finish coat (paint, varnish, or lacquer)	Provides surface protection	May need occasional renewal

Interior wood should be stored in dry, heated conditions before it is installed. New, exterior wood should be primed and painted as soon as possible. Do not paint immediately after rain, or in fog. Often, the first step in coating wood is to sandpaper with the grain to smooth the wood and remove dirt. (See Preparing Wood, page 199.)

WEATHERING AND DETERIORATION

Weathering is wood degradation caused by exposure to natural and artificial chemical, mechanical, biological forces and radiation. These forces can alter the molecular structure and mechanical qualities of wood. The first effect of weathering is usually a color change due to the ultraviolet (UV) portion of sunlight. The checks and cracks become pathways for moisture and microorganisms to enter. A layer of loose fibers forms on the surface, and the grain raises and loosens. As weathering continues, boards cup and warp, and they gradually lose structural integrity. Fungi (mold) invades, increasing the gray color. Once a rough, gray surface has developed, degradation usually slows down.

The rate of degradation depends on many factors. Less dense woods in serious exposure are likely to degrade fastest. In softwoods like pine, about 1/4 inch will erode every century. Oak degrades at about half that rate. UV radiation is especially harmful to earlywood, which is softer than latewood. This effect leaves peaks of latewood and valleys of earlywood typical of weathered wood. Sunny exposures and low, humid locations weather quickly. Northern exposures and high spots protected by overhangs weather slowly.

You can minimize grain raising and checking by using edge-grained lumber and low-density species. Warping and cupping are least likely if a board is not more than eight times as wide as it is thick.

Decay caused by "dry rot" fungus can destroy wood. Dry-rotted wood is dry and crumbly, but the term is misleading because wood must be wet for this fungus to grow. Wood that is badly dry-rotted should be replaced, not painted. Prevent decay by keeping wood dry, using heartwood rather than sapwood, and using preservative treatments.

The second major enemy of wood is insects, such as carpenter ants and termites. Paint does not help protect against these perils, although carpenter ants prefer wet wood and can be deterred by keeping wood dry.

Slight weathering reduces wood's ability to hold paint, but it greatly increases the uptake and protection of penetrating stains and clear finishes.

Sometimes weathering is desired for decorative purposes. You can mimic weathering with bleaching oil, bleaching stain, or weathering stain. (For a technique to match new wood shingles to weathered shingles, see page 210.)

PREPARING WOOD

To prepare new wood for coating, set nails and screws below the surface. Perform other necessary repairs (see Part E, Patching). Then clean, sand, seal, and fill as indicated.

CLEANING

If wax, grease, oil pencil marks, etc., are present, remove them with one of three solvents: a) a combination of toluol, methyl alcohol, acetone, and other chemicals; b) alcohol; or c) lacquer thinner. Remove the solvent residue with denatured alcohol. Use good ventilation and an organic cartridge in the respirator with these chemicals. If you wash with water, you will raise the grain and need to sand again (although this will increase the smoothness).

Remove rust stains with a solution of 2-percent oxalic acid (or 5-percent phosphoric acid) in water.

Mildew is a surface fungus that harms the appearance of paint (and signals excess moisture that can lead to other problems). Mildew is found in areas that do not dry out thoroughly (such as shady or low-lying spots), particularly in damp climates.

Mildew is a blotchy and usually powdery deposit. If the spot bleaches out with liquid household bleach, it's probably mildew. To kill mildew before painting, see Shingles and Shakes, page 209.

SANDING

Most wood can benefit from sanding with the grain before painting. Use 150 grit, followed by 220 grit. For curved surfaces, use paper with a soft backing and flex the paper so it can follow the surface. After sanding, remove dust with a painter's duster, compressed air, or a tack rag.

Raise small depressions by moistening them and applying a hot iron. Allow the wood to dry before sanding.

TABLE D6 Exterior wood finishes

Finish	Initial treatment	Appearance of wood	Cost of initial treatment	Maintenance procedure	Maintenance period of surface finish	Maintenance cost
Preservative oils (creosotes)	Pressure, hot and cold tank steeping	Grain visible. Brown to black color, fading slightly with age. Pungent odor.	Medium	Brush down to remove surface dirt.	No maintenance required; color will fade with age.	Nil
	Brushing	Same	Low	Same	3–5 years	Low
Waterborne preservatives	Pressure	Grain visible. Greenish color, fading with age.	Medium	Brush to remove surface dirt.	No maintenance required, painting or staining optional.	Nil, unless stains or paints are chosen.
	Diffusion plus paint	Grain and natural color obscured.	Low to medium	Clean and repaint.	7–10 years	Medium
Organic preservatives[1]	Pressure steeping, dipping, brushing.	Grain visible. Colored as desired.	Low to medium	Brush down and reapply.	2–3 years or as preferred.	Medium

Finish	Initial treatment	Appearance of wood	Cost of initial treatment	Maintenance procedure	Maintenance period of surface finish	Maintenance cost
Water repellent[2]	Best method: dipping. Acceptable: one or two brush coats of clear material.	Grain and natural color visible, becoming darker and rougher textured.	Low	Clean and reapply sufficient material.	1–3 years or as preferred.	Low to medium.
Stains	One or two brush coats.	Grain visible. Color as desired.	Low to medium	Clean and stain bleached areas.	3–6 years or when preferred.	Medium.
Clear varnish	Four coats (minimum)	Grain and natural color unchanged if maintained adequately.	High	Clean and stain bleached areas, then apply two more coats.	2 years or when breakdown begins.	High
Paint	Water repellent, prime, and two topcoats.	Grain and natural color obscured.	Medium to high.	Clean and apply topcoat. If damaged, remove and repeat initial treatment.	7–10 years[3]	Medium to high

COURTESY U.S.D.A. FOREST PRODUCTS LABORATORY

[1] Pentachlorophenol, bis(tri-n-butyltin oxide), copper napthenate, copper-8-quinolinolate, and similar materials.
[2] With or without added preservative. Addition of preservative helps control mildew and gives better performance.
[3] Using top-quality acrylic latex topcoats.

TABLE D7 Characteristics of wood for painting and weathering

Wood	Ease of keeping painted: 1 = easiest; 5 = most exacting[1]	Weathering		Appearance	
		Resistance to cupping: 1 = best; 4 = worst	Conspicuousness of checking 1 = least; 2 = most	Color of heartwood (Sapwood is always light)	Degree of figure on flat-grained surface
Softwoods					
Cedar					
Alaska	1	1	1	yellow	faint
California incense	1	-	1	brown	..
Port-Orford	1	-	-	Cream	..
Western red	1	1	1	brown	distinct
White	1	-	-	light brown	..
Cypress	1	1	1	light brown	strong
Redwood	1	1	1	dark brown	distinct
Products overlaid with resin-treated paper[2]	1	-	1	-	-
Pine:					
Eastern white	2	2	2	cream	faint
Sugar	2	2	2	..	..
Western white	2	2	2	..	..
Ponderosa	3	2	2	..	distinct
Fir					
Commercial White	3	2	2	white	faint

| Wood | Ease of keeping painted: 1 = easiest; 5 = most exacting[1] | Weathering | | Appearance | |
		Resistance to cupping: 1 = best 4 = worst	Conspicuousness of checking 1 = least 2 = most	Color of heartwood (Sapwood is always light)	Degree of figure on flat-grained surface
Hemlock	3	2	2	pale brown	''
Spruce	3	2	2	white	''
Douglas fir (lumber and plywood)	4	2	2	pale red	strong
Larch	4	2	2	brown	''
Luan (plywood)	4	2	2	''	faint
Pine: Norway	4	2	2	light brown	distinct
Southern (lumber and plywood)	4	2	2	''	strong
Tamarack	4	2	2	brown	''

TABLE D7 (continued)

| Wood | Ease of keeping painted: 1 = easiest; 5 = most exacting[1] | Weathering | | Appearance | |
		Resistance to cupping: 1 = best 4 = worst	Conspicuousness of checking 1 = least 2 = most	Color of heartwood (Sapwood is always light)	Degree of figure on flat-grained surface
			Hardwoods		
Alder	3	-	-	pale brown	faint
Aspen	3	2	1	"	"
Basswood	3	2	2	cream	"
Cottonwood	3	4	2	white	"
Magnolia	3	2	-	pale brown	"
Yellow poplar	3	2	1	"	"
Beech	4	4	2	"	"
Birch	4	4	2	light brown	"
Cherry	4	-	-	brown	"
Gum	4	4	2	brown	"
Maple	4	4	2	light brown	"
Sycamore	4	-	-	pale brown	"
Ash	5 or 3	4	2	light brown	distinct
Butternut	5 or 3	-	-	light brown	faint
Chestnut	5 or 3	3	2	-	distinct
Elm	5 or 4	4	2	light brown	"
Hickory	5 or 4	4	2	brown	"
Oak, white	5 or 4	4	2	light brown	"
Oak, red	5 or 4	4	2	brown	"

COURTESY U.S.D.A. FOREST PRODUCTS LABORATORY

[1] Woods ranked in group 5 for ease of keeping well painted are hardwoods with large pores that need filling with wood filler for durable painting. The second classification in the table applies to woods filled in this manner.

[2] Plywood, lumber, and fiberboard with overlay or low-density surface.

TABLE D8 Suitability of finishing methods for exterior wood surfaces[1]

Type of wood	Water-repellent preservative		Stains		Paints	
	Suitability	Expected life (yr)[2]	Suitability	Expected life (yr)[3]	Suitability	Expected life (yr)[4]
Siding: Cedar and redwood						
Smooth (vertical grain)	high	1-2	moderate	2-4	high	4-6
Rough-sawn or weathered	high	2-3	excellent	5-8	moderate	3-5
Pine, fir, spuce, etc.:						
Smooth (flat grain)	high	1-2	low	2-3	moderate	3-5
Rough (flat grain)	high	2-3	high	4-7	moderate	3-5
Shingles						
Sawn	high	2-3	excellent	4-8	moderate	3-5
Split	high	1-2	excellent	4-8	-	-
Plywood (Douglas fir and Southern pine)						
Sanded	low	1-2	moderate	2-4	moderate	3-5
Textured (smooth)	low	1-2	moderate	2-4	moderate	3-5
Textured (rough-sawn)	low	2-3	high	4-8	moderate	3-5
Medium-density overlay[5]	-	-	-	-	excellent	6-8
Plywood (red cedar)						
Sanded	low	1-2	moderate	2-4	moderate	3-5
Textured (smooth)	low	1-2	moderate	2-4	moderate	3-5
Textured (rough sawn)	low	2-3	excellent	5-8	moderate	3-5

TABLE D8 (continued)

Type of wood	Water-repellent preservative		Stains		Paints	
	Suitability	Expected life (yr)[2]	Suitability	Expected life (yr)[3]	Suitability	Expected life (yr)[4]
Hardboard (medium density)[6]						
Smooth						
Unfinished	–	–	–	–	high	4-6
Preprimed	–	–	–	–	high	4-6
Textured						
Unfinished	–	–	–	–	high	4-6
Preprimed	–	–	–	–	high	4-6
Millwork (usually pine): windows, shutters, doors, exterior trim	high[7]	–	moderate	2-3	high	3-6
Decking						
New (smooth)	high		moderate		low	2-3
Weathered (rough)	high		moderate		low	2-3

TABLE D8 (continued)

Type of wood	Water-repellent preservative		Stains		Paints	
	Suitability	Expected life (yr)[2]	Suitability	Expected life (yr)[3]	Suitability	Expected life (yr)[4]
Glued-laminated members						
Smooth	high	—	moderate		moderate	3–4
Rough	high	—	high		moderate	3–4
Waferboard	—	—	low	1–3	moderate	2–4

COURTESY U.S.D.A. FOREST PRODUCTS LABORATORY

[1] This table is a compilation of data from the observations of many researchers. Expected life predictions are for average continental U.S. location; expected life will vary in extreme climates or exposure (desert, seashore, deep woods, etc.).

[2] Development of mildew on the surface indicates a need for refinishing.

[3] Smooth, unweathered surfaces are generally finished with only one coat of stain, but roughsawn or weathered surfaces, being more adsorptive, can be finished with two coats, with the second coat applied while the first coat is still wet.

[4] Expected life of two coats, one primer and one topcoat. Applying a second topcoat (three-coat job) will approximately double the life.

[5] Top-quality acrylic latex paints will have best durability.

[6] Medium-density overlay is generally painted.

[7] Semi-transparent stains are not suitable for hardboard. Solid color stains (acrylic latex) will perform like paints. Paints are preferred. Exterior millwork, such as windows, should be factory treated according to Industry Standard IS4-81. Other trim should be liberally treated by brushing before painting.

Earlywood can be compressed during planing at the sawmill. Grain affected by this "machining stress" will rise after it absorbs moisture. If you dampen new wood, then sand it, you will remove the machining stress and prevent the grain from rising again when the wood absorbs environmental moisture.

FILLING

Filler (not "hole-filler") can be applied to close the pores of open-pore wood after sanding and before staining. Be sure to select an exterior filler material for use outdoors. Interior products are not suited to exterior temperature and/or moisture. Use this procedure:

1. Brush filler into the wood, working across the grain.

2. After the sheen is dull, remove surplus filler. Wipe first across the grain (to push filler into the pores), then with the grain.

3. Allow the filler to dry completely, sand lightly, and finish.

SEALING

Seal (or stain and seal) wood before filling cracks or holes. This prevents the wood from absorbing oil or solvent from the patching material, which reduces durability and leaves voids for dirt to gather. Seal wood with pronounced soft spring growth and hard summer growth (such as fir plywood) to prevent uneven buildup of topcoats. Uneven buildup can weaken the surface, and some areas will be lighter and others darker. Seal with one or two coats of acrylic primer-sealer, oil or alkyd primer, or thinned varnish.

To seal bleeding pitch or knots, use aluminum paint or regular sealer. For the best job, spot seal the bleeding spots first, then seal the entire surface.

PLYWOOD AND PARTICLE BOARD

Rough-sawn plywood, commonly used for exterior walls, can be protected quite effectively with penetrating stain. Sanded plywood is only recommended for mild exposures like soffits. Both sanded and rough-sawn plywood can develop surface checks and cracks, which can cause early failure of oil and alkyd paints. Acrylic latex primer and topcoat systems are good for rough siding, but penetrating stains are best because they can seep into the grain.

Both particleboard and fiberboard are manufactured into siding. Some of these materials are factory-primed or coated with resin-treated cellulose sheets. Paints and opaque stains are best for particleboard and fiberboard.

SHINGLES AND SHAKES

Wood shingles and shakes are durable roofing and siding materials, but they need some preventive maintenance to reach maximum lifespan. Remove leaves and plant debris occasionally to prevent wet spots, moss, and fungus. If the dampness is extreme, trim trees to increase sunlight and air circulation.

Kill moss, mildew, and other plant growth with this treatment:

3 ounces trisodium phosphate or 1 ounce laundry detergent
1 quart of 5-percent sodium hypochlorite (laundry bleach)
3 quarts warm water

Use this procedure:

1. Apply the solution at full strength. Keep off trees and shrubs; rinse any plants that are doused with the solution.

2. Brush into the surface with a soft brush.

3. Rinse thoroughly with fresh water.

PRESERVATIVES

Wood shakes and shingles can be treated with water-repellent preservative to extend their life. Copper naphthenate, copper-8-quinolinolate, and 3-iodo-2-propynl butyl carbamate have all proven effective for preserving shingles. Apply only to a dry roof. Wear eye, hand, and respiratory protection and apply with brush or sprayer. Using this treatment every few years will greatly extend the life of wood roofing.

MATCHING WEATHERED SHINGLES

Patched-in shingles can be blended with old work by spraying a solution of 1 pound baking soda dissolved in 1/2 gallon of water. After a few hours in sunlight, a permanent chemical reaction will turn the shingles a weathered gray color. An alternative is to use a bleaching stain.

WOOD FLOORS

Oak is the most common wood flooring material, but ash, pecan, maple, walnut, and certain softwoods are also used. Flooring should be kiln dried, stored in a heated building, and protected from moisture during and after installation. The atmosphere in the new building must be stabilized before a wood floor is installed, with temperatures above 65°F. All plaster, masonry, and concrete should be fully cured.

If an unprotected floor absorbs moisture, the expansion will crush the wood cells against adjacent boards. When the boards dry out, this "compression set" will leave permanent gaps between the boards. This is why a new or freshly-sanded floor must be finished immediately.

The major categories of finish for wood floors are penetrating sealers and surface finishes. Some penetrating sealers can be coated with a surface finish (wax, for example) to prevent damage to the surface.

Penetrating sealers are essentially thinned varnishes that seep into the top layer of wood and leave a low-gloss finish. Two coats of penetrating sealer are generally needed, with occasional renewals. Slow-drying sealers are usually preferred due to lap-mark problems with fast-drying sealers. Because a penetrating finish is below the surface of the wood, traffic marks are usually subtle. The finish only wears when the wood does; it is not prone to chips and scratches.

Surface finishes, including polyurethane varnish, are relatively easy to apply, and can provide good protection against abrasion, dirt, and water. Polyurethane is available in matte, semi-gloss, or full-gloss finish. Make sure not to shake the can, and apply it in a manner that does not cause bubbles.

APPLYING FLOOR FINISH

To prevent moisture from swelling the wood, apply floor finish immediately after sanding:

1. Remove dust and dirt from window frames, doors, walls, and floor with a vacuum.

2. Remove any wax with wax stripper or a solvent such as mineral spirits. Apply the chemical with gloves and fine steel wool.

3. Remove grease if present with solvent or TSP. Rinse off TSP. (Use of any water will raise the grain and necessitate sanding. Try to avoid using water—use a solvent instead.)

4. Keep the room at about 70°F for application and drying. Low humidity will promote drying.

5. Strain old finish to remove chunks.

6. Allow plenty of ventilation, and apply penetrating sealer with a clean string mop or a long-handled applicator with a lamb's wool pad. Make the final strokes parallel to the grain. Remove excess sealer with a clean cloth, and allow to dry.

7. Apply polyurethane varnish with a lamb's wool pad or a varnish brush. Work with the grain. To avoid lap marks, do not let the leading edge dry out. The first coat of varnish may be thinned (1/2 to 1 quart mineral spirits per gallon varnish) to help it penetrate and seal the wood.

8. When dry, buff the first coat of varnish with steel wool to remove bubbles. Then remove the dust and apply the second coat.

REPAIRING FLOOR FINISH

The best rule in repairing wood floor finishes is to start the repair when you can see wear, and before the wood is exposed. If the floor is made of boards, examine lengthwise sections as defined by the boards. The joints between boards can make practically invisible joints between old and new finish. A section of floor that is 50 percent damaged should be totally sanded and refinished.

Make sure to strip wax with a rag dampened in mineral spirits or other paint thinner before applying new finish. Remove the last wax with water and detergent, working quickly to keep the floor as dry as possible.

Penetrating sealer can be repaired rather easily. Apply the sealer only to the repair area, and mop up any spills on good floor. Blend the new work with the old after the new area is almost complete.

Repairing varnish requires a bit more work. If polyurethane will be used over an uncertain surface, apply a coat of oil-base varnish to increase adhesion. Use this procedure to repair varnish:

1. Sand off the problem area to increase tooth and remove damaged finish. Try to define the repair area by the joints between boards.

2. Apply a first coat to the problem area only, ending brush strokes at joints if possible.

3. Sand the new area lightly.

4. Apply a coat to the entire floor to blend in the patch.

WINDOWS

Examine windows before painting. If the wood is so rotten that you can stick a screwdriver into it, the window should be replaced.

Windows may stick due to paint sealing, moisture swelling, or general deterioration. If you are asked to open a stuck window, make sure the client understands that damage may result. You may be able to open a stuck window by forcing a putty knife, trowel blade, or window saw between the sash and the frame. Do this in several places and keep prying or pushing up until the window slides free.

To free a truly stuck double-hung window:

1. Use a window saw to clean dried paint from cracks. This tool has a triangular blade with teeth on two sides; insert the point into a crack and work from side to side.

2. With a nail set, punch the nails through the trim strip holding the sash in place. Remove the trim. (One side should be sufficient).

3. Pull the window out of the track, making sure the ends of suspension ropes do not disappear into the jambs.

4. Scrape the paint from jamb, sash, and trim. Sand or plane mating surfaces.

5. Replace the sash, and check its operation.

6. Renail the trim strip, making sure it does not bind the window.

7. Set the nails.

Before painting the outside of a wood window, clean out deteriorated glazing, remove glazier's points, and sand smooth. To prevent the mullion from absorbing solvent from the glazing compound, coat with a paintable water-repellent preservative, thinned exterior paint, or linseed oil. When dry, apply and smooth a paintable glazing compound. Use special glazing or gasketing as needed for steel or aluminum windows. Wait as long as necessary before painting.

Many painters use a systematic approach to painting windows. You can mask the glass with tape, but for brushing it may be easier to scrape the glass when the paint is partly dry. Be careful not to break the seal between the glass and the glazing, as this will allow moisture to penetrate into the sash.

For most wood windows, a 2 1/2-inch angle sash brush is a good all-around tool. If you wish to get specialized, use an angle brush for cutting-in sash, an oval brush for flat areas, a round brush for metal sash, and a small angle or flat brush for French sash.

To paint a double-hung window:

1. Raise the bottom sash, and lower the top sash. Paint parts that will be hidden when the window is closed. Dip the brush lightly in the can to prevent overfilling.

2. Close the window to within 1 inch of fully closed. Face to the left, and paint all parts of the sash facing you. Let the paint seal the glass to the putty or glazing strips.

3. Face right, and paint all parts of the sash facing you.

4. Paint all the tops of the sash. Wiggle the brush into the corners to paint them without damaging the bristles.

Figure D6 Painting windows and doors

a) window terminology

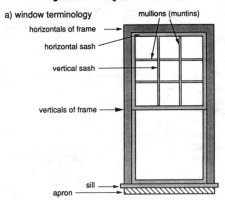

horizontals of frame

horizontal sash

mullions (muntins)

vertical sash

verticals of frame

sill

apron

b) painting order for doors
remove or mask knob
and lockset first

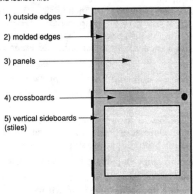

1) outside edges

2) molded edges

3) panels

4) crossboards

5) vertical sideboards
(stiles)

5. Paint all the bottoms of the sash. (Paint the underside of the upper sash with exterior paint.)

6. Paint the verticals and horizontals of the frame. To prevent sticking, keep the brush dry where the frame meets the sash.

7. Paint the sill and apron.

8. Finally, slide the window up and down and check for holidays.

9. Leave the window open slightly to prevent paint sealing between the sash and the sill. Slide the sash open once or twice during drying to prevent sealing.

DOORS

Because interior doors need occasional cleaning, paint them with semi-gloss or satin enamel. For top durability, apply a paintable, water-repellent preservative to an exterior door before painting. Paint exterior doors with exterior trim enamel and interior doors with interior trim enamel. Enamels will show the slightest dust, so cleanliness is vital in painting doors. Avoid raising dust, and use clean brushes and strain old paint.

The best practice is to remove all hardware except hinges, but masking tape is a faster way to protect hardware. A beer or soda can with one end cut off will mask many door knobs rather nicely. If the knob and hardware remain in place, brush away from them to blend the area near the knob into the field of the door. Examine the door for cracks and dents, and fill with putty. Patch deep holes in hollow-core doors with a procedure for plaster or drywall (see Part E, Patching). Sand and seal new doors and trim. If the floor is carpeted, apply 2-inch masking tape to the carpet near the jambs. Push the tape flat with a patching knife when painting the bottom of the jamb.

Once you start a door, allow no interruptions until it's finished—otherwise you risk leaving lap marks. Wedge a doorstop under the door to keep it stationary. Use a roller or brush on flush doors. Use a brush alone or in combination with a roller on contoured doors. (To avoid the stippled appearance of a roller while taking advantage of its speed, roll on the paint and immediately lay it off with a brush.) Paint the top and bottom of exterior doors to retard moisture absorption and prevent warping and rotting. Paint the lock edge with exterior paint if the door opens out. Paint the hinge edge with exterior paint if the door opens in.

Paint a panel door in this order:

1. Edges (then wipe off hinges with a rag under a putty knife blade)

2. Molded edges of face

3. Panels

4. Crossboards

5. Vertical sideboards

6. Leave the door wedged open until completely dry.

Brush a flush door in three parts—top, middle, and bottom:

1. Use a 3-inch brush to apply vertical strips of paint. Leave a 3-inch gap between the strips.

2. When one-third of the door is applied, begin brushing horizontally to cover the area completely.

3. Repeat for the rest of the door.

4. Lightly lay off the whole door in the direction of the grain. Work rapidly so you can coat the whole door before it gets tacky.

CABINETS AND FURNITURE

If they are painted at all, most cabinets are painted with enamel. Cabinet insides may be painted with a brush with a short handle. Start by inspecting for damage and removing or masking hardware. Repair surface damage with painter's putty or wood filler. Clean inside shelves with detergent or TSP, then rinse with warm water. Remove drawers, and stand them on end. Plan to continually inspect for drips and runs, which are quite visible on enamel. When the cabinet is dry, use this procedure:

1. Dust the entire surface.

2. Cut in inside corners with a brush. Use a lightly loaded, 7-inch roller on a short handle to complete the inside. If a stipple finish is unacceptable, lay off with a wall brush.

3. Inspect the inside for holidays and drips.

4. Paint the frame, then the door insides and outsides.

5. Paint the sides of the cabinet with the roller, and lay off.

6. Paint the drawers.

To paint tables and cabinets with feet, use this procedure:

1. Turn the object upside down, and drive a small nail into each foot. The nails will let paint dry on the legs without sticking to the dropcloth.

2. Finish the bottom structure and legs.

3. Turn the object right side up, and finish the top.

TRIM

Inspect trim closely before painting. Fill nail holes with putty. Fill cracks with latex caulking, then smooth with a moistened finger. Stain patched areas to match if necessary. Sand bare wood with fine paper, and dust with a tack rag. Let the dust settle before priming.

A trim guard can be used to temporarily mask edges. The tool is handy, but you must wipe it clean frequently or it will smear paint just where you want it least.

In the "French method" of painting trim, the outside edge of the trim is painted with trim enamel. In the "Hollywood method," the edge is painted with wall paint. This takes slightly more work.

PREVIOUSLY COATED SURFACES

The amount of preparation required for previously coated surfaces depends on the condition of the existing coating and its compatibility with the new coating. If the new coating is incompatible with the existing one, either remove it completely or select a different new material. Painting over an existing coating can reduce the life of the new coating, but that's often better than stripping the paint. To check compatibility of new paint with existing paint, apply about 2 square feet and allow to dry thoroughly. Then try to scrape the new paint off.

A solid, nonglossy coat of paint may need nothing more than a good inspection and cleaning. A glossy coat must be abraded with sandpaper or steel wool to give tooth for the new coat. Repainting is particularly difficult if the film failed at the bottom or throughout its thickness. For example, after cracking or loss of adhesion, you must do a great deal of preparation before repainting. Scraping, flame-cleaning, wire brushing, or other techniques may be needed over deteriorated coatings. Kill mildew with the preparation described in Shingles and Shakes, page 209.

To coat a stained surface, first test whether the stain will bleed or not. Apply a little enamel to an inconspicuous area, and look for discoloration when it's dry. If you see discoloration, the stain is a "bleeding type." Dull the finish with sandpaper, apply a stain-sealing material like shellac, then apply primer. If you must apply paint over varnish, consider adding a softener (such as 2 to 3 ounces of toluene) to the paint to increase adhesion.

PAINTING OVER WALLPAPER

Painting over wallpaper offers a short-term savings of time, but its long-term costs can be great. Strippable wallpaper is best removed, because the water in latex paint can seep into the joints between the hangs and soften the adhesive. A coat of paint will also make it that much harder to remove the wallpaper in the future.

If you plan to leave the wallpaper, test that its dyes do not dissolve in the primer you will use. It's best to seal the surface with solvent-based primer-sealer, because water-based primer can loosen the paper. Apply the primer to an inconspicuous spot, and examine the surface after it dries. If the dyes are soluble, coat the paper with shellac, or strip it.

Some vinyl wallpaper in good condition can be painted, but this material is notorious for disliking paint. Apply an oil or alkyd primer in an inconspicuous spot, let the primer dry, and try to scrape it off with your fingernail.

Enamel paint is likely to show every defect in the wallpaper beneath it, so it's best to strip down to sound paint or plaster. If you must leave the paper on, make sure it is smooth and flat.

PAINTING TREATED WOOD

Contrary to a common misconception, some treated wood can be painted or stained. Follow these guidelines:

Wood treated with *creosote* or other oily preservatives is generally not paintable because the preservative tends to bleed through. A coat of stain-killing sealer or aluminum paint may help. (Wood that has extensively weathered may be paintable. Try a penetrating finish.)

Wood treated with *pentachlorophenol* cannot be painted until all solvents have evaporated. If the treatment contained heavy solvents, the rate of evaporation may be too slow, and the wood can never be effectively painted.

Wood treated with *water-borne preservatives* can be painted or stained if the wood is clean and dry. A weathering period is usually recommended before painting. Special stains are sold for some types of treated wood. Consult the manufacturer of the wood; a bleach may be recommended first.

Special Techniques

STAINING

Staining has both decorative and protective uses. The primary problem with stain is ensuring even penetration, which is needed for thorough protection and good appearance. A thin coat of sealer may be needed on softwoods or end grain before staining to prevent a blotchy appearance or excess penetration. You may need as many as five parts of thinner to one of part of sealer to seal softwood. Test the sealer first on a scrap—it could prevent all penetration—then have the customer approve the result.

Stain often brings out blemishes, such as glue or grease spots, which are otherwise invisible. These spots can be seen if you spray the surface with alcohol. Once the alcohol evaporates, sand off the blemish before applying the stain.

Select a stain by whether you wish to accentuate or hide the grain. Pigmented (wiping) stains hide the grain, and penetrating stains show off the grain. If necessary, you can thin stain or tint it with universal colors. Be sure to make enough for the whole job.

Apply stain with brush, carpet pad, or rag. Rags seem to work about as well as anything, as stain is likely to drip off a brush. The darkness of the stain is determined by how long it rests on the surface before being wiped off. The nature of the wood will help determine how much area to wet. On very porous wood, apply to a small area so you can wipe the stain off before it gets too dark.

If you notice blemishes in the wet stain, sand them out before the stain dries. If the stain beads up over an oily spot, wipe off the stain and remove the oil with lacquer thinner and sandpaper. Then reapply the stain.

Wipe penetrating stain with a clean cloth to reveal the grain, and work the stain into light areas. Let the stain dry as long as the label indicates, then seal, sand, and finish. Sealing protects the stain from sandpapering until the finish is applied.

To stain *previously stained surfaces*:

1. Give the surface a good cleaning with TSP and rinse off.

2. Sand worn-out finish with fine paper.

3. Test some new stain on an inconspicuous area to check color and penetration. Remove this stain with a rag soaked in mineral spirits if it doesn't work.

4. If stain soaks into the damaged area too fast, it will be darker than the existing finish. In this case, seal and stain the damaged areas by blending some color into a little sealer.

5. If the penetration is adequate, blend the damaged area into the existing finish with the staining rag.

6. When the stain or sealer is dry, sand the entire area.

7. Then stain the entire surface, paying attention to achieving even coloration.

An alternative repair method would be to use spirit stain, which can cut into many surface materials.

━━━

CLEAR FINISHES

Clear finishes—varnish, lacquer, and shellac—present a set of unique problems, primarily because defects in the substrate and finish will be visible. Applying a good clear finish may require co-ordination of substrate, filler, stain, sealer, and finish. Wood doors, windows, and trim that will be stained should be "stain-grade," a grade of wood with no finger joints. Use the cleaning and sanding suggestions above.

Clear finishes require a clean room, and this may take some co-ordination with other trades. Some painting contractors prefer to shut off electric power in the building before they start clear finishing work. Many painters prefer to apply stain before trim is fastened to a building.

When you start a day of finishing, begin on the most obvious areas, such as entry doorways. Then work your way toward less conspicuous areas, ending up with baseboards. It's a good idea to strain varnish midway through the workday. Make sure the finish can and the brush stay clean.

Sanding sealer can be applied after stain. Consider the sealer the first coat of varnish—it serves the same purpose but is easier to sand. Smooth the sealer with fine sandpaper, steel wool, or the green "stripping pad" manufactured by 3M Company. Because this pad contains no steel, it leaves no particles to rust.

OLD FINISHES

Old finishes can pose big problems because you can rarely be exactly sure of their makeup. In many cases, the safest course is to strip the finish, but that's also expensive and can damage wood.

Some old varnish can be restored without being stripped. Remove wax buildup with alcohol or commercial wax remover. Wash the finish in mild detergent, mild TSP, or a nonwaxing, nonfoaming soap such as Dirtex. The right treatment will remove the yellowing that darkens old wood.

An alternative is to go over the finish with mild steel wool or sandpaper. As usual, test a hidden section first. When the scratches are gone, touch up and seal, then apply a final coat of varnish or shellac (lacquer will usually not work on existing finish).

BLEACHING

Bleach is used to remove stains (such as moisture stains on a floor), lighten a wood's natural color, or remove deep discolorations. Strip off any coatings first. Protect adjacent areas by taping down plastic sheeting; protect your hands with rubber gloves. Bleach will raise the grain, so you can figure on sanding afterwards.

Laundry bleach straight from the bottle can be used. Powdered bleach is available for use before staining pressure-treated wood. Commercial wood bleach is available at paint stores; follow manufacturer's directions. To use the oxalic acid crystals sold at drugstores, dissolve 1/2 cup of crystals in 1 quart of hot water. Apply the hot solution liberally with brush or sponge, allow to dry, and brush off.

Several applications of bleach may be needed to get the desired shade. When you reach that color, neutralize with a solution of 1 part household ammonia in 10 parts water. Wash with clean water and allow to dry before finishing.

RESURFACING

To resurface furniture, you must generally strip it down to bare wood, perform repairs, and start a new finish. Follow stripping instructions in Surface Preparation, page 154, or take the piece to be dip-stripped. Dipping is harmful to the wood, glue, and patina, but it's effective and much faster and safer for you.

After stripping, examine the piece and make necessary repairs. Then begin sandpapering, working to a progressively finer grade. Finish with steel wool or extra-fine sandpaper until the whole piece feels smooth.

Use this procedure to refinish furniture:

1. Test a small amount of stain on an inconspicuous area. Time how many minutes you need to produce the color you want.

2. Begin working on the main piece, staining a small area at a time. Make sure to blend in the edges.

3. If further coats are needed, apply them.

4. Wipe the piece down with a clean rag. If you see light spots, restain them.

5. Let the stain dry about 24 hours, wipe again, and polish with steel wool.

6. Apply the finish, and build up as many coats as you want.

PLASTER TEXTURES

When restoring walls, you may have to match various surface textures. Sand finish is a popular type of finishing coat plaster that contains sand. You can match sand texture by mixing the sand finish additive sold in paint stores into primer or topcoat. If you start with slightly less additive than directed, you can always add extra sand to subsequent coats if needed.

Texture paint has a thick body that retains brush marks and other texturing effects. Texture paint is good at hiding imperfections in drywall and plaster. Apply with a stiff brush or roller. While wet, texture with a brush, texturing roller, sponge, whisk broom, comb, crumpled newspaper, or anything else that will give you the desired texture. Clean off the peaks with a straightedge or trowel if you wish. Topcoat per manufacturer's instructions.

STENCILING

Stenciling is a process for transferring a pattern from a stencil to a surface. The technique may be used to transfer an outline or an entire pattern. Stencil designs may be placed atop each other.

A stencil is a thin sheet of paper or metal. Use prepared stencils, or cut your own from stiff oiled paper, cardboard, or tagboard. If using nonoiled paper, apply mineral oil, shellac, or lacquer to the stencil to help preserve it. Cut stencils with sharp knife or razor blade.

Paint may be applied with a brush, roller, or spray. The paint can be latex, oil, or almost any other base. If you are interested in stencil work, a course of study is recommended.

Use this procedure:

1. Place the paint in a saucer.

2. Tape the stencil tightly to the surface.

3. Tap a stencil brush (a round brush with short bristles) into the paint, remove as much paint as possible from the brush, then tap it into the stencil. Hold the stencil down with your hand during this step, and make sure no paint gets under the stencil edges.

4. If using a spray can, make sure the masking is adequate. Begin spraying, making the application light enough to prevent sags.

5. Remove the stencil unless applying another coat.

6. If you will reuse the stencil elsewhere, make sure the back is dry before taping it into place.

7. Store stencils between wax paper to prevent them from sticking together.

STRIPING

Striping is a process of painting a thin line for decoration or to separate two colors. Paint for striping must be thin enough to flow but not so thin that it runs. These techniques can be used for striping:

- Apply masking tape to both sides of the line. Mark long lines first with a chalkline and charcoal, which is easy to wash off and will not bleed through paint. Place the masking tape on each side of the line, and press into place with a burnishing tool or roller. If spraying, tuck the edge of a strip of newspaper under the tape to enlarge the masking. Brush or spray the paint. If brushing, make paint slightly dry to prevent runs. Remove the tape before the paint is fully dry.

- A striping tool works like a miniature paint roller. Place a straightedge along the line and slide the tool's guide against it. Practice first, and use steady strokes.

Figure D7 Striping

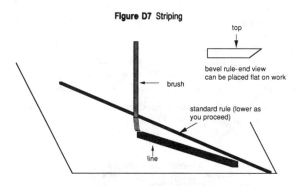

top

bevel rule-end view
can be placed flat on work

brush

standard rule (lower as
you proceed)

line

- A striping brush is a high-quality brush with soft bristle. Dip the brush halfway into the paint, and use a straightedge as a guide. If possible, use a bevel lining rule, which has a bevel on one side so capillary action cannot draw paint under it. Otherwise, tilt the straightedge so the brush slides against it about an inch above the surface. Lower the straightedge as you move the brush farther from the point where the straightedge touches the surface. Make sure the lower end of the straightedge does not wander.

STIPPLING

Stippling techniques leave a dotted effect on the surface. Usually, the stippling coat is applied over a contrasting background color. The equipment for stippling can range from folded-up newspaper to a block stippling brush. Latex paint dries too rapidly to serve as stippling paint, so it's best to use alkyd paint.

Stippling should usually be uniform across the entire surface, but in some cases it should be heavier in the center and fade out near the edges, or vice versa.

Use this technique:

1. Paint the background color and let it dry.

2. Apply a thick coat of the stippling color to a scrap of plywood or metal.

3. Slightly dampen a sponge, newspaper, stippling roller, or brush, and press it into the stippling color, then press it against the wall. Practice the application on a scrap first.

4. Continue until you have achieved the desired appearance.

You can also stipple a single coat by going over it with a stippling roller or brush while it's wet. Or roll on a second coat and stipple it to create gaps so the basecoat can show through.

TROUBLESHOOTING

Troubleshooting is a way of learning from other people's mistakes—and of preventing your own. (See troubleshooting sections under air-atomization and airless spray topics also.) Trouble-shooting here is divided into drying problems and problems of dried paint.

DRYING PROBLEMS

Drying problems show up before the paint is dry, and they should be corrected as soon as possible, generally by scraping off and painting correctly. As a rule, the previous coat must be dry before the next coat is applied. Temperature, humidity, and air circulation all affect drying and curing rates. Because each product has a recommended curing temperature and recoat time, be sure to follow manufacturer's directions.

Drying problems can result from:

- Improper surface condition (moisture, contamination, or poor quality materials)
- Improper mixing of two-component coatings
- Improper application technique (applied too thick, for example)
- Inadequate drying or curing time
- Wrong humidity or temperature

The following drying problems generally show up during or immediately after application.

- *Crawling* is the drawing of wet paint into globs or bubbles. Stop painting until you have isolated and corrected the cause: weather too cold or too humid; poor mixing of paint; painting over a greasy surface; or painting over incompatible coating.
- *Wrinkling* results from the surface of the paint drying too fast, while the bottom layer remains soft. Wrinkling is likely if paint is applied to a cold surface on a warm, dry day. Scrape off the wrinkled paint, and wait for better conditions before repainting.
- *Slow drying* can be traced to old paint, cold weather, or poor ventilation. If the paint truly refuses to dry, scrape it off and correct the problem before repainting.
- *Insects* can be a problem with slow-drying exterior paint. Do not leave a light on near wet paint, as it can attract insects. If the

problem is serious, consider adding Japan drier to increase speed drying of solvent-based paint.

FINISHED COATINGS

Painting over a failed coating can be dangerous—because the same problem may return to ruin your work. Troubles of dried paint are generally caused by one or more of these factors:

- Poor quality paint
- Paint not designed for its environment, such as soft material exposed to heavy traffic
- Paint incompatible with primer
- Improper surface preparation
- Improper application procedures
- Wrong environment during or after drying
- Moisture on the surface (during application or afterward)
- Deterioration caused by aging

Moisture is the predominant cause of paint failure, and it can damage substrates as well as coatings. Moisture can travel through wood and appear on the other side. As can be seen from Table D9, many failures result when moisture migrates from a warm building to a cold exterior. This condition is hard or impossible to correct by repainting (although vapor barrier paint on the interior can help). Structural changes, such as installing vents and vapor barriers, can prevent moisture from moving and destroying another coat of paint. (On metal surfaces, you can assume that the moisture comes from the outside.)

Check these sources of moisture when analyzing external paint failure on frame buildings:

- Water vapor migrating through walls, especially from unvented kitchens and bathrooms
- Water trapped in the wall due to a vapor barrier erroneously applied to the exterior
- Rain penetrating cracks, uncoated surfaces, or faulty caulking or flashing

• Overflowing gutters too close to the fascia, letting water run down the wall

TABLE D-9

Paint failure

Problem	Description	Solution
Peeling	The lifting of sheets of paint due to moisture, grease, chalk on the substrate. Also caused by painting over glossy paint or heavy buildup.	Scrape off loose paint. Ventilate the wall if moisture is the problem. Remove heavy buildup, dull glossy surfaces, clean thoroughly and prime the surface. If chalking is the problem, use primer that can wet chalky surface (not latex).
Flaking	Large chips have loosened due to swelling and contraction from moisture in the wood.	Scrape off loose paint. Ventilate the wall. Clean thoroughly, prime the surface, and paint. Consider a penetrating stain instead of paint.
Cracking (alligatoring)	Crazed appearance caused by not drying first coat before applying second coat. Surface was too glossy. Paint was applied too thickly.	Scrape off paint, clean surface, dull if glossy, prime, and paint.
Blistering	Balloons of paint on surface. Caused by moisture within the wall or solvent evaporating too quickly during drying.	Scrape off loose paint. Ventilate the wall. Repaint with a permeable latex primer and topcoat. (Do not paint in direct sunlight or in conditions above 90°F.)

TABLE D9 (continued)

Problem	Description	Solution
Chalking	Whitish film gathers on the surface and may damage surfaces below. May be natural aging. Abnormal chalking can result from thin first coat.	Scrub with stiff brush and detergent before repainting. Prime severe cases with oil- or alkyd-base material.
Scaling	Separation of large areas due to air pollutants building up on protected surfaces.	Scrape off paint, rinse, and prime. In future, clean surface occasionally with water and detergent.
Mildew	A blotchy growth of fungus; grows best in warm, damp conditions.	Kill mildew with mixture of bleach, detergent, and water. Prime and repaint with paint containing mildewicide. Trim trees to increase sunlight and air circulation.
Sagging and wrinkling	Ripples of wet paint caused by gravity. Caused by excessively thick application.	Scrape and repaint. Do not allow coats to go on too thick—thin paint when needed. Keep paint cans closed when idle.
Discoloration	Caused by rust, bleeding stains, or exudate from substrate.	Find the source of rust—clean and prime nail heads or other rusting metal. Control bleeding stains with a stain-blocking primer. Control exudate from wood with aluminum paint or another primer that seals wood resin.

TABLE D9 (continued)

Problem	Description	Solution
Peeling on concrete porches and steps	Caused by moisture wicking up from the ground (only a problem with impermeable paint).	Interrupt moisture flow by diverting surface water and installing drainage tile. Or strip the paint and repaint with permeable coating (though it may have a shorter life span).
Crumbling of concrete and paint at the same time	Caused by painting concrete when it is too wet.	Scrape clean, remove all rotten concrete. Patch, and repaint when completely dry.
Paint peeling on masonry	Impermeable paint prevents moisture from escaping.	Scrape clean and repaint with a permeable coating such as latex.
Premature paint removal and rusting from ferrous metal	Metal was not cleaned sufficiently before painting.	Clean off paint, and blast or wire brush to remove all rust. Use a primer able to wet the surface.
Separation between coats	Incompatible coatings were used, or solvent in an upper coat dissolved the lower coat, or second coat was applied too soon.	Scrape, prepare, and repaint using a compatible material and proper procedures.
Uneven color or gloss	Inadequate primer coat allowed uneven penetration of surface by topcoat. Moisture on surface caused flat spots.	Scrape, prime thoroughly, and repaint.
Gas discoloration	Caused by chemical reaction, usually in industrial area. May be caused by natural gas, methane, or zinc.	Consult paint manufacturer.
Dirt collection	Dirty spots not caused by another paint problem	Clean thoroughly and repaint.

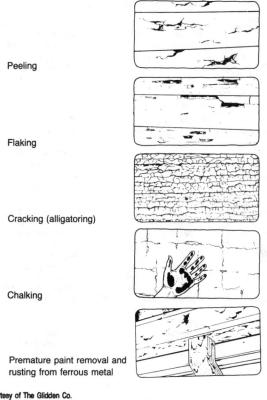

Peeling

Flaking

Cracking (alligatoring)

Chalking

Premature paint removal and
rusting from ferrous metal

Courtesy of The Glidden Co.

PART E

PATCHING

This section describes how to patch interior and exterior materials: wood, drywall, plaster, wallcovering, masonry, and concrete. In addition, the basic techniques for installing drywall are explained. Tools for patching are described in Part A; materials in Part B.

The major difficulties in many patching operations are preventing old cracks from recurring and new cracks from appearing around the repair. Sometimes the hardest job is figuring out what caused the problem in the first place, but if this problem is not corrected, it is likely to reappear.

The goals of patching are to create a strong, durable repair that is level with the existing surface and matches it in texture and appearance. Creating the right texture usually depends on controlling the moisture level (and thus the consistency) of the wet patching material. Often you must wait until the patching begins to dry before starting to texture, because the surface can be gouged if you texture when it is too soft. But if you wait too long, the texture will be too shallow because the material is so stiff. Sometimes, as in float and trowel finishes, you must sprinkle water on the surface before texturing. To make the best textures, learn to creatively use various types of brushes, rollers, stipplers, trowels, and sponges.

You must also ensure that the patch has the correct color (unless it will be painted). Mortar and wood patching material can be purchased in several shades (see Part B for instructions for tinting mortar). Tinting colors can be added to many materials.

The following principles are applicable to most patching situations.

- Remove all crumbling, rotted, or degraded material, but do not damage the surroundings.

- Scrape or sand anything that rises above the surface. Otherwise, small ridges or burrs will be magnified by the patching material.

- Choose the patching material to match the surface texture. If the patch will not receive an opaque coating, the patching should also match the surface color.

- Moisten the edges of the damaged area before applying many water-based patching materials. This prevents the abrupt removal of water that can dry patching before it sets. Moistening is not necessary with a material like drywall joint compound. Do not moisten nonabsorbent surfaces, like cured plaster, because this can prevent patching from adhering. (You can also seal the damaged area to control the suction and give the patching time to hydrate.)

- Some patches should be kept moist after installation to ensure enough water for hydration. This is true of portland cement and mortar, especially when applied to highly absorbent material, in thin layers, and/or during hot weather. Lime-based finishes and drywall joint compound set by drying, so this is not a concern.

- Patching material should be formulated to set relatively quickly.

- Fill deep holes with several layers of fast-setting material.

- Thick consistency is appropriate to deep holes. Thin consistency is better for thin and finish coatings.

Wood

Several types of wood putty and filler are used to repair cracks, holes, and nail- and screw-heads. Many of these absorb less stain than the base wood, so they stain lighter than the surroundings. (See Part B, Wood Putty and Hole Filler.)

Because wood filler can shrink during drying, the wet patching should be slightly higher than the surroundings (you can sand it flush later if necessary). Fill holes early in the finishing process, but after the wood is sealed. If filler is applied before sealer, the wood can absorb solvent and shrink the filler.

To create an inconspicuous repair, keep the filler off undamaged areas. The standard method for doing this is to sand off filler that spills, but because filler is harder than wood, it is difficult to remove without injuring the wood. It's better to prevent as much spillage as possible by using the following method to fill a small gouge, nail hole, or screw hole:

1. Lightly sand the edges of the hole to remove burrs and blow out crumbs.

2. Use two trowels, one to hold the filler and the other to apply it. Withdraw a small amount of filler on one trowel and close the container (some of these materials dry very quickly).

3. Using the second trowel, force the filler deep into the hole. Do not fill to the surface. Work rapidly to prevent the filler from drying out, and make sure the filler firmly contacts the wood.

4. After about 3 to 5 minutes, when the filler is partly hardened, return to the hole and scrape off extra filler. Remove as much filler from the surroundings as possible.

5. Let the patch set hard.

6. Apply a second coat to the level of the surrounding wood. After a few minutes, scrape off again.

7. When the patch is set again, dab in a bit of filler to bring the patch up a bit above the surface. Let the filler set.

8. Sand the patch down to the surface with a sanding block. You should need almost no sanding, and the surrounding wood should be free of filler.

Another option for filling or repairing holes in wood is to use shellac or lacquer sticks, which are available in various colors. These sticks are melted and applied with a knife. They are quite useful for small, quick patches in paneling.

PANELING

Wood paneling can be damaged, splintered, or broken in various ways. Slight damage can be repaired with wood filler using the above technique.

For a larger hole in paneling, saw out the damaged portion and try to replace it. Spare paneling may be stored in the attic or basement. If not, you may have to stain up something similar. Let the homeowner make the final decision about whether the match is adequate. If the damage is large enough, and matching paneling can be found, replace the entire sheet.

The key to removing and replacing damaged paneling is careful cutting and sizing. A circular saw is a must for a decent job:

1. Locate the center of the studs adjacent to the damage. Using a level, mark a vertical line on the center of each stud.

2. Use the level to make horizontal lines above and below the hole so you have marked out a rectangle. To reduce splintering, place good masking tape over the rectangle, then re-mark on top of the tape.

3. Cut the hole with a fine-toothed plywood blade on the circular saw. Cut with the blade set shallow so it does not cut into the studs (this also reduces splintering).

4. Remove the cutout, and measure the hole for the patch.

5. To avoid splintering the surface with a circular saw, mark and cut the panel from the reverse. (Mark and cut from the top with a table saw, which cuts downward.) Cut so you barely remove the line, using a plywood blade.

6. Sand the edges of the cut paneling and patch. Hold the sandpaper perpendicular to the surface, and sand from the face toward the back to avoid damage.

7. Stain raw edges and face of the patch, and raw edges of the cutout, to match the surface.

8. Install the patch into the hole, nailing with 1-inch paneling nails tinted to the proper color.

Patching Plaster and Drywall

DRYWALL DEFECTS

The first problems with drywall generally show up at fasteners and on joints. Corrective measures depend on a proper analysis of the following defects shown in Table E1.

TABLE E1
Drywall troubleshooting

Problem	Appearance	Possible causes	Solutions
Fastener problem	Protruding fastener or bulging drywall, local cracking, depression, dark spot.	Misaligned framing.	Repair framing if possible, fasten panel, and recoat.
		Fastener not square or proper depth.	Be sure proper length of fastener is applied squarely into framing at proper depth, then recoat with compound.
		Face paper punctured.	Recoat with compound.
		No hand pressure was applied during fastening.	Use screws to bring drywall flush to framing, and recoat with compound.
		Lumber shrinkage after fastening.	Refasten and recoat.

TABLE E1 (continued)

Problem	Appearance	Possible causes	Solutions
Fastener problem (cont.)		Drywall core damaged during fastening, bulging due to absorbing moisture.	Dig out damaged gypsum, and fill with patching compound.
Joint defect	Ridge, blister, darkening, or depression at joints.	Edges of sheets damaged.	Remove severely damaged areas, and patch.
		Framing twisted, pulling out fasteners and raising panel.	Screw panel down and recoat.
		Panels fitted poorly and bulging.	Remove panel and replace with right size.
		Tape blistered due to poor taping procedure.	Slit tape, press joint compound underneath, then finish.
		Sanding sealer may have a filler component.	Sand crowned joint until level.
		Delayed shrinkage of joint compound due to conditions during and after jointing.	Apply additional coat of compound until joint is flat.
		See "Fastener problem."	
Loose panels	Sheet not tight against framing.	Poorly fitted panels are bulging.	Remove panel and replace with right size.

TABLE E1 (continued)

Problem	Appearance	Possible causes	Solutions
Loose panels (cont.)		Lumber shrinkage after fastening.	Use screws and hand pressure to bring drywall flush to framing. Recoat screws with compound.
		See "fastener problems."	
Joint cracking	Cracks along center or margin of joints.	Framing twisted.	Screw and repair joint.
		Panels fitted poorly and bulging.	Remove panel and replace with right size.
		Rapid drying; improper taping or covering; or cold, wet conditions during application.	Scrape loose material, coat small cracks with cut shellac, and recoat with compound; or cover cracks with complete taping system and coat.
	Stress cracks in center of joint due to building movement.	Structural movement.	Isolate and cure stress problem, then retape, feather down to a wide edge to hide buildup.
		Angle cracking due to excess compound.	Sand excess compound and fill cracks.
		Tape cut during installation.	Replace tape and recoat.

TABLE E1 (continued)

Problem	Appearance	Possible causes	Solutions
Joint cracking (cont.)		Ridging due to moisture and thermal variations (panels were applied frozen).	Allow ridge to develop fully, sand ridge down, fill voids with thin film of compound over whole area.
Field cracking	Diagonal crack from corner of partition or over structural element.	Heavy blows or abuse to framing during or after installation.	Patch as needed.
		Panel attached directly to flat grain of wide wood framing.	Patch or repair as a joint ridge (above).
		Structural shifting.	Isolate and cure movement problem, then retape and feather down.
		Expansion and contraction due to thermal or moisture changes.	Correct environmental problem, isolate panel from stress, and repair.
Bead cracking	Crack along edge of corner bead.	Rapid drying; improper covering; cold, wet conditions during application.	Scrape loose material, coat small cracks with cut shellac, and recoat with compound; cover large cracks with complete taping system and coat.

TABLE E1 (continued)

Problem	Appearance	Possible causes	Solutions
Bend cracking (cont.)		Corner bead not fastened properly during installation or knocked loose afterwards.	Scrape away loose compound, refasten corner bead if loose, and recoat.
Wavy surfaces	Panels bowed or undulating.	Panels fitted poorly and bulging.	Remove panel, and replace with right size.
		Framing misaligned.	Repair framing if possible, replace panel, and recoat.
		Cracks along center or margin of joints. May be caused by structural movement or twisted framing.	Relieve stress if possible, then screw panel down and repair joint.
Board sags on ceiling	Usually worst in high humidity. Panels fitted poorly and bulging.	Framing too far apart.	Repair framing, or use thicker panel.
		Board too long or thin.	Remove and replace with right length or thickness.
		Insulation too heavy.	Replace insulation, provide support, or use thicker drywall.
		Vapor barrier faulty.	Install vapor barrier in proper position, and replace panel.

TABLE E1 (continued)

Problem	Appearance	Possible causes	Solutions
Board sags on ceiling (cont.)		Nails unseated due to poor technique or wood problem.	Replace with screws and recoat.
Surface defects, discolored, water damage	Fractured, soft, or crushed boards caused by abuse or lumber shrinkage.	Panels damaged by water before installation.	Repair or replace damaged panels.
		See "field cracking" above.	
		Variations in suction magnified by use of high-gloss paint.	Redecorate with high-nap roller, and flat paint.
		Joint darkening due to painting in humid weather or before joints are fully dry.	Treat darkened area with diluted bleach solution. Prime with undiluted latex with high solids content, repaint when thoroughly dry.

ADAPTED FROM U.S. GYPSUM COMPANY'S *GYPSUM CONSTRUCTION HANDBOOK.*
(U.S. Gypsum recommends the use of Sheetrock® brand gypsum panels and joint treatment products. Any substitution of brands may affect application and appearance.)

PLASTER DEFECTS

Some plaster defects resemble drywall defects (see page 237). Other problems can stem from the following factors.

- Poor job conditions causing excessively slow set or drying before setting
- Poor quality materials, aggregate, or mixing
- Lath or structure incorrect
- Application procedure or thickness improper
- Mixing or pumping equipment dirty or worn

The above problems can cause the following types of defects:

- Cracks
- Blemishes, surface stains, and color variation
- Weak or soft surfaces
- Bond failure between coats
- Disintegration caused by moisture

The solution depends on the nature and extent of the defect. Patching operations must attack the cause of the problem to be successful. In extreme cases, an entire wall must be replaced.

Rotten spots are often caused by plumbing or roof leaks. If caught in time, they may be repaired before the lath rots, too. Otherwise, the job must be torn down to the lath and replastered.

Wood lath needs repeated moistening before being plastered; otherwise it may curl up as the plaster sets and damage the patch. Moistening will establish this curl before the plaster is applied. To get around this problem, nail metal lath over the wood lath, or replace the wood with gypsum lath.

REPLACING PLASTER OR DRYWALL

Before repairing a plaster or drywall surface, make sure the substrate is sound. If it is not, the choices are:

- to remove the entire surface and treat it as a new installation
- to tear the plaster down to wood lath, renail the lath, and apply two or three coats of plaster

• to cover the existing surface with plaster or drywall

Two techniques can be used to cover damaged or unpaintable drywall or plaster without removing it:

• Apply 1 × 3 furring strips 16 inches on center. Make the nails penetrate 1 3/4 inches into the studs. Screw the drywall, and treat as a new installation.

• Cover the surface with 3.4-pound, self-furring metal lath fastened with barbed, galvanized roofing nails. Use galvanized wire to tie ends of metal lath so it stays below the final surface. Apply three coats of heavyweight (not lightweight) plaster. Add 2 to 3 cubic feet of sand per bag of gypsum plaster.

CRACKS

Plaster and drywall cracks can be caused by structural strain, poor materials, or careless workmanship. It's important for customers to realize that patching cannot compensate for structural problems, and even a good patch will fail if the true cause of the problem is not cured. Drywall cracking is covered in detail in Table E1, Drywall Troubleshooting.

Plaster suffers from two types of surface cracking:

Chip cracking, a complex of short cracks on the surface, is a defect of the finish coat caused by excess suction and/or slow drying. Extensive chip cracking must be removed and refinished. Small areas can be filled with joint compound or finishing plaster (wet the cracks before applying finishing plaster).

Map cracking is a series of fine cracks resembling the borders on a map. This defect can be caused by weak basecoat, vibration, structural loads on a ceiling, or metal lath subjected to great temperature changes. Pull off the surface, or treat with the techniques below for patching cracks.

PATCHING CRACKS

All the books suggest that you undercut the edges when cleaning out damaged areas, so the wound is wider at the back. This supposedly allows the repair material to key into the crack. However, if you can figure out how to do this in brittle old plaster without pulling off half the wall, you should be writing books for builders, not reading them. Fortunately, patching material chemically bonds to plaster and mechanically bonds to rough edges, so there is no need to undercut. But be sure to remove all questionable material.

Plaster-based patching materials need water to set, so they should be formulated to harden as quickly as possible. When using these materials, moisten the substrate (especially for small repairs) to prevent it from sucking moisture from the patch. Do not wet gypsum lath before plastering.

Patch a shallow crack in one step, using a material that will leave the desired surface texture, such as drywall compound or finish-coat plaster. (Recipes for finish-coat plaster are found in Part B, Materials.)

Use this procedure to patch a wide, deep crack in plaster:

1. Remove all deteriorated plaster. Large expanses that are only slightly loose can sometimes remain, but all fragments must go.

2. If the crack is large, remove about 6 inches of plaster on each side and fasten a strip of wire lath into the crack to reduce the chance of future cracking.

3. Clean out all dust with a brush or compressed air.

4. If using basecoat plaster for the first coat, flick water at the edges of the crack with a sponge, wide paintbrush, or wetting brush. If using quick-setting compound, consult the label about wetting the surroundings.

5. Apply the patching, leaving the surface about 1/8 to 1/16 inch below the surroundings.

6. Allow the basecoat to partly set, and scratch with a wire brush to leave a good tooth for the finish coat.

7. When the basecoat is fully set, apply the finish coat. Use drywall compound, plaster of paris, or finish-coat plaster. Add sand or

other aggregate if needed to match the surface. When partly set, flick water at the surface and float the patch to blend it in with the existing work.

PATCHING HOLES

Many techniques can be used to repair holes in drywall or plaster. The choice of technique depends on the size of the hole and the availability of patching materials.

STUFFING WITH PAPER

The easiest technique, suitable for small holes, is to reinforce the hole with paper, then apply patching:

1. Remove all loose material.

2. Stuff the hole with balled-up stiff paper, making sure the paper is below the surface.

3. Fill the hole with quick-setting compound to about 1/8 inch below the surface. Make sure some compound gets between the paper and the rear of the surface, to cement the paper into place.

4. Let the compound set.

5. Apply a final coat of joint compound, spackling, or finish-coat plaster.

COVERING WITH TAPE

A small hole can be quickly covered with several layers of drywall tape and joint compound. The mound on the surface left by this procedure may be obvious, but the technique is fast and easy:

1. Clean off all loose and ragged material.

2. Smear joint compound about 4 inches past the hole in all directions.

Figure E1 Repair with fiberglass tape

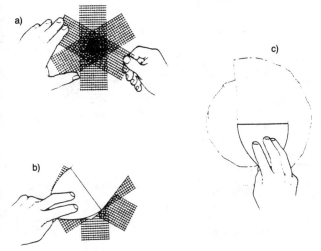

Courtesy of Hyde Tool Company

3. Cut several strips of drywall tape (paper or fiberglass), and embed in the compound. Add new compound on top of each strip, but make the patch no higher than necessary.

4. When everything is dry, feather the edges with a new coating of drywall compound.

5. When dry, sand thoroughly.

PATCHING WITH WIRE LATH AND QUICK-SETTING COMPOUND

This technique is best suited for patching relatively small holes (up to about 6 inches diameter). It makes a good, inconspicuous patch.

Figure E2 Patching with wire lath

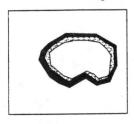

a) apply patching plaster to rear of hole

b) cut wire lath

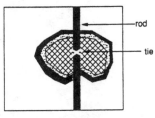

c) fasten wire lath inside hole, bring up tight to wet plaster and allow to set

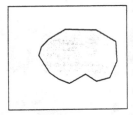

d) fill with patching plaster or spackling

1. Cut away loose material, and remove anything above the surface.
2. Cut a piece of stiff wire lath or wire screen about 2 inches larger than the hole in each dimension.
3. Dampen the edges of the hole, and push back any insulation.
4. Apply a coating of quick-setting compound to the rear of the wall.
5. Feed a wire or string through the lath so you can hold on to it.

6. Maneuver the lath inside the hole, then pull it toward you to embed the lath in the wet compound.

7. While the compound is still soft, tie the wire or string to a dowel or rod on the surface. Make sure the lath remains below the surface.

8. After the compound sets, cut the wire or string and remove the dowel.

9. Build up the patch with quick-setting material, leaving it about 1/8 inch below the surface.

10. Scratch the surface of the setting compound to allow the finish coat to adhere. Make the final coat with joint compound, spackling compound, or finish-coat plaster, and float into place.

PLUGGING A RECTANGULAR HOLE WITH DRYWALL

1. Make a rectangular cardboard template larger than the damaged area, and use it to mark a hole around the damage. Cut along the lines with a drywall saw. Hold the saw so it slants in, leaving the outside of the cutout larger than the inside. This will allow the patch to wedge into place.

2. Use a rasp or sanding block to smooth the sides of the hole.

3. If the back side of the panel is accessible, cut a bridge of drywall to reinforce the patch. Cement this bridge into place with joint- or quick-setting compound, and allow to set fully.

4. Use the template to mark a plug of drywall. Cut the plug about 1/4 inch smaller than the hole in each dimension. The plug should have the same taper as the cutout.

5. Butter the sides of the patch with joint- or quick-setting compound, press it into place so it is flush with the surface, and allow to set.

6. Complete the repair with normal drywall jointing procedures.

CUTTING BACK TO THE STUDS AND NAILING DRYWALL

1. Cut out the damaged area back to the centerline of the adjacent studs. Use a level to make the cuts plumb and level. Cut drywall with a drywall saw or utility knife. Plaster is more difficult to cut. Special blades for a reciprocating saw cut on forward and backward strokes to minimize damage. The best way to protect surrounding plaster is to cut with a circular saw. However, this will create a dust storm and will quickly dull all but the hardest blade.

2. Nail the remaining drywall (plaster is too brittle to nail) around the edges of the cut.

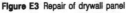

Figure E3 Repair of drywall panel

Courtesy of USG Corporation

3. Cut a piece of drywall as thick as the wall material and about 1/4 inch smaller in each dimension. To repair plaster, you may

have to shim the drywall with strips of wood or asphalt shingle to bring it flush with the surface.

4. Nail the patch into place.

5. Apply joint compound to the four sides. Embed drywall tape over the joints, and complete as a normal drywall joint.

FINISHES

The finish coat determines the final appearance of a repair job. Either drywall compound or finish-coat plaster can be applied to make many textures. Recipes for finish coats are found in Part B, Materials. Observe these general limitations:

- The temperature should be held above 55°F during and after application.

- Basecoats should be roughened before fully set to give the finish coat a key for good adhesion.

- Allow good ventilation after the material has set. If moisture cannot escape, the plaster will be weak and may rot.

- If the basecoat is very dry, it will draw too much water from the finish coat. Spray such a surface with water before applying the finish coat. Or, better, apply the finish coat while the basecoat is still damp.

Trowel finish is a smooth, hard, easy-to-maintain foundation for paint and wallcovering. To prevent blistering, use a quick-setting material. Various degrees of hardness can be achieved by altering the recipe. Sand can be added to make a rougher texture.

To apply a trowel finish, wait until the basecoat is dry. Mix the finish, and apply it to the wall, then double back to make a coat no more than 1/16 inch thick. Wait until the wall sucks out some moisture from the finish, then sprinkle a little water on the surface. Make circular motions with a narrow, rectangular plaster-finishing trowel to distribute the finish, taking care not to let the trowel dig into the surface. Fill the voids as they appear with finish that builds up on the trowel.

Float finish is more crack-resistant than trowel finish, and is easier to apply. A float is a soft, rectangular rubber tool used to manipulate plaster as it sets. Controlling the moisture allows you to control the resulting texture. The wetter the surface, the deeper the texture will be. Using too much water or waiting too long before floating will reduce the strength of the surface. Note that floating is also an excellent way of blending portland cement plaster and many other repair materials against the edges of a hole. A floated repair can be almost invisible.

Put a float finish on walls or ceilings with this procedure:

1. Apply a float finish to a set, partly dry basecoat, and double back to make a coat no thicker than 1/8 inch.

2. Wait until the coating dries a little, and moisten a soft rubber float. Flick water from a brush onto the surface.

3. To make a *swirled float finish*, only go over each section once. Float with arc-shaped motions so each swirl covers only the start of the preceding swirl. Work backwards across the ceiling. To make a *patternless float finish*, make large oval motions without removing the float from the surface.

Spray finish can be applied by machine to match a variety of textures. Test the finish technique before applying to a large area.

Notes on surface finishes:

• Lime putty does not set adequately unless it contains gauging plaster.

• Do not use trowel finish over lightweight aggregate applied to metal lath.

• Do not use gypsum- or lime-based materials, including Keene cement, over masonry or any material made with portland cement.

Wallcovering

Wallcovering can be harmed by improper application, soiling, or surface damage. The following suggestions can be used to repair

Figure E4 Swirled float finish

Start in corner, use stroke order shown, leave only part of each stroke visible.

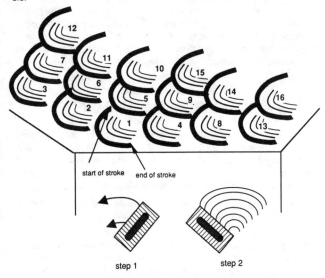

start of stroke   end of stroke

step 1   step 2

wallcovering if it is on a sound surface. If the substrate is damaged, refer to the information on patching plaster or drywall.

In all wallcovering repairs, make sure the paste is compatible with the covering. Vinyl coverings should always be pasted with vinyl paste. Use vinyl-to-vinyl paste to paste vinyl over vinyl.

To deal with a *blister* after paste has dried, cut it at an angle with a razor blade. Try to cut an inconspicuous part of the pattern, using one or more straight or curved cuts, whatever is least obvious. Use an artist's brush to apply white cement behind the paper, then press into place.

Repair *small tears* by applying white glue to the area and pressing into place.

Curled edges at seams can be tough to paste back, especially if they have been curled for a long time. If the paper is brittle, you may be able to moisten it to increase flexibility. Do not use too much water or you might loosen adjacent paste or damage the covering. In some cases, remoistening the paste is enough to bring it back to life. If there is too little paste under the curled section, add some of the original type of paste if possible. After repairing the seam, flatten evenly with a seam roller.

PATCHING WALLCOVERING

Patch small areas of wallcovering with: a) rip-and-cover method, or b) double-cutting method. Ripped edges may be less visible than cut edges. Method b) takes more work, but the patch it leaves is hard to see.

Use this procedure for a *rip-and-cover* patch:

1. Feather jagged edges of the damaged area lightly with sandpaper. Locate a scrap of wallcovering having the correct pattern elements.

2. Tear out a piece of covering big enough to cover the damage and containing the correct pattern element. Tear so only the decorative surface (not the backing) is visible at the edges.

3. Apply paste to the rear of the patch with a small artist's brush, and place it over the wound. The patch should exactly match the wallcovering pattern.

4. Carefully smooth and remove excess adhesive.

To patch with the *double-cutting* method:

1. Tape a piece of covering that's slightly larger than the patch into position so it duplicates the existing pattern.

2. Double-cut around the damaged area with a new razor blade and straightedge. (In some cases it's less obvious if you cut free-hand, because you can avoid cutting pattern elements.) Cut through both layers of wallpaper, but cut the drywall as little as possible. Make sure the patch does not wander during cutting.

Figure E5 Wallpaper double-cut patch

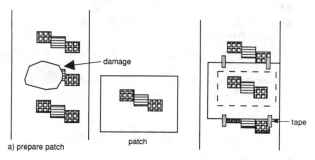

a) prepare patch

damage

patch

b) tape patch in position and double-cut on dotted line

tape

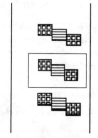

c) remove damaged area and paste patch into position

3. Mark the top of the patch (if it's not obvious), then take the piece down.

4. Remove wallpaper within the cuts by pulling, scraping, or using wallpaper remover.

5. Paste the patch (or apply paste to the damaged area), and slide the patch into place.

6. Roll the margins lightly, and sponge off the excess adhesive. Return in a few minutes, and press down the patch again.

Masonry and Concrete

Masonry and concrete can be patched with a number of compounds. As with all patching operations, the keys are to clean the surface well, choose the correct material, and apply and cure it properly.

Standard, medium-gray mortar is often used to repair masonry, even if the mortar is white or another color. The result is a hodgepodge that can hardly be called professional work. See Part B, Materials, for techniques for coloring mortar.

PATCHING STUCCO

Stucco, a coating of portland cement and aggregate, is made in several varieties. Rough stucco is sometimes spray-applied. It can be difficult to match this material, but the old mason's trick explained below can make a nearly invisible repair. The smoother ("Southwest") type of stucco is easier to patch. Patch exterior stucco with prepared stucco mix, or a mixture of sand and portland or mason's cement.

As with all repairs, start by correcting the cause of the problem (structural shifting, water damage, etc.). Never allow portland cement products to dry before setting. In hot, dry conditions, fog stucco occasionally for the first forty-eight hours of setting.

To patch stucco, follow steps 1 to 4, then go to the individual directions for the type of stucco being patched.

1. Remove all loose material, and brush out the hole.

2. For a large hole, the substrate must be rough enough to hold the patch. If not, fasten galvanized metal lath into the hole.

3. Moisten the edges and bottom of the hole.

4. If the hole is deep, apply a basecoat of stiff mortar and scratch it during setting.

For rough stucco:

5. Apply a second basecoat of mortar tinted the correct color. Save some of this mortar for the third coat. Allow the second coat to set until fairly stiff.

6. Soften up the mortar in the pail or wheelbarrow into a soft finish coat.

7. Flick water onto the second coat now that it has stiffened.

8. Mash a stiff-bristled brush into the pail of finish coat.

9. Fling the softened material against the repair. If the second coat is still somewhat soft, it will deform just enough to give the right texture, and the patch will be almost invisible.

For Southwest-style stucco:

5. Apply a second coat if needed to bring the basecoat flush with the bottom of the finish coat.

6. Apply a finish coat colored to match the old stucco, making the trowel strokes to mimic the existing work.

7. If the stucco is uneven on the surface, do not trowel it. Follow the instructions for floating under "Finishes" in Patching Plaster and Drywall, page 250. If you need to alter the color after the finish coat has set, apply colored portland cement paint.

PATCHING EXPOSED AGGREGATE

Masonry with exposed aggregate can be matched only if you can find similar aggregate. If this is possible, follow these directions.

1. Wash the entire wall with a strong detergent to remove as much dirt as possible.

2. Chip out all damaged material so the area has straight sides.

3. Mask the edges of the repair.

4. Apply a mortar basecoat (3 parts sand and 1 part mason's cement) up to the level of the surrounding mortar, but below the exposed aggregate.

5. Push new aggregate into the soft basecoat.

6. Remove the tape, and touch up the edges.

TUCKPOINTING

Tuckpointing is the repair of eroded or damaged joints in brick, block, or stone, without replacing the units. Joints are usually damaged after water invades and freezing weakens the mortar. Damage can also result from mortar that was improperly mixed or cured, structural movement, or other causes.

First clean the joint thoroughly with a hammer and chisel or a tuckpointing raker. Remove mortar at least 1/2 to 3/4 inch deep. If the decay extends deeper, remove that mortar also. On a large job, consider using a tuckpointing grinder. A grinder may damage the edges of nearby masonry units and is not suggested for preservation work. Wear eye protection while removing mortar.

Then clean out dust with compressed air, water, or a stiff brush. If water was not used in washing, wet the joint now to prevent surrounding masonry from absorbing too much water from the new mortar.

Tuckpointing mortar should be drier than normal mortar and should shrink as little as possible. Buy special tuckpointing mortar, or see Part B for a recipe for preparing tuckpointing mortar (and hints on coloring mortar to match existing masonry).

Place the mortar on a hawk or the bottom of a brick trowel, and force it into the joint with a tuckpointing trowel of the proper width. Fill deep joints gradually, giving the mortar time to set so it will not sag or shrink excessively. When the joint is full, let it set slightly, then tool to match the surrounding wall with a jointer, a piece of rubber hose, or a trowel.

BRUSHING JOINTS

Brushing joints after the mortar starts setting is one of the best tricks of the masonry trade. Brushing removes the scraps of mortar and trowel marks. Many people have tried to smooth these scraps with a trowel, but this is almost impossible and usually unnecessary.

Bristles should be 3 inches long and slightly stiffer than a whisk broom. Brushes sold for general cleaning chores may be suitable. In Wisconsin, where the author lives, the best brushes are sold for cleaning equipment in dairy barns. Do not use a paint brush—the bristles are too soft.

The trick in brushing is to treat the joint when it has set just the right amount. Wait until the mortar has stiffened from loss of water, which can take as little as five minutes or an hour or more in cold weather. When the mortar is ready, the brush will not leave streaks, but will remove high spots and trowel marks. You may want to give a harder scrubbing when the joint has set further; this will remove nearly all traces of mortar from around the joint.

◼ GROUTING

Grouting is a method of repairing small cracks in brick, tile, or block. Use powdered grouting mortar if available. Smear the mortar across the entire surface and into all cracks and voids. Rough walls cannot be cleaned very well after grouting. Clean mortar from a smooth wall before it has time to set. A coat of clear sealer may be applied to the entire surface afterwards.

◼ FILLING A LEAKING CRACK

Hydraulic cement, which sets quickly under water, can repair cracks in basements, tunnels, and shafts. In cold conditions, warm the repair area and mixing water to hasten the set. For warm conditions, use cold water to retard the set.

Compare the following procedure to manufacturer's specific directions:

1. Prepare the surface. Remove defective mortar and concrete from the crack. Cut cracks at least 3/4 inch wide and deep. Remove any tie wires or other metal embedded in concrete to a depth of 3/4 inch.

2. Mix the hydraulic cement with water, and force it into the crack. If water is streaming out, hold the cement until it becomes warm in your hand, indicating that it is starting to set. Then force it into the crack, and hold it with a trowel until it hardens (usually within three to five minutes).

3. Cut off the repair flush with the surrounding surface.

4. Scratch the surface before its final set if you plan to apply a finish coat to the patch.

CLEANING EFFLORESCENCE AND STAINS

Masonry can be discolored by: a) efflorescence, mineral salts that leach from masonry or mortar, or b) stains, which include rust, dirt, and just about anything else. To keep matters confusing, the term "stain" is used to describe certain efflorescences.

Both water and salts are necessary for efflorescence to take place. Water comes from leaks or condensation inside the building. Salts can come from masonry units, mortar, or other building elements. The best remedy for efflorescence is to close off the source of the water (so more salts cannot migrate), then remove the stain. Sometimes efflorescence can be prevented by sealing the front of the wall to prevent water from entering. However, this sealing will cause further problems if the water is actually entering from the rear, so it is vital to know the source of the problem.

Use these suggestions for removing efflorescence and stains:

Brown stain may be caused by deposits of manganese salts leaching from mortar or brick. The problem may result from muriatic acid used for cleaning. Manganese salts are usually removed with oxalic acid or other compounds.

White stain (also called "bloom") may be caused by water soluble salts. Old white efflorescence can be very resistant to removal. Clean by washing with clear water and a stiff brush. Wash during warm, dry weather so the cleaning water does not cause more bloom.

Green stain is caused by the vanadium salts found in some bricks. To remove, flood the wall with water, then spray on a mixture of sodium hydroxide (1/2 pound per quart of water). Leave the solution on the wall for a few days, and flush it off.

Smoke may be removed with a scouring powder containing bleach or an alkali detergent with an emulsifying agent. Smoke can be difficult to remove.

Dirt can be tough to remove from textured surfaces. Try scouring powder and a stiff brush. High-pressure steam cleaning is an alternative for large areas or resistant dirt.

Moss can be a problem in areas that are constantly damp. Moss can be killed by a commercial weed killer or an ammonium sulfate solution.

PATCHING CONCRETE

Concrete walls can be patched with mortar, hydraulic cement, or proprietary acrylic or portland-cement materials. If you expect adhesion problems, use a bonding agent or portland-cement paste (see Step 4 in the procedure for patching a concrete floor below).

Unfinished concrete has a rough, gravelly surface. The purpose of finishing concrete is to raise the sand-cement paste to the surface. The result is to increase hardness, attractiveness, and resistance to weather and abrasion.

To finish a horizontal slab of concrete, follow these steps:

1. Screed the concrete with a 2 × 4; slide the 2 × 4 from side to side along guides or adjacent concrete until it is flat. Screeding aligns and settles the gravel and starts raising the sand and ce-

ment to the surface; it does not just strike off the excess concrete.

2. Allow the concrete to rest a while (the time depends on the weather and the composition of the concrete).

3. Begin floating with a wooden float. When the concrete is set enough for this step, the float will glide on the surface, not dig in. Floating raises more paste and helps bury the gravel. (A homemade concrete float is described in Part A, Tools.)

4. Allow the concrete to rest, then trowel with a concrete finishing trowel or plaster trowel. The purpose of troweling is to densify and flatten the paste. If the trowel makes big swirls in the surface, the concrete is too green. Try again later on.

5. When the surface is evenly textured, stop troweling. If you want a finer surface, trowel again after a while. The greater the degree of set, the finer the pattern left by troweling.

Special compounds are available for patching defects in concrete floors—follow manufacturer's directions. The following technique for patching a concrete floor uses regular concrete and shims to flatten the patch to slightly above the surroundings. This allows the patch to shrink to the proper level after setting:

1. Remove all loose material to at least 1 inch deep. Make the edges of the patch as square as possible.

2. Clean out all loose particles.

3. Soak the patch area and surroundings with water for several hours to cut suction. No pools of water should be present when you start applying the patching material.

4. Prepare a paintlike slurry of portland cement and water. With a brush or broom, smear the slurry into the hole. Brush out to remove thick spots.

5. Place shims around the edge of the patch.

6. Load in the patching concrete and screed.

7. Allow the patch to settle and shrink for an hour or two before troweling. In hot weather, cover to slow the drying.

Figure E6 Patching concrete floor

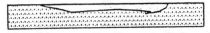

a) incorrect patch--feathered edges will fail

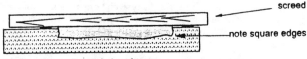

screed

note square edges

b) correct screeding technique leaves
flat patch after shrinkage

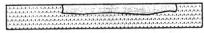

c) correct patch--1" min. depth

SLABJACKING

Concrete that has settled can be raised with a technique called slabjacking. Slabjacking is helpful for intact slabs that were built on poor soil or unstable fill; the technique cannot repair broken slabs. Slabs anchored to a foundation are not good candidates for jacking. In general, the procedure is about half as expensive as a new slab.

Slabjacking is a specialty trade, not something to be attempted by an amateur. Basically, the crew drills holes in the slab and pumps in a gravel-free cement grout. When the voids below the slab are filled with grout, the pumping begins to raise the slab. Control is crucial, because there is no way to settle a slab that has been raised too much.

APPLYING CLEAR MASONRY COATINGS

Clear, water-repellent coatings for masonry are based on silicon or other chemicals. Detailed application instructions are provided by manufacturers. The following is a general guide to application:

1. Select the proper coating for the type and orientation of masonry. Limestone may need special coating material. Coverage per gallon will vary greatly depending on coating material, surface porosity, and texture.

2. Prepare the surface. Allow new work to age as the manufacturer specifies. Clean and repair old surfaces.

3. Observe weather limitations during application.

4. Cover shrubbery and adjacent buildings.

5. Apply the coating with a low-pressure spray or brush. Flood the surface so the material runs down the wall as far as the manufacturer specifies.

6. Apply a second coat after the proper curing period.

APPLYING CEMENTITIOUS WATERPROOFINGS

Many waterproofing products on the market combine portland cement and aggregate. These long-lasting, strong-bonding materials can be troweled or brushed on a surface. Following is a general description for using these materials. Consult manufacturer's directions for specific products:

1. Prepare the surface. Old structures must be clean. Chip, sandblast, or grind defective material. Remove coatings, efflorescence, fungus, and other foreign matter. Repair all cracks and voids. Mortar must be fully cured before it is coated. Add a bonding agent to coatings applied to extremely dense concrete or masonry. Observe temperature limitations on the package.

2. Mix the coating to a thick batter. A brush should stand up in the material when it is ready to apply.

3. Dampen the surface ahead of the application. If the coating pulls off the wall, dampen the wall again. Apply little or no water in damp, cool conditions.

4. Apply the coating with a brush or trowel. A special brush may be recommended; otherwise use a 6-inch tampico brush, not a paintbrush. A long handle will speed the application and reduce fatigue. Brush or trowel on a heavy coat per instructions. Greater water pressure behind the wall calls for a heavier coating.

5. If two coats are needed, apply the second coat before the first has fully set—after about twenty-four hours in average conditions. For some applications, a different material, such as acrylic paint, can be used for the second coat.

6. Allow the coating to set. In hot, dry conditions fog the surface every few hours during setting.

WALLCOVERING

Wallcovering is just about anything that can be pasted to a flat surface: paper, various types of cloth, vinyl, wood, cork, even leather. Each material has strengths and weaknesses, and each has special handling requirements that must be observed. This part explains how to purchase, cut, paste, and apply these materials. See Part B, Materials, Section 3 for a description of materials and supplies.

The basic pitfalls of wallcovering installation are:

- Starting at the wrong place
- Failing to use guidelines
- Wasting the covering
- Failing to shade (minimize the effect of printing variations)
- Failing to cut inside corners; failing to wrap outside corners
- Mismatching patterns or failing to keep them straight
- Leaving paste on ceiling, woodwork, or wallcovering

Pattern Types

The pattern, or relationship between the repeating visual elements of a covering, is an important consideration in deciding how to hang material. The three possible types of pattern are random, straight across, and drop.

RANDOM

Strips in *random match* will work no matter where they are placed. Vertical stripes, for example, are okay no matter how they are arranged vertically. Each hang wastes only the 4-inch total top and bottom allowance.

Random texture is a slightly more complicated style that wastes as little material as random match. If the material is slightly darker on one side, the wall can end up with a dark-to-light jump at every seam if all strips are applied in the same orientation (the outside of the roll always at top or bottom). Solve this problem by reversing every other strip: hang all odd-numbered strips with the outer end of the roll at the top; hang all even-numbered strips with the outer end to the bottom. This is easier if you take alternate strips from different rolls. To prevent confusion, mark the top of each hang as you cut it as "R" or "L," or "1" or "2."

Grasscloth is a variety of random texture that needs special consideration. Examine the material, and place seams to complement rather than detract from the architecture. Grasscloth can be trimmed to reduce its width or straighten the edges.

STRAIGHT-ACROSS

As the name implies, a straight-across pattern is hung with the same elements next to each other. Examine the paper, noticing especially any elements on the border (some manufacturers print elements on the border to help installers align strips). Once you locate an element on the border, check with a framing square that the other part of the element is directly opposite, on the other edge. If so, the paper is straight across.

A pattern may still be straight across, even if no element is on the border. If you see sequences of elements repeating horizontally (such as element–space or element 1–element 2), the pattern is also straight across. The repeating element is placed at the same distance from the ceiling on every hang.

DROP

Patterns are said to "drop" when elements that are split by the border are found at a different height on each edge. Drop patterns have less waste than straight-across patterns. In half-drop paper, every other strip is identical at the ceiling break. In multiple-drop paper, the identical strips repeat less frequently.

Determine the type of drop with this procedure:

1. Find an element that is cut by the left edge, and measure to its next appearance on the same edge. This is the "vertical pattern repeat."

2. Square from the upper element on the left edge to the right edge.

3. Measure down to where the element you are seeking is cut by the right edge. This gives the length of drop (not the *type* of

Figure F1 Hanging alternate strips

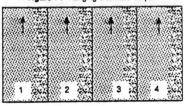

a) wrong way—emphasizes imperfections

b) right way—minimizes imperfections

Figure F2 Pattern styles

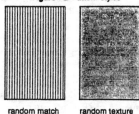

random match   random texture

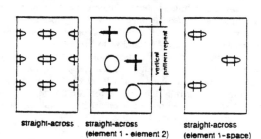

straight-across   straight-across   straight-across
                   (element 1 - element 2) (element 1 - space)

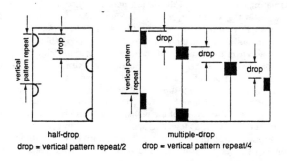

half-drop   multiple-drop
drop = vertical pattern repeat/2   drop = vertical pattern repeat/4

drop). If the length of drop equals half the vertical pattern repeat, the paper is half-drop. Otherwise, it is multiple-drop.

4. To figure how many separate types of strip are needed for multiple-drop, divide the vertical pattern repeat by the drop. For example, if the vertical pattern repeat is 32 inches and the drop is 8 inches, 32 ÷ 8 = 4. Four types of strip will be needed, and the fifth strip will be identical to the first.

To analyze a design with no divided elements on the border, locate a repeating sequence of elements, such as element A, space, element B. Consider this sequence a single component of the design, and use the technique above to determine the type of drop.

When applying half-drop paper, develop a notation for the strips, such as "R" and "L." For multiple-drop, use as many numbers as needed ("1," "2," "3," and so forth).

Before cutting drop pattern, determine which elements you want at the ceiling line. Lay out a trial hang, see how it looks, and mark the starting point. Often you will get the best economy by cutting from alternate rolls. Lay out the rolls on the floor, and line up the patterns, then take odd-numbered hangs from one roll and even-numbered hangs from the other.

Estimating Coverage

Estimating coverage is not the easiest part of wallcovering, but accurate estimates save time, money, and headaches. The best rule is to buy slightly more than you expect to need. Otherwise, you may run short and find that the correct dye lot is unavailable. Ask the dealer about return policies; if the covering is returnable, it's always best to err on the side of caution and buy extra material—and not to cut a roll until you are sure you will need it.

An estimate may reflect the type of drop, the vertical pattern repeat, the width and length of rolls, the availability of double or triple rolls, and the layout of the walls. Double and triple rolls usually minimize waste, as fewer scraps are created on each bolt.

The type of drop helps determine the amount of waste. Random drop has the least waste, while long drops have the greatest. A good rule-of-thumb is to figure 30 square feet of usable paper per 36-square-foot roll, or 22 square feet from a 28-square-foot European (metric) roll. Estimating tables are available from manufacturers, or use the following methods.

Take care to use inches *or* feet and inches when estimating and hanging. Do not mix the two types of measurements.

A simple way to estimate coverage is to divide the total wall area by estimated coverage per roll. Use this procedure:

1. Multiply the length of the wall by the height that will be covered plus 1/2 foot (both in feet) to find gross area in square feet.

2. Divide gross area by 30 (22 for European rolls) to find gross number of single rolls.

3. Subtract 1/2 roll for each standard window or door.

4. Round up to the next whole number.

The *strip method* will estimate covering needs for paper with a drop pattern more precisely. The example uses a 20-inch covering, available in single rolls 21.6 feet long with an 18-inch vertical pattern repeat:

1. Measure the height that will be covered plus 6 inches.   120″

2. Divide this amount by the vertical pattern repeat.   120″ ÷ 18″ = 6.67

3. Round up to find the number of full repeats per hang.   = 7

4. Multiply this number by the length of the repeat to find the gross length per hang.   7 × 18″ = 126″

5. Convert this measurement to feet, and use it to recalculate wall area and material needs with the above procedure.

To estimate heavyweight vinyl, which is usually sold by the square yard from bolts 54 inches wide:

1. Find the perimeter of the room in feet.

Figure F3 Estimating with strip method

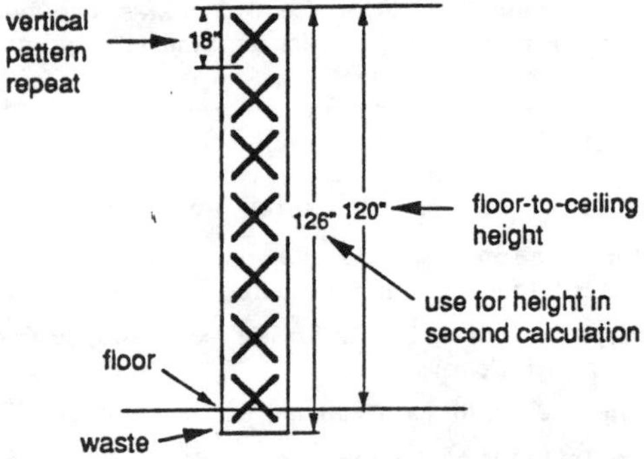

2. Multiply by height from floor to ceiling (in feet) plus 1/2 foot to find square footage.

3. Divide total square footage by 9 to find square yards needed.

ESTIMATING STAIRWAYS

Stairways can be estimated with the square-foot method (best for random patterns) or the strip method (best for straight-across or drop patterns).

To estimate a stairway using the *square-foot method*, first calculate the area of one wall. Do this by calculating the size of a rectangle above the top of the top full tread and adding the area of the triangle below that tread:

Step	Calculation	Total
1. Sketch the elevation, as seen facing a well wall.		
2. Find the area of the triangle under the top tread = 1/2 × Base × Height. (Do not measure to the landing.)	$1/2 \times 5'6'' \times 6' =$	16.5 sq. ft.

	Step	Calculation	Total
3.	Find the square footage of the rectangular part of the well wall (from the top tread upwards).	8' × 5'6" =	44 sq. ft.
4.	Add lines 2 and 3 to find the area of one well wall.	44 + 16.5 =	60.5 sq. ft.
5.	Figure the second well wall, if present. Add the above figure for an identical wall, or make a separate calculation for a different wall.		60.5 sq. ft.
6.	Calculate the area of the head wall.	3'6" × 6 =	19.5 sq. ft.
7.	Total the area of the head wall and well walls.		140.5 sq. ft.
8.	Divide by 30 (or the usable size of a bolt).	140.5 ÷ 30 =	4.7
9.	Round up to find how many bolts are needed.		5 bolts

Figure F4 Estimating stairways by forming a rectangle

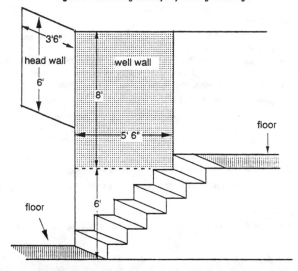

To estimate a stairway using the *strip method*:

1. Examine one well wall, and determine the starting point.

2. Lay out guidelines for each hang.

3. Determine the requirement for each strip, as measured to the lowest point within the guidelines.

4. Write down the requirements, and calculate what combination of rolls or bolts will make the best use of the material.

Fundamentals

The following suggestions are applicable to most steps of wallcovering installation:

- Do not trust your eye to get things right—use rulers and plumblines.

- If you use chalk for guidelines, use a light-colored chalk and apply it lightly. Place the guideline 1/4 inch to the side of the actual seam location to prevent the chalk from being visible if the seam pulls apart.

- Use charcoal in the chalkline to eliminate the problem of show-through and to allow you to locate guidelines directly under the seam. If any charcoal bleeds through, it can be removed when the seam is sponged. Using charcoal may increase accuracy because there is no need to estimate the 1/4-inch clearance.

- Use your judgment if the ceiling, chair rail, or floor is out of level.

- Use plenty of razor blades, especially on light, delicate, or expensive materials. Dull blades are guaranteed to rip, usually when you are about to finish a job and have no spare covering.

- Take care not to cut through drywall. Consider using a pad beneath both hangs when double-cutting on drywall.

- Always use vinyl-to-vinyl adhesive to paste overlaps in vinyl covering.

- Sponge off seams after they have grabbed. Avoid using excess water, or the seams could pull apart because the paste is not fully set. The sponging will help remove traces of charcoal that have seeped through the seam.

Preparing the Wall

In wallcovering, just as in painting, surface preparation is the key to a good mechanical and chemical bond. Skimp on this step, and the covering is likely to have problems at some point. The first step in preparing a wall is patching (see Part E).

Dull glossy surfaces before applying the first coat of sizing. Clean, dull surfaces in good condition may need no preparation, or just a coat of sizing, depending on the manufacturer's instructions. To hang a very dark color over a light wall, it may help to apply a dark primer-sealer.

NEW PLASTER

Use this procedure to prepare new plaster:

1. Allow the plaster to dry until it registers about 15 percent on a moisture meter. This may take ninety days or more.

2. To remove *acid spots*, prepare a mix of lime and water. Wash the problem areas with this solution, then rinse with vinegar to neutralize the lime.

3. Test for *excess alkali* on the wall. Prepare a solution of 1 gram phenolphthalein in 15 cc denatured alcohol, and spread it over the entire wall. Pink spots indicate alkali; the degree of pinkness corresponds to the concentration of alkali. (You can also mix the phenolphthalein into sizing.)

4. If the wall indicates alkali, neutralize with one of these procedures:
   a) Wash with 4 pounds zinc sulfate in a gallon of hot water.
   b) Wash with 8-percent acetic acid until the pink disappears. After either treatment, rinse with clear water and allow to dry.

5. Apply primer-sealer, let dry, and apply the wallcovering.

Saltpeter is a deposit on plaster that destroys the adhesion of wallcovering and paint. Saltpeter is similar to efflorescence in masonry: moisture dissolves the saltpeter in the wall and carries it to the surface. When the moisture evaporates, saltpeter is left on the surface.

You can recognize saltpeter by its effects: blistering wallcovering or flaking paint. The best way to deal with saltpeter spots is to replace the affected plaster and eliminate the source of moisture in the wall. Otherwise, remove the saltpeter by washing the wall with muriatic acid and water. A few modern coatings can stick to saltpeter, and it may be easier to use them than to replace the plaster. If you cannot determine whether a problem is being caused by saltpeter, consult an expert at a paint store or paint company.

NEW DRYWALL

The only preparation needed for new drywall that has been properly taped and sanded may be a coating of primer-sealer. Check with the wallcovering manufacturer—sizing may also be required. Make sure to choose a sealer that does not raise the nap. Do not use shellac-type coatings for sizing.

PAINTED WALLS

Use this procedure to prepare a painted drywall or plaster wall for wallcovering:

1. Wash with TSP or equivalent to remove dirt and grease.

2. Check that the paint is good quality and soundly adhered to the wall. If the paint was permanently darkened by the washing, or if it has softened from absorbing water, it is unsuitable for covering. Remove softened paint with water and steel wool. Then seal the porous surface with an approved primer-sealer or glue sizing—whichever the covering manufacturer specifies.

3. Dull glossy paint by hand-sanding with medium paper or a chemical washing agent.

4. Scrape sand finish or other textures with a broad knife or other scraper until smooth.

5. Patch all voids and cracks, and allow to set and dry.

OLD WALLPAPER

The best treatment for a previously papered wall is to remove the paper (see Surface Preparation in Part D) and start fresh. If the paper is in good shape, you may be able to avoid the trouble of stripping. Inspect for tight seams and good adhesion in trimmed areas, such as around baseboards, ceilings, and openings. Then run your hand over the walls and listen for the slight crackling that indicates loose paper. If the paper passes this test, verify that it is securely adhered:

1. Get a 2-square-foot sample of the new paper.

2. Paste half of the paper, allow it to relax, and apply to the surface.

3. When the paste has dried completely, try to pull the unpasted half from the wall.

4. If the old wallpaper pulls away, the wall must be stripped. Otherwise, the surface is probably adequate. It's generally wise to prime before hanging.

PLYWOOD AND PANELING

Wood should be sealed to prevent the paste from raising the grain. First prepare the surface by countersinking nail heads. Then inspect for: a) a waxy surface, which will prevent adhesion, and b) grooves between sheets, which may be visible through the wallcovering.

Use either of these tests for wax:

- Scrape wax from the surface with your fingernail (only detects a heavy coat).
- Lightly clean the surface with ammonia or a weak solvent. If wax is visible on the rag, or the surface is duller after cleaning, wax is present.

Remove wax by sandpapering or washing with alcohol or wax stripper.

To prevent grooves, joints, and knotholes from showing through, spackle and cover with fiberglass mesh and patching compound, such as the proprietary Pro-Kote.

An alternative for dealing with these depressions is to "railroad" liner paper:

1. Fill joints between the sheets with spackling (these are too large to bridge with liner).
2. Stretch liner over the wall tightly so it cannot sink into the grooves.
3. Spackle any remaining depressions, allow to dry, and sand lightly.

MASONRY

Masonry must be chemically and mechanically ready for wallcovering. Clean with detergent, wire brush, or hammer and chisel. If you have a rough, unpainted masonry surface, apply a very smooth coat of portland-cement plaster with a trowel. Coat painted masonry with drywall compound, again applied very smoothly with a trowel. Liner paper is a good measure for smoothing any masonry surface.

Laying Out the Room

Room layout, or "engineering," is the process of determining where the application will start and end, and where the pattern elements will be placed.

Because you have the greatest control over appearance at the starting point, it is generally located at the room's focal point. Above a fireplace, around a large window, or in front of a conversation area are all common focal points. It is usually possible to work in both directions from the starting point.

Because the pattern will not match at the ending, or "kill," point, locate it at the least obvious place, such as behind a door casing, over a door or window, or in a corner.

Note: Accurate engineering requires that you find out the actual relaxed width of the covering. Paste up a scrap as wide as the paper, or dunk it in a water tray for about ten seconds. Allow the scrap to relax for ten minutes and measure. Use this amount for the actual hang width in all figuring and measuring.

Once you have located the starting and kill points, decide how the pattern elements will be placed. For fine patterns and stripes and textures, this is not a problem. If the material has a large design, place it so the entire pattern is visible at the focal point. If the pattern contains an animate object (an animal or something moving), do not cut it near the focal point. If you are unsure, let the owner decide what to place at the focal point.

If a whole wall is a focal point, there are two possible locations for the first seam (see Figure F5, Starting and Kill Points). Center the seam if the strips at the corners will be wider than 6 inches. Otherwise, center the first strip on the wall.

A pattern with strong horizontal elements is troublesome on a building with a sloping ceiling. You cannot keep the hangs vertical and still have a patterned paper follow a nonhorizontal ceiling. Use these techniques to mask the discrepancy:

1. Hang the covering true level and plumb, but use a pattern that does not emphasize horizontal lines. Strong vertical lines and

Figure F5 Starting and kill points

a) center the seam

7 6 5 2 | 1 3 4 8

if greater than 6", center the seam. Otherwise, see b).

←— 14' —→

centerline

b) center the strip

6 5 4 1 | 2 3 7

greater than 6"

←— 12' —→

centerline

c) room layout

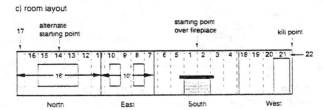

17 | alternate starting point | 16 15 14 13 12 11 | 10 9 8 7 | 6 5 1 2 3 4 | 18 19 20 21 | kill point ←22

←— 16' —→   ←10'→   starting point over fireplace

North | East | South | West

random patterns minimize the eye's ability to see that the building is not level.

2. Use the sloping element as the guideline. Draw a guideline about 6 inches below the ceiling, and square off it to establish false vertical "plumblines" to guide the installation.

Once the starting point is identified, follow these steps to make the guideline for the first strip:

• If the starting point is the center of a wall, simply make a vertical guideline with chalkbox, plumb bob, or spirit level.

• If the starting point is a building element, like a door frame, measure one width plus 1/8 inch away from it at three points. Use a chalkbox, plumb bob, or spirit level to draw a vertical line through the mark closest to the starting point.

With straight-across paper, it may help to snap a horizontal guideline at the height of an element cut by the edge of the paper, to ensure that the element is applied at the same height from the ceiling. With drop paper, you can make a horizontal guideline for every other hang, for the same reason.

Techniques

TRIMMING SELVAGE

Practically all modern wallcovering is sold pre-trimmed. If you run across untrimmed paper, you can trim it before or after pasting. Trim one strip at a time. Trimming a stack may save time, but it sacrifices quality.

Materials like metallic foil and sculptured or delicate papers are tough to trim, so use extra care and replace the blade after every cut. It may help to weight the opposite side of the material on the table. Make sure the straightedge does not slip while you cut. If you must trim foil, cut it in small sections, and do not fold the material.

Use the following procedure to trim selvage.

1. Move the strip to the edge of the pasting table, and make sure it is lying flat and straight.

2. Determine the amount to be trimmed.

3. Place a T square or straightedge on the cut, and hold it firmly in place.

4. Cut the edge at 90°. Be especially careful with dark papers—if they are cut at an angle, the lighter middle layers may be obvious on the wall.

PASTING

Uniformity, speed, and cleanliness are the goals of the pasting operation. Any paste on the table will wind up on the face of a sheet. Use this procedure:

1. Place the hangs on the table with the tops to the left. Fan out the sheets so they cover most of the table top.

2. Move the first hang so one long edge lines up with one edge of the table. Slide the hang so its top lines up with one end of the table. This placement prevents paste from getting on the table because waste paste will end up on the next sheet. (It may help to use a spring clamp to hold one end of the hang on the table.)

3. Apply the paste with brush or roller (you may have to experiment to see which works best for a particular paste). Use a figure-eight motion with the brush. Brush or roll toward the edges, and lift the applicator as you return it to the paper. Make sure the entire strip is pasted.

4. Make a large fold across the width, starting from the top of the strip. Do not crease.

5. Make a second fold, so the top and bottom edges almost butt in the middle. The sheet is now booked.

6. Remove the hang from the table if you will paste another hang. Let the hang relax for a few minutes before applying it. Make sure the folds are not creased.

Figure F6 Pasting and booking

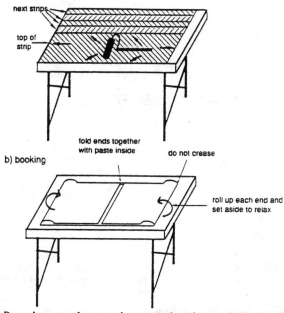

a) pasting
roll or brush toward edges
lift on return stroke

next strips

top of
strip

fold ends together
with paste inside

do not crease

b) booking

roll up each end and
set aside to relax

Paper has a tendency to dry out at the edges, and this impairs adhesion at the seams. You can prevent drying by placing booked sheets in a plastic bag while they relax. It's a good idea, if working alone, to paste only two strips ahead. This reduces the time pressure and allows you to do a better job.

It's vital to allow the pasted covering to expand (relax) before application. Do this by letting the covering rest in booked form for about ten minutes. (Book prepasted paper after soaking.) Failing to allow relaxing time is almost guaranteed to cause wrinkling when

Figure F7 Smoothing down

a) strip #1

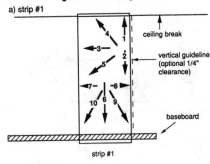

ceiling break

vertical guideline
(optional 1/4"
clearance)

baseboard

strip #1

b) strip #2

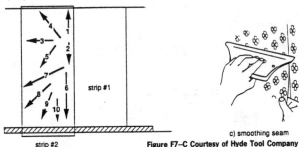

strip #1

strip #2

c) smoothing seam
Figure F7–C Courtesy of Hyde Tool Company

the covering expands on the wall. (The need to relax explains why
paste is usually applied to the covering, not the wall.) If the manufacturer specifies that the covering is nonexpanding, the paste may
be applied to the wall or covering.

APPLYING COVERING

Once the vertical guideline is marked, and the first strip is relaxed,
it's time to hang paper. During this process, remember that sliding

paper on the wall is likely to stretch and ruin it. Apply it as accurately as possible to begin with:

1. Grasp the pasted and booked strip by its center (so it folds over like a saddlebag), and bring it to the starting point.

2. Unbook the top (keep the bottom booked), and apply the top next to the guideline. Leave any allowance you figured in advance between the edge and the guideline.

3. Check that the desired pattern element is correctly located at the ceiling or near the horizontal guideline, then begin smoothing with a smoothing brush or tool. Make the first smoothing stroke upward, and the second one downward.

4. Continue smoothing to press air from the sheet, stroking away from the guideline as shown.

5. When the top portion is accurately hung, unbook the bottom and align it to the guideline. Make the first smoothing stroke directly down, then stroke away from the guideline.

6. Begin applying strip #2 with a similar technique. First align the top next to strip #1. Make sure the top is pasted accurately, then smooth. If you slide a strip into position, you are asking for trouble. The paper may rip or the seam may come apart.

7. Unbook the bottom, and use the smoothing pattern shown for strip #2. Roll the seam between the two strips. Repeat the procedure for subsequent hangs.

APPLYING LINING PAPER

Liner is generally railroaded onto the wall, which speeds the application and creates a "cross-seaming" effect. If the liner and facing paper will be applied in the same direction, do not locate the seams one on top of the other. You may need to apply a half-strip of lining paper to start off, to ensure that the seams wind up at different locations.

The wall should be prepared, patched, primed, and sealed as usual, to allow for good adhesion and easy removal. Apply the adhesive recommended by the manufacturer to the wall or liner as specified. It's best to use butt seams for the liner.

To apply lining paper:

1. Get stepladders and/or planks ready so you can apply the whole strip at one time.

2. Determine the application pattern. Then measure and paste the liner. Allow to relax if specified by the manufacturer.

3. Gather the pasted paper in accordion folds of a reasonable size.

4. Apply the first strip near the ceiling. Smooth the first yard back toward the starting point.

5. Continue applying, smoothing now towards the finishing point. Do not make vertical smoothing strokes, as this would force the liner into grooves. Keep the liner tight to bridge minor gaps and depressions in the wall.

6. Apply more strips until the wall is completed.

7. When done, examine for gaps, and spackle.

Seams on lining paper may show through foils and other light-bodied coverings. To prevent this, make overlapped seams on the lining paper and sand them smooth. Keep paste off the edge of the upper sheet, and overlap the seam about 1/2 inch. After the paste has dried, carefully sand each seam. The seam should be nearly invisible.

SEAMS

Seams can make or break an installation. The major problem, of course, is pulling apart. The primary goal of installing is to align the seams perfectly and then convince the paste to set up quickly near them. Once the paste has hardened, the seam should stay perfectly aligned. The basic seam types used in wallcovering are butted, overlapped, wired, double-cut, and mitered.

BUTTED SEAM

In the butted seam, adjacent sheets are applied so their edges just touch. This seam is simple to make but can present problems with pull-away. To increase the chance that this seam will remain tight, make it as a wired seam (with only 1/64-inch overlap). Then pull the edges apart so the upper sheet will drop level with the lower sheet. The seam should then have enough "spring" to remain in position.

OVERLAPPED SEAM

This seam is commonly used to correct out-of-square corners, and/or to conceal the corner in case of structural shifting. One hang overlaps the other by an amount that can vary with the application. The overlapped seam can also be used for liner paper (see Applying Liner Paper, above) and borders on inside corners.

WIRED SEAM

In the wired (ridge) seam, about 1/16 inch of the second strip is lapped over the first strip. This avoids the problem of seams pulling away or uneven edges, but it does leave a ridge on the wall. The overlapping sheet should "point" away from the room entrance, to make the seam less prominent. The seam can be used to correct for scalloped edges on the paper, or for its visual effect. If the light source is very close to the wall, the wired seam will make prominent shadows and should be avoided.

DOUBLE-CUT SEAM

A double-cut seam is used to make a perfect joint between two hangs. The second strip is applied slightly overlapping the first, and both strips are cut through to leave a practically invisible seam. Because the second strip temporarily overlaps the first, it's necessary to protect the first strip from adhesive. This can be done with a 4-inch "slip-sheet" of white wallcovering, lining paper, heavy

Figure F8 Seam types

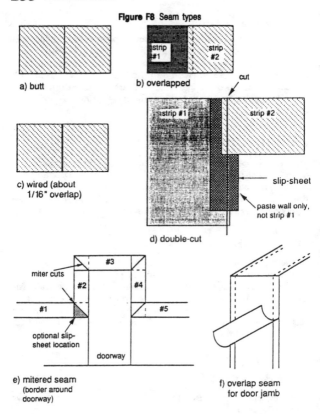

a) butt

b) overlapped

strip #1

strip #2

cut

c) wired (about 1/16" overlap)

strip #1

strip #2

slip-sheet

paste wall only, not strip #1

d) double-cut

miter cuts

#3

#2

#4

#1

#5

optional slip-sheet location

doorway

e) mitered seam (border around doorway)

f) overlap seam for door jamb

plastic, or wax paper. You can make plenty of 4-inch strips of plastic by hacksawing a roll of 4-mil contractor's plastic into 4-inch cylinders. Do not use masking tape, newspaper, or colored wallpaper due to the chance of staining. You can protect drywall from the razor knife by placing another pad beneath both hangs, or by using a 30/30 trimmer.

Use this procedure to make a double-cut seam:

1. Paste the wall a few inches beyond strip #1 to hold the slipsheet. Keep paste off the face of strip #1.

2. Apply the slip-sheet onto this adhesive so it protects the face of strip #1.

3. Apply strip #2 to the wall to overlap strip #1. To avoid pattern mismatches, minimize the width of overlap.

4. Double-cut the seam with straightedge and razor knife or 30/30 trimmer.

5. Pull out the slip-sheet and both pieces of cut-off wallcovering.

6. Smooth and roll the seam. Sponge paste from the surface.

MITERED SEAM

The mitered seam is a double-cut, 45° seam that is often used where a border changes direction at a window or door. Follow this procedure:

1. Apply strip #1 up to the door jamb or other obstruction.

2. Overlap strip #2 clear to the bottom of strip #1. Use a slip-sheet if desired (on the bottom left in the drawing) to protect the face of strip #1 from paste.

3. Double-cut through both strips at 45° to horizontal, starting the cut from the jamb. Remove scraps, smooth, and sponge off paste.

Figure F9 Rolling seams

Courtesy of Hyde Tool Company

KEEPING SEAMS TIGHT

Several techniques can be used to increase adhesion at seams:

- Press paste away from the seam with a seam roller.
- Run a squeegee or broad knife along the seam to press out excess adhesive.
- Use the "swatching" technique.

Swatching must be performed several hours before the covering will be applied. First apply adhesive under the future seam locations, and let it dry. The dry paste will blot up water from adhesive on the covering and increase adhesion near the seams.

1. Mark out the location of all seams with a light pencil, chalk, or charcoal.
2. Mix clay-based adhesive with 50-percent more water than usual.
3. Apply the mixture to the seam lines with a brush (a roller will leave visible marks), and allow to dry.

These tricks will also help make good seams that stay tight:

• Make sure the paste is still wet and "live" over the whole sheet. Edges are usually the first to dry, especially if the paste is applied thinly or the weather is hot and dry. If drying is a problem, relax the booked strips in a plastic bag.

• Do not try to slide sheets into position. Align the seams first, then apply the rest of the strip.

• Do not overwork the paper or you will stretch the fibers more than they can bear, and the result will be visible in the seams.

• Do not press seams too hard—this pushes out too much paste.

• Do not roll embossed or flocked seams—the impression can destroy the texture. Use a sponge or brush instead.

• Inspect seams about ten minutes after first rolling. Reroll questionable seams at this point.

• If edges were not cut square at the factory, the backing can show through at the seams. Apply a very dilute watercolor to these areas, and wipe it off after about ten seconds—just long enough to allow the paint to soak into the backing. You can also use this technique to hide seams that have pulled apart.

CEILINGS

Arrange sufficient scaffold planks and stepladders before starting a ceiling. A pocket for holding the smoothing brush is a necessity for working a ceiling. Remove smoke alarms and as many fixtures as possible (or see below for a method for hanging without completely removing fixtures). An assistant on the floor can feed the pasted strips to you and smooth the material with a floor broom.

To prevent damage to sidewalls, always paper (or paint) a ceiling before decorating the walls. When engineering a ceiling, arrange the pattern as an extension of the focal wall. If the pattern allows,

Figure F10 Ceiling application

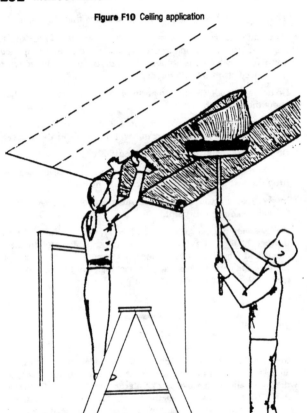

orient the ceiling paper across the narrower dimension of the room. Shorter strips are easier to handle.

Locate the first seam according to two factors: the presence of a central lighting fixture, and the type of seam used at the ceiling break.

Use either of these approaches to begin establishing the guideline for the first strip:

- Run a seam through the central lighting fixture. This allows you to notch one side of each adjacent strip for the fixture and eliminates the need to disconnect the fixture wiring. Once this seam is located, measure over as many widths as necessary to locate the guideline for the first whole strip near one wall.

- Begin papering along one short wall. Snap a chalkline 1/4 inch from the seam location, and hang the paper. Disconnect the fixture and paper over it, then slit the paper and reconnect the fixture.

The location of the starting guidelines also depends on whether you will cover the walls:

- If walls will be covered, plan on overlapped seams at the ceiling break. The ceiling paper must hang down about 1/2 inch at all ceiling breaks, and you must account for this 1/2 inch when locating the first seam. Also make a square cutout in each corner of the ceiling so the paper will reach all the way to the corner. When pasting the wall hangs, trim the tops with scissors to avoid cutting the overlap from the ceiling.

- If the walls will not be covered, trim into the ceiling break with a razor knife and locate the first guideline accordingly.

Once the guideline for the first strip is established, cut the hangs 4 inches longer than the ceiling dimension, and apply. After the ceiling is completed, mark plumb lines on the wall from each ceiling seam. This allows the wall seams to meet ceiling seams.

CORNERS

The goals in making corners are: a) to have a tight-adhering covering, b) not to lose too much of the pattern, and c) to maintain a vertical application after rounding the corner. Outside corners are usually quite prominent in a room and should receive extra care, both in workmanship and pattern placement.

If you are working on a perfectly square and plumb building, no special techniques are needed to go around a corner. Otherwise, follow these directions to make a clean corner and start the next wall with a vertical guideline.

INSIDE CORNER

1. When you have applied strip #1 to within one width of the corner, measure at three points from the strip to the corner.

2. Cut strip #2 to the longest of these dimensions, and hang it to the corner.

3. The cut-off makes strip #3. Measure at three points the width of strip #3 from the corner. (If you use chalk, add 1/8 inch to the width of strip #3 to find these three points.)

4. Make a plumb line through the mark closest to the corner, and hang strip #3 to this line. Make a butt or slightly overlapped seam in the corner.

5. Continue working down the wall as usual.

OUTSIDE CORNER

Outside corners are made with an overlapped seam placed about 2 to 3 inches from the corner. If the seam is nearer the corner, the covering could be rubbed loose over the years. (If the corner is plumb and true, you may not need the overlapped seam.)

Figure F11 Corner technique

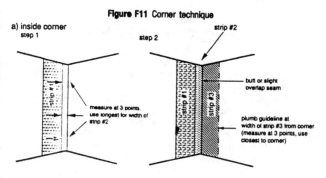

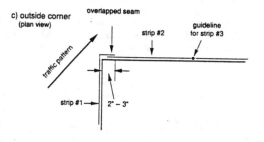

Locate the seam as far as possible from the traffic pattern. To reduce the prominence of the overlapping edge, make the overlap face away from the traffic. Slit strip #2 from the top and bottom corners so the paper can fold around the corner. To preserve the pattern, make strip #2 from the cut-off of strip #1.

Make a guideline for strip #3. If the corner is quite crooked, it might be a couple of strips before you are perfectly vertical again.

WINDOWS AND DOORS

You can usually cover near a door or window without changing seam locations. Before pasting the strip next to a door or window, hold it against the woodwork and mark 2 inches beyond the trim. To minimize paste smearing on the door frame, cut off the covering past this point, then paste the hang.

Because door and window frames project from the wall, "relief cuts" are needed to allow the paper to lay flat to the wall. A relief cut is a 45° slit that starts from the exact corner of the trim and works toward the waste. Make the cut by hinging the paper back from the trim and cutting at 45°—perpendicular to the miter cut on the molding.

Apply the header next, then establish a new plumb line for the strip beyond the door. Again, remove all but 2 inches of the paper that will overlap the door, then paste. Make a relief cut as you start hanging. Smooth the strip into place, working downward and away from the door. Use the guideline so the hanging remains vertical.

Figure F12 Applying near a door

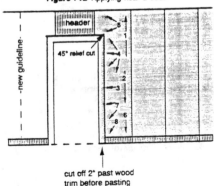

cut off 2" past wood
trim before pasting

RECESSES

Recessed windows can be tackled with this procedure:

1. Locate seams guidelines. Make sure strip #1 will be long enough to overlap the window trim by 2 inches. (Add 2 inches to the depth of recess to determine how far the strip must extend beyond the front corner of the recess.)

Figure F13 Recessed window

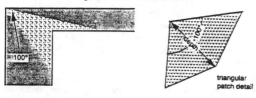

a) triangular patches in corners

triangular patch detail

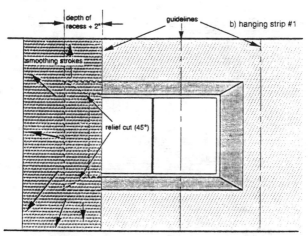

2. Mark the remaining guidelines.

3. Cut two triangular patches (note that the angle that is placed into the front corner must be greater than 90°), and paste them into position in the first two corners. Trim the excess at the window molding. (With planning, you may be able to take the patches from the waste created in step 6.)

4. Place strip #1 in position on the wall, and smooth. Make relief cuts at 45° from the front corners of the recess.

5. Apply into the recessed area, bring it up to the molding, trim, then smooth carefully. Double-cut or make overlapped seams with the corner patches placed in step 3.

6. Hang strip #2 as a full piece (to maintain the pattern on top and bottom). When top and bottom are smoothed into place, mark the cuts so the folded sections will overlap the window molding by 2 inches. Remove the center section. Smooth, and trim to the molding trim.

7. Cut two more triangular patches, and paste into position in the last two corners. Then cut the last hang, making miter cuts as before.

Figure F13 (continued)

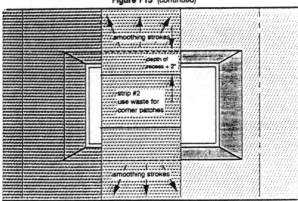

c) hanging strip #2

SLANT WALLS

The following technique can be used to apply covering to dormer walls and other walls with abrupt angles. The amount of work required will depend on the accuracy of the walls. For extremely long knee and slant walls, hang the upper and lower pieces as separate strips, making them match at the junction.

1. Snap vertical guidelines on the slant and knee walls.
2. Cut strips long enough for the slant and knee walls combined.
3. Begin hanging at the top of the slant wall, keeping close to the guideline.
4. Bring the strip down to the knee wall, and smooth it.
5. Begin applying onto the knee wall. If this section does not apply straight, cut a separate strip for the knee wall and make a double-cut or overlapped seam at the joint between the slant and knee walls.
6. Check that the joints are tight, and complete the smoothing process.

STAIRS

Plan your application so you will not need to lean a ladder against freshly applied wallcovering. Take into account the possibility of injury, and use sufficient ladders and planking. Don't paste too many strips ahead, or you will be tempted to rush and might have an accident.

Depending on the configuration, you may want to hang toward the head wall or away from it. Because it's handy to lean a ladder against the head wall for scaffolding, it is usually papered last. If you start at the intersection of head and well walls, work toward the top of the stairs, hang the opposite well wall, and return to the head wall. You may have to book and apply the tops of two hangs to the head wall while the scaffold is in the upper position. Once the tops are smoothed, remove the ladder, put the plank into the lower position, and complete smoothing.

Figure F14 Stairway scaffold

a) upper scaffold
  use to hang well walls
  and top of head wall

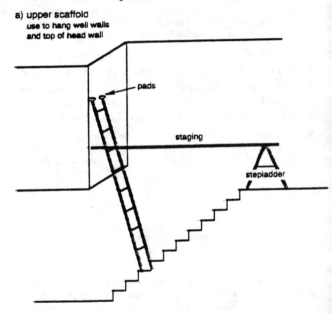

Figure F14 (continued)

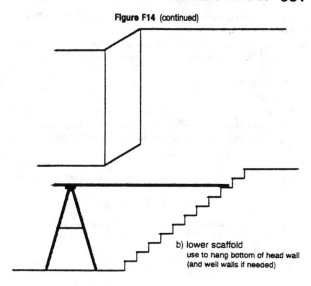

b) lower scaffold
use to hang bottom of head wall
(and well walls if needed)

ARCHES

The general procedure for papering around a curved arch is to cover the flat walls with hangs that are slightly oversized, and to tooth their edges so they can fold around the curve. A curved arch can be the focal point of a room. To center the seams on an arch, make it the starting point.

Use this procedure to cover an arch:

1. Position strip #1 to overhang the opening.
2. Establish guidelines for strips #2 and #3.

3. Paste and hang strips #2 and #3. Cut the middle hang short to save paper.

4. Trim the excess from the inside corner of the arch. Leave about 1/2 inch for overlap seams at the jambs and any straight horizontal section of the arch. Leave 1 inch for the toothed strips in the curved section.

5. Paste down these tabs.

6. Cut two strips for the inside and underside of the arch. Each must reach from floor to slightly past the apex. To prevent peeling back, make each strip 1/4 inch narrower than the arch depth.

7. Paste the strips into place, making sure they cover the tabs from the wall hangs. Double-cut at the apex, and smooth carefully.

Figure F15 Curved arch

a) application

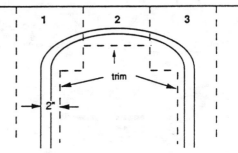

Figure F15 (continued)

b) toothing

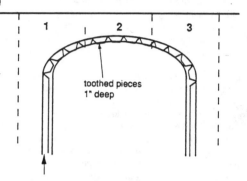

toothed pieces
1" deep

leave 1/2" for
overlapped seam, then cut and apply
2 strips to bottom and inside of arch

BORDERS

Borders are narrow materials used to accent the transition between materials. Borders are commonly used at the top of a wall, around openings, and at the height of a chair rail. Borders can shrink the apparent size of a room, and should be chosen to complement the furnishings and other wallcovering. Because they attract attention, borders should not be used near ceilings that are badly out of level. For rooms like these, any border would be better at the height of a chair rail. (The chair rail is commonly centered on one-third the ceiling height.)

When hanging border over a patterned wallcovering, make sure it harmonizes with the main covering. A little time examining the border and main covering should reveal any problems with harmony. If possible, allow about 1 to 2 inches "breathing room" between pattern elements in the main covering and the border.

Borders are sold in spools or by the yard. For small repeats or random patterns, estimating is a simple matter of determining the length of wall to be covered, then adding about 10 percent for waste and pattern matching. For longer repeats, you can use standard estimating techniques. When estimating mitered openings, measure all the way to the trim and add about 1 foot for each miter cut.

Before hanging, determine how wide the border will be after it has expanded. Paste or wet a short length, allow it to relax, and measure. To join a border when a roll runs out, overlap the new border, match the pattern, and double-cut.

Borders can be hung over existing wallpaper or a prepared wall. Apply vinyl borders over vinyl covering with a vinyl-to-vinyl adhesive. Borders can also be double-cut into the edge of new wallpaper, but only if the paste on the new covering has not fully set.

The steps in hanging borders are similar to those for hanging regular covering, except that inside and outside corners are joined with overlapped seams to prevent pulling away:

1. Reroll the border to inspect it and take out the curl.

2. Measure the width minus 1/2 inch down from the ceiling, or wherever the border will be. If the ceiling line is uneven, measure at 2-foot intervals so the border will parallel the ceiling. In square and true construction, establish the guideline with a chalkline.

3. If the border will be applied to a painted wall, apply primer-sealer to the area marked out. Keep the primer 1/2 inch back from the edge, to prevent it showing through. (Primer is not needed to apply border over new wallcovering.)

4. When the primer has dried, paste the border and book it. Book in accordion-fashion, with the starting point marked or remembered.

5. Begin the border 1/2 inch before the starting point. Paste the border along the wall.

6. Extend the border 1/8 inch past an inside corner, and cut vertically. Start the next section of border exactly in the corner.

7. Make an overlapped seam about 1/2 inch wide on an outside corner.

OTHER SITUATIONS

Try to engineer your work to avoid placing seams behind obstacles like toilet tanks and radiators. It's best to turn off a radiator before hanging, as the heat can dry the paste too quickly. To apply behind a toilet tank or radiator, smooth with the brush as far as you can reach, then use a straightedge to complete the smoothing. Apply extra paste on the wall to increase adhesion. Toilet tanks can be removed relatively easily (though replacing them can be more of a problem).

To cut around a switch or outlet, first shut off the circuit at the service panel. Cut a pair of slits in the shape of an "X." Let the paper overlap the switch box by 1/4 inch. Fold the tabs back, and trim if needed.

To paste paper to a switch or outlet cover plate, use this procedure:

1. Locate a scrap matching the pattern around the switch. Make the scrap 2 inches larger than the switch plate in each dimension.

2. Hold the scrap against the wall so the pattern matches. Cut along a horizontal line 1 1/4 inch above the top of the opening.

3. Hold the switch plate and scrap against the wall in the correct location. Loosely fold the scrap under the top of the plate (if it's too tight, you will not have room to adjust it).

4. Remove the assembly from the wall, and cut the other three sides at about 3/4 inch beyond the plate. Fold these edges loosely over the plate.

5. Return the assembly to the wall, and adjust so the pattern matches perfectly. Then turn the plate over, make the folds tighter, and trim excess paper from the scrap.

6. Screw the plate into place, taking care to make any final adjustments to the pattern location.

Figure F16 Cutting around a switch

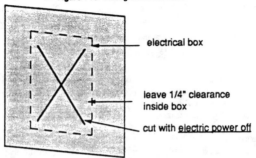

electrical box

leave 1/4" clearance
inside box

cut with <u>electric power off</u>

a) cut out inside electric box

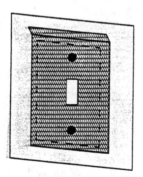

b) adjust paper around
switch plate, cut away
corners on back, fold,
position, and fasten plate

HEALTH AND SAFETY

Health

In the past decade or so, painters and occupational health specialists have become more aware of the hazards caused by chemical exposure in the painting industry. Although solvent-based paints pose the biggest hazard, even some latex paints are now known to carry a risk of mercury poisoning. For their own health, painters must identify the hazards facing them and understand how to avoid or minimize them.

ASBESTOS

Asbestos is a mineral fiber that was widely used in pipes, siding, sheets, floor tiles, coatings, sealants, and insulation due to its resistance to heat and chemicals. In 1987, OSHA estimated that hundreds of thousands of construction and industrial workers were being exposed to the mineral.

Inhaled asbestos fibers become lodged in the lung's air sacs, and they cannot be removed. Years of exposure to asbestos has caused disabling and fatal diseases, including asbestiosis, a condition like emphysema; lung cancer; and cancer of the membranes covering the lungs and other organs.

307

The current OSHA standards for asbestos are:

Permissible exposure limit (PEL): 0.2 fiber per cubic centimeter of air, averaged over an eight-hour day. This limit cannot be exceeded, except thirty minutes' exposure to 1 fiber per cubic centimeter of air is permissible.

Action level: 0.1 fiber per cubic centimeter of air, averaged over an eight-hour day. If this level is exceeded, employers must begin compliance activities, such as air monitoring, employee training, and medical surveillance.

If you suspect asbestos is present in a building, it's best to test whether the material actually is asbestos. If the test is positive, remember that asbestos is only dangerous if it is "friable" (able to become airborne). Undamaged asbestos may be left in place if it will not be disturbed by construction or repairs.

If asbestos must be removed, OSHA suggests calling in a specialist contractor, who knows the many personal protection, isolation, and cleanup procedures needed to safely remove asbestos.

CHEMICAL HAZARDS

The numerous chemicals used in the painting trade can cause a distressing variety of problems. Some difficulties, including skin irritation and respiratory problems, show up right away. These short-term effects may be just annoyances or they may signal major, long-term damage. Other symptoms, including cancer or neurological difficulties, may not appear for many years after exposure.

Suppliers are required to provide Material Safety Data Sheets (MSDS) for all hazardous chemicals they provide, and employers must make these sheets available in the workplace. MSDS list the toxic properties of the chemical and necessary precautions. A smart worker will read these sheets and check that precautions are followed.

Your sense of smell is not a good guide for detecting hazardous chemicals because it can be deceived in the following ways.

- Many solvents are dangerous at levels that most people cannot smell.
- Some poisons, including carbon monoxide, have no odor.
- The sense of smell may "fatigue" after a few minutes. The odor disappears even though its concentration remains the same.
- Some hazardous chemicals, including benzene, smell good.

As a guideline, something that irritates your nose is likely to cause problems in your lungs and elsewhere.

Coworkers can give you some clues about hazards. If it takes new workers some time to be able to withstand conditions in which you routinely work, the problem may not be their lack of "toughness." The real problem may be that you have found a way to force yourself to work in unhealthy conditions. If a high percentage of newcomers complain about conditions and quit, an environmental problem may need addressing.

One of the first effects of many toxic chemicals is a feeling of drowsiness, "highness" or dizziness. Do not ignore this warning sign—it may be caused by nerve damage that could become a permanent disease. Toxic chemicals can cause paralysis, loss of feeling, intense pain, tremors, Parkinson's disease, and other diseases of the central or peripheral nerves. Studies of painters have found abnormally slow reflexes and other neurological symptoms. These effects are bad in themselves, but they can also impair judgment, attention, and balance, and cause accidents.

Some scientists think long-term exposure to solvents causes "solvent syndrome," a group of neurological problems including fatigue, dizziness, and tremors. The key principle of hazardous chemical exposure is this: If the exposure is severe enough, and it lasts long enough, permanent damage is likely.

WHAT ARE PAINTERS' OCCUPATIONAL ILLNESSES?

Long-term exposure to chemicals like benzene can cause cancer. Chemicals can also damage vital organs, including the liver (which breaks down chemicals in the blood) and the kidneys (which remove chemicals from the blood for elimination through the urine). Sufficient damage to either organ can kill. The deadly scarring of the liver called cirrhosis can be caused by drinking alcohol or by chemical exposure.

Anemia, a reduction in the oxygen-carrying cells of the blood, is a common problem among painters. Anemia can be caused by lead or benzene. Though serious in itself, it can also signal the start of leukemia, an often-fatal blood cancer.

The most common occupational illness, dermatitis, can be caused by many substances. Dermatitis is a reddened, blistered reaction to an irritant. Contact dermatitis is an allergic reaction to foreign substances. Poison oak and ivy cause a form of this disease, as do epoxy resins. Repeated exposures can sensitize the skin to the foreign agent. From that point, smaller and smaller amounts are needed to cause the reaction.

Dermatitis can be prevented by keeping the skin clean with gloves, clothing, and barrier creams. Change your clothes to avoid bringing contaminants home. Ideally, you will have one locker for clean clothes and another for dirty ones.

Painters are subject to chronic bronchitis, a low-level infection of the lungs. One study found that 30 percent of painters suffer from this disease, which causes constant coughing. Bronchitis is especially prevalent among smokers and abrasive blasters. Painters are also prone to emphysema, a degeneration of air sacs in the lungs. Asbestos and silicon can fatally injure the lungs (see Asbestos, page 307.)

FOUR FACTORS FOR EXPOSURE

The effects of chemical exposure depend on four factors:

The *nature* of the chemical: whether it can penetrate the skin, how it travels through the body, what parts it affects, and how quickly it can be eliminated.

The *concentration* of the substance: some substances seem to be hazardous only above certain concentrations, while others (such as asbestos) are hazardous at virtually any dose.

The *duration* of exposure: In general, the longer the exposure, the more severe the results. Exercise can also affect the intensity of exposure. Heavy exertion causes you to breath harder and inhale more.

The *physical* state of the substance: solids can be ingested (swallowed), liquids can be absorbed through the skin or ingested, and vapors can use any route. You must consider the physical state when deciding what type of protection you need.

ROUTES OF ADMINISTRATION

Hazardous substances can enter the body in three ways: inhalation, absorption, and ingestion. The nature of the substance and the working conditions will determine which route is the most hazardous for a particular situation. In general, inhalation is the most serious risk for most painters.

INHALATION

Gases, fumes, mists, dusts, particles, and vapors can all enter the body through the nasal passages and lungs. The substances can damage the airways directly or be taken up in the blood so they can travel through the body. Inhaled substances can also go directly through nerve cells in the nose to the brain.

When discussing inhalation, one point must be stressed over and over: YOU MUST USE THE CORRECT TYPE OF VAPOR OR DUST CANISTER FOR THE HAZARD TO WHICH YOU ARE EXPOSED, AND YOU MUST REPLACE IT WHEN NEEDED.

Look for these signs that your respiratory protection is inadequate:

- Many workers cough up phlegm, even the nonsmokers.
- Mucus from your nose is the same color as the material you are applying.
- You have a frequent sore throat or cough.
- You experience feelings of dizziness, fatigue, or nausea.

ABSORPTION

A surprising number of chemicals can be absorbed through the skin, including most of the organic solvents used in paints. From the skin, these substances can enter the blood stream and reach vital organs. Gloves and protective clothing must be chosen to match the hazardous substance. The possibility of skin absorption is an excellent reason not to wash hands in solvent.

INGESTION

Substances can enter the digestive tract through the nose or mouth. The substance may directly damage the nose, mouth, or digestive tract, or it may enter the bloodstream and cause injury elsewhere. Chemicals can be trapped in nasal mucus and swallowed. Dirty hands can also carry contaminants to food. Keep your lunch protected at the job site, and wash your hands before eating, drinking, or smoking.

ACUTE OR CHRONIC POISONING

Chemicals can cause either acute or chronic poisoning. Acute poisoning is ingesting enough of a toxic chemical to immediately endanger health or life. Acute poisoning can show up as dizziness, grogginess, nausea, or unconsciousness.

To respond to acute poisoning, call a doctor or emergency service immediately. Try to find out what the chemical was. Ask the victim or coworkers, or look around for containers. Call a poison hot line, especially if you have identified the chemical.

Do not induce vomiting in someone who is groggy or unconscious or who has ingested an acid, base, or petroleum product. Milk can reduce the rate of absorption of an acid, base, or petroleum product. Do not give any liquid to an unconscious person.

Chronic poisoning results from prolonged, repeated exposure to a chemical. Chronic effects may not appear for years after exposure begins, but they can be more serious than acute effects and may not be treatable. Chronic problems among painters can affect most of the major organs, including lungs, nerves, brain, and kidneys.

AIR CONTAMINANT LEVELS

OSHA and other organizations have set several types of levels for controlling chemical and physical contaminants. These levels are expressed in parts per million (ppm) or milligrams per cubic meter (mg/m³). In general, measurements must be taken in a worker's "breathing zone."

The following jargon is used to regulate acceptable levels of contaminants. More detailed information, including levels for hundreds of substances, can be found in OSHA publication 3112: Air Contaminants—Permissible Exposure Limits.

The *permissible exposure limit* (PEL) is set by OSHA to "substantially reduce significant risk of material health impairment among workers." Limits must, however, be "technologically and economically feasible." The new PELs are intended to protect against cancer, narcosis, and damage to the liver, lung, kidney, cardiovascular, and nervous systems. PELs should also help prevent respiratory and sensory irritation.

The *short-term exposure limit* (STEL) is the employee's fifteen-minute, time-weighted average exposure; it shall never be exceeded.

The *ceiling value*, set by OSHA, shall never be exceeded.

The *time-weighted average* (TWA) value is the employee's average airborne exposure in any eight-hour work shift in a forty-hour work week. It shall not be exceeded.

The *recommended exposure limit* (REL) was developed by the National Institute of Occupational Health and Safety as an independent limit on contaminant levels.

The *threshold limit value* (TLV), set by the American Conference of Government Industrial Hygienists, may differ from the PEL.

Increased understanding of the health hazards of pollutants has caused a general lowering of all these standards. But for economic or political reasons, OSHA may fail to sets its levels low enough. No standard can guarantee safety.

INFORMATION ABOUT HAZARDS

Painters have two good sources of information about hazards from the materials they use: Material Safety Data Sheets (MSDS) and the container label. Manufacturers of paints and other industrial chemicals must give MSDS to their customers, and employers must make them available to everybody who works with the chemicals. MSDS and labels generally include this information:

- Product identity, manufacturer's name, and emergency telephone number for more information
- Hazardous ingredients and exposure limits, generally in parts per million for an eight-hour shift
- Flammability and explosion information
- Health hazards and first-aid data
- Requirements for ventilation, personal protective equipment, and waste disposal

SELF-TEST FOR NEUROLOGICAL SYMPTOMS

Some of painters' worst occupational diseases affect the nervous system. Often, the symptoms are mistaken for "old age," fatigue, or lightheadedness, even though the damage is caused by chemicals in the workplace. Scientists in Sweden have developed a

Figure G2 Screen for nervous problems

Question	Yes	No
Do you have a short memory?	☐	☐
Have your relatives told you that you have a short memory?	☐	☐
Do you often have to make notes about what you must remember?	☐	☐
Do you often have to go back and check things you have done, such as turning off the stove, locking the door, etc?	☐	☐
Do you generally find it hard to get the meaning from reading newspapers and books?	☐	☐
Do you often have problems with concentrating?	☐	☐
Do you often feel irritated without any particular reason?	☐	☐
Do you often feel depressed without any particular reason?	☐	☐
Are you abnormally tired?	☐	☐
Are you less interested in sex than what you consider normal?	☐	☐
Do you have palpitations of the heart even when you don't exert yourself?	☐	☐
Do you sometimes feel pressure in your chest?	☐	☐
Do you perspire without any particular reason?	☐	☐
Do you have a headache at least once a week?	☐	☐
Do you often have a painful tingling in some part of your body?	☐	☐

Source: Christer Hogstedt, Swedish National Board of Occupational Safety and Health, Solna, Sweden.

screening questionnaire to detect nervous problems caused by chemicals. This questionnaire (see below) is no substitute for good medical attention, but it's cheap, easy to use, and harmless.

There is no exact "scoring," but anyone with more than six positive responses should probably be evaluated by a doctor. Some people with real neurological problems have "passed" the questionnaire. And some people who "failed" it actually had no problems. But the scientists who developed it found it can detect most people who have nerve problems caused by occupational chemical exposure.

There are several benefits of early diagnosis. Most disorders are easier to treat at an early stage. Peripheral nerves (those outside the brain and spinal cord) can sometimes recover if exposure ceases. A worker can choose to reduce or eliminate further exposure, which should lessen the chance that the condition will get worse. The worker can also avoid chemicals like pesticides, glues, cleaners, and other household products, which can intensify the problem.

CONTROLLING HEALTH HAZARDS

Four basic methods can be used to reduce hazardous exposure to safe levels. In order of decreasing desirability, they are: substituting other materials, engineering controls, administrative procedures, and personal protective equipment.

SUBSTITUTION

From a health standpoint, the best way to avoid toxic exposure is to substitute nontoxic or less-toxic materials. Do not substitute something of unknown toxicity—it might be worse than the original material. Product labels should list the ingredients, but not every manufacturer complies perfectly. Then check MSDS for the permissible exposure limits for the various materials; in general, safer materials have higher limits.

Abrasive blasters can reduce the danger of silicosis by substituting slag, grit, or shot for sand. Water-based paints are much less hazardous than solvent-based paints.

ENGINEERING CONTROLS

Engineering controls are process changes designed to keep hazardous substances out of your lungs and mouth, and off your skin. Ventilation, enclosures, and automation are the primary engineering controls. Covered containers and ventilated solvent cabinets are two common engineering controls.

General ventilation is the provision of fresh air throughout the workplace. General ventilation is not enough to control very hazardous substances. Most general ventilation systems use blowers, ducts, and controls to move air. The system must have an inlet so "make-up" air can replace the exhausted air. Make-up air should enter at the least contaminated point; exhaust air should exit at the most contaminated point. The make-up air must come from a fresh source that is far from a toxic exhaust or vehicle exhaust.

Local ventilation is the use of big vacuum devices to remove contaminated air near the point of contamination. This system is better than general ventilation for removing toxic gases or dust because it prevents the substance from mixing with room air.

In local ventilation, hoods or duct intakes are placed as close as possible to the source of contamination. Air must flow quickly and away from the painter's breathing zone. To prevent particles from settling out in the duct, light dusts may need 2,000 feet-per-minute air flow. Heavy mists or moist dusts need at least 4,500 feet-per-minute.

Ventilation systems must be designed and maintained properly. Filters must be replaced. Make-up air must be sufficient. Ducts should be round and their bends gradual. Kinks and gaps must be fixed. Clean-outs must be provided in areas where dust can settle.

ADMINISTRATIVE PROCEDURES

Administrative procedures are methods to reduce exposure to any one worker. The primary procedure is job rotation, which is used to spread the risk to many workers in the hope that this is safer than having one worker face the entire risk. Scientifically, it is not clear whether rotation works.

PERSONAL PROTECTIVE EQUIPMENT

Personal protective equipment—masks, respirators, and hoods—is considered the least desirable form of protection, but in reality is often the most effective, and cheapest, protection for painters. See Part A, Tools and Equipment.

Safety

Construction is a dangerous occupation, and workers and management are obliged to help ensure a safe workplace. The following information is intended as minimum requirements, not a comprehensive guide to job safety.

Some conditions greatly increase the chance for accidents in any working environment: crowded work areas, blocked passageways, overloaded platforms and hoists, inadequate support for scaffolds, elevators without proper guards, damaged tools or power cords, poor ventilation or lighting, defective or worn-out protective equipment and clothing, and improper storage or use of fuels and other chemicals.

Some types of behavior also increase the odds of accident and injury, including poor attention to the task (especially when working with power equipment), creating sparks or flames near flammable materials, creating toxic fumes in unventilated areas, riding equipment not designed for personnel, removing guards from machinery, stacking materials unsafely, and neglecting to wear protective clothing. Other dangerous habits include horseplay and working when very tired.

The Occupational Safety and Health Administration is responsible for establishing and enforcing health and safety standards at workplaces. Although the detailed regulations are complex, OSHA offers simple booklets summarizing the agency's operations, listing standards that are frequently overlooked, and giving other helpful information.

OSHA has a free "Onsite Consultation Program" available to all employers. This program provides workplace inspections to recognize and correct hazards; it will not issue citations. The program is primarily targeted to small businesses that want to fulfill their requirements under the OSHA law. The employer's only obligation is a commitment to correct serious hazards found during the inspection.

OSHA booklets	
number	*name*
2056	All About OSHA
2201	General Industry Digest
2202	Construction Industry
2098	OSHA Inspections
3077	Personal Protective Equipment
3079	Respiratory Protection
3084	Chemical Hazard Communication
3088	Emergency Response in the Workplace
3091	Safety and Health Guide for the Chemical Industry
3096	Asbestos Standard for Construction
3097	Electrical Standards for Construction
3112	Air Contaminants—Permissible Exposure Limits

These are some OSHA standards and other safety information applicable to painting, patching, and wallcovering:

ACCIDENT REPORTING

The employer must maintain a log and summary (OSHA Form no. 200 or equivalent) of all recordable injuries and illnesses for each work site. Reportable events are those that result in fatality, hospitalization, lost workdays, medical treatment, job transfer or termination, or loss of consciousness. Incidents must be entered in the log within six days after the employer learns of them. An annual summary of this log must be compiled each year and posted at the work site from February 1 until March 1.

ELECTRICITY

OSHA requires compliance with the 1971 National Electric Code in most cases. Fifteen- and 20-amp, single-phase, 120-volt circuits at construction sites must use ground fault interrupters or an assured

Figure G3 OSHA offices

U.S. Department of Labor Regional Offices
for the Occupational Safety and Health Administration

Region I

(CT, MA, ME, NH, RI, VT)
16-18 North Street
1 Dock Square Building
4th Floor
Boston, MA 02109
Telephone: (617) 223-6710

Region II

(NJ, NY, Puerto Rico, Virgin Islands)
1 Astor Plaza, Room 3445
1515 Broadway
New York, NY 10036
Telephone: (212) 944-3426

Region III

(DC, DE, MD, PA, VA, WV)
Gateway Building, Suite 2100
3535 Market Street
Philadelphia, PA 19104
Telephone: (215) 596-1201

Region IV

(AL, FL, GA, KY, MS, NC, SC, TN)
1375 Peachtree Street, N.E.
Suite 587
Atlanta, GA 30367
Telephone: (404) 881-3573

Region V

(IL, IN, MI, MN, OH, WI)
230 South Dearborn Street
32nd Floor, Room 3244
Chicago, IL 60604
Telephone: (312) 353-2220

Region VI

(AR, LA, NM, OK, TX)
555 Griffin Square Bldg.
Room 602
Dallas, TX 75202
Telephone: (214) 767-4731

Region VII

(IA, KS, MO, NE)
911 Walnut Street, Room 406
Kansas City, MO 64106
Telephone: (816) 374-5861

Region VIII

(CO, MT, ND, SD, UT, WY)
Federal Building, Room 1554
1961 Stout Street
Denver, CO 80294
Telephone: (303) 837-3061

Region IX

(AZ, CA, HI, NV, American Samoa
   Guam, Pacific Trust Territories)
Box 36017
450 Golden Gate Avenue
San Francisco, CA 94102
Telephone: (415) 556-7260

Region X

(AK, ID, OR, WA)
Federal Office Building
Room 6003
909 First Avenue
Seattle, WA 98174
Telephone: (206) 442-5930

equipment grounding program unless they are part of permanent structural wiring. One or more employees at the job site should make daily inspections of temporary wiring and electrical equipment.

Other guidelines for electrical safety are as follows:

- Check electrical equipment before using. Equipment must be grounded. Don't use if it has frayed cords, damaged insulation, or exposed wires.

- Never operate electrical equipment when standing in wet or damp areas.

- Electric cords must be three-wire type. Do not hang cords from nails or wires. Splices must be soldered and adequately insulated.

- Keep electrical wires off the ground. Never run over wires with equipment.

- Plug receptacles must be the approved, concealed contact type.

- Exposed metal parts of electrical tools that do not carry current must be grounded.

- Shut off power in case of a problem or accident.

- Do not touch anyone who is in contact with live electrical current. Instead, first shut off the power. Then move the person by pushing him or her with a dry piece of lumber. Give mouth-to-mouth resuscitation if the victim is not breathing. Call an ambulance.

FIRE

On larger jobs, a fire-fighting program must be followed throughout the construction work. The job site must have an alarm system to alert employees and the fire department of a fire.

Follow these fire prevention measures:

- Store oily or greasy rags in a tightly closing metal container.

- Remove all flammable waste daily.

- Maintain adequate clearance between heat sources and flammable materials.
- Keep fire extinguishers of the proper type handy.
- Each floor of a building must have two separate fire exits to allow quick exit if one is blocked for any reason.

FLAMMABLE LIQUIDS

Flammable liquids pose both fire and explosion dangers. Pour gasoline with an approved gooseneck filler. Keep the spout in contact with the metal tank opening to prevent sparks from static electricity. Do not smoke while filling. Never fill a machine while it is running. Store gasoline in approved cans away from any possible fire, sparks, or mechanical hazard.

Do not store more than 25 gallons of flammable or combustible liquids inside a building except in an approved storage cabinet. Not more than 60 gallons of such liquids may be stored in any one cabinet.

Outside storage areas may contain no more than 1,100 gallons of fuel in each area. The storage area must be free of other combustible materials and at least 20 feet from any building. "No smoking" signs must be posted in the area.

HAND TOOLS

Wear safety glasses or goggles when using any striking tools. Check that the handle is securely attached before using a hammer. Throw out a hammer, chisel, or set with dents, cracks, chips, or mushrooming.

Electric hand tools must have double insulation, proper grounding, or a ground fault circuit interrupter. Dead-man switches, which require constant pressure on the trigger to operate, are required for electric tools on construction sites.

LADDERS

Ladders are the source of many accidents. Use only industrial- or commercial-grade ladders, and keep them in good condition. (See Part A, Tools and Equipment, for information on ladder selection and use.)

- A ladder used for access to a roof should extend about 3 feet above the eaves.
- Do not paint wood ladders; this hides damage. Use a clear linseed-oil finish. Keep all ladders free of grease and oil.
- Store wood ladders dry.
- Support ladders along their entire length in storage to prevent warping. Never store a ladder with objects on it.
- Never sit on side rails.
- Store ladder ropes in a dry, dark place. Take special care with manila ropes.
- Inspect the ladder before use. Do not use damaged equipment.

LADDER SETUP

- Do not use a metal ladder near electrical wiring. Always look up for wires before raising a ladder.
- Do not extend or level a ladder on boxes or other supports.
- Do not set up a ladder on a scaffold unless it is compatible with the scaffold system.
- Use spike shoes on ice.
- Have someone brace a foot against the bottom rung while setting up an extension ladder (or brace the bottom of the ladder against a building).
- Do not set up in front of a door or passageway unless it is sealed or guarded.

- Stepladders should be opened completely, with the braces locked into place.
- The correct angle for a ladder against a wall is about 75°. (The distance from the feet to the wall should be 1/4 the working length.) If the feet must be closer to the wall, tie the top to the building. If the feet must be farther from the wall, nail a cleat or have someone hold the feet to prevent slippage.
- Make sure the top rests firmly against a solid support.

LADDER USE

- Keep grease, dirt, and mud off the rungs and shoes.
- Climb and stand with feet at the center of rungs.
- Never stand on the top rung.
- Move the ladder instead of leaning to reach your work.
- Face the ladder when climbing.
- Use a hoist when possible instead of lifting items up a ladder.
- Do not leave tools or material on top of a ladder.
- Never tie two short ladders together.
- Allow only one person on the ladder except in an emergency.
- If you feel faint or dizzy, do not climb down immediately. Drape your arms between the rungs, and rest until you feel better, then slowly climb down. Ask for help if you need it.

LADDER JACKS

Ladder jacks are devices that suspend a plank between two ladders that lean against the same surface. Jacks are an acceptable scaffold for light-duty work as long as the working height is less than 20 feet. If the device bears only on the rungs (and not on the side rails) it should have at least a 10-inch purchase on each rung. Heavy-duty ladders are required, and they must be secured to prevent shifting. Ladders must not be more than 8 feet apart. The minimum platform width is 18 inches. Planks must be of 2-inch nominal lumber and must overlap the supports by at least 12 inches. Only two people are allowed on each 8-foot section of planking.

———

SCAFFOLD, PLATFORMS, AND RAILINGS

Scaffold, platform, and railing safety is a complicated topic, and the following are only minimum guidelines.

Do not work on a scaffold that lacks a solid footing. Examine the scaffold and staging before using it. Make sure the equipment is designed for the job and is used as designed.

Railings are required on all platforms that are 10 feet or more above a surface. Railings are also required on exposed edges of platforms that are narrower than 45 inches and 4 feet or more above the ground. Standard railings have a top rail 42 to 48 inches above the floor and an intermediate rail centered between the top rail and the floor. The top rail must be smooth-surfaced, and any point along it must withstand 200 pounds' pressure in any direction.

A *toe board* at least 4 inches high is required at floor level to keep tools and materials from falling.

Floor openings may have standard railings or be covered with planks or steel plate. Do not cover floor openings with plastic.

Ladderway openings require standard railings except at the entrance. Passage through the entrance must be guarded. Use a swinging gate, or offset the path so a worker cannot walk directly into the opening.

Ramps and inclined walkways, used to move workers and materials, are generally constructed of 2 × 10 or 2 × 12 lumber. Make sure the wood is well-seasoned and free of knots and defects. Fasten the planks with cleats to reduce springing. A typical ramp angle is 15°. Ramps must be secured top and bottom, and at the middle if needed. Protective railings, 42 inches high, are used on both exposed sides of a ramp where it is more than 4 feet high. Install uprights every 4 feet.

STEEL SCAFFOLD

Steel scaffold sections may be used up to 125 feet high. Observe these minimum guidelines:

- Inspect all parts before using. Use parts from one manufacturer only.

- Watch out for electrical wires. Ask the utility to shield or disconnect wires that are in the way before erecting the scaffold.

- Establish a solid footing. Use adjustable legs rather than placing boards or bricks under the feet.

- Make sure the entire structure is plumb, level, square, and rigid.

- Use all braces, including horizontal cross braces, to prevent flexing.

- Secure scaffold to the building at least every 30 feet.

- An unsecured scaffold must be no higher than four times the smaller base dimension.

- Set up planks and guard rails (required for scaffolds over 10 feet high) when you reach working height.

- Set up a ladder for climbing to the platform.

LIFELINES

Use a lifeline to protect yourself when using a swing stage or bosun's chair. Do not use a lifeline or lanyard for any purpose except employee safeguarding. Make sure to inspect this equipment personally before using it. The lifeline should be designed and used so it provides a completely separate means of support. That way, if any element of the primary support fails, the lifeline can still function safely.

STRAIN AND PAIN

According to OSHA, repetitive motion injuries are the fastest-growing type of work injuries. These problems (also called cumulative trauma disorders) are caused by repeatedly making the same movement. Carpal tunnel syndrome, tendonitis, bursitis, and tenosynovitis are the most common of these injuries.

Due to the repetitive nature of the work, the painting trade is subject to repetitive motion injuries. Many factors may be involved in causing these injuries: the worker's medical condition, physique, skill, training and experience, the tools, the layout of the workplace, and the pace of work.

Look for the following symptoms in any part of the neck, shoulder, arm, or hand:

- tenderness

- swelling

- pain

- clumsiness or weakness

- aching, tingling, or numbness, especially at night

- disturbance of sleep

(For further information, see Occupational Disease Surveillance, Carpal Tunnel Syndrome, in the *Journal of the American Medical Association*, 1989 vol. 262, p. 886–889.)

The best way to prevent repetitive motion problems is to listen to your body. Repetitive motion problems have a way of getting worse with time, and they can incapacitate you as they have thousands of others. When pain announces a problem, take steps to identify and correct it. Seek medical advice before the pain gets overwhelming. Remember that many problems are not caused by your physical weaknesses, but by working conditions. The best solution is to correct the source of the problem, not to treat the symptoms alone.

Protect yourself from repetitive motion injuries with the following measures.

- Use tools with a comfortable handle—neither too small nor too large. Grasp as much of the hand as possible—avoid holding it with just two fingers and thumb.

- Work in a comfortable position. Avoid overhead work if possible.

- Use the wrist in a neutral position—not bent backward nor forward.

- Make repetitive motions with all joints of the arm, rather than just one or two.

- Change the job and tool to suit your needs, not vice versa.

- Take rest and stretch breaks to relax your body.

- Avoid doing one motion all day, day after day. Rotate to other jobs, or find equipment to reduce the repetitive motion.

GLOSSARY

Additive process. The rule governing interaction of colors of light beams (see Subtractive Process).

Bodied oil. Oil in which some molecules have been polymerized to reduce drying time without increasing viscosity too much.

Book. To fold pasted wallcovering face-to-face so it has time to relax.

Box. To mix several cans of paint together to ensure even blending and coloration.

Brown coat. The first coat in a three-coat plaster system.

Calcine. To heat a substance like lime hot enough to drive off water from its crystal structure.

Ceiling break. The joint between wall and ceiling.

Chalking (self-cleaning). The gradual decay of exterior paint from the top down.

Color joint. The intersection of two colors of paint.

Colors-in-oil. Pigments dissolved in oil used to tint solvent-based paint.

Companion wallcovering. Two or more materials whose patterns and colors are compatible.

Cornice. A molding at or near the ceiling break.

Cross-seaming. To apply the facing layer of wallcovering perpendicular to the backing layer.

Dado (in wallcovering). The area between the baseboard and chair rail.

DFT. Dry film thickness (usually measured in mils).

Dry rot. A fungus that destroys wood; can only grow if moisture is present; looks dry afterward.

Earlywood. Wood that formed early in the growing season; softer than latewood.

Egg-shell. A surface sheen between matte and semi-gloss.

Enamel. A tough topcoat paint, usually formulated as semi- or full-gloss.

Float. A rectangular tool used to manipulate a material (plaster, concrete, or mortar) while it sets; may be wood, metal, or rubber.

Float finish. A finish coat of plaster (or occasionally mortar) that receives its final treatment from a float.

French sash. A window with many lites.

Fungus. A category of simple plant organisms that includes mold and mildew.

Hiding power. The ability to obscure lower layers. Expressed in terms of square feet of a standard black-and-white surface that can be hidden by a pound of the pigment dispersed in a linseed-oil vehicle.

Hue. A pure color on a color wheel (not toned, tinted, or shaded).

Hygroscopic. Likely to take up moisture.

Iodine number. A number reflecting the ability to dry. Higher iodine numbers usually dry faster.

Kill point. The ending point in wallcovering, where the pattern will not match.

Laitance. A deposit of fine cement on the surface of concrete.

Latewood. Wood that formed during the later part of the season; tougher than earlywood.

Lay-off. To finish a brushing job by stroking lightly across the freshly painted area; helps ensure smoothness.

Lite. One pane of glass in a window.

Matte (flat). The lowest gloss available in a paint.

Mil. One-thousandth of an inch, used to measure thickness of a coating.

Mildew. A form of fungus that disfigures painted surfaces.

Mill scale. A tough coating of rust that is formed in the steel mill.

Muntin. The wood strip between the lites in a sash.

Opacity. The ability to resist the passage of light.

Overlapped seam (lap seam). A seam in which the strip applied first lies below the strip applied second.

Painter's holiday. A gap in a new coating.

Pickle. To treat metal with acid to remove corrosion and etch its surface.

Pigmentary process (See Subtractive Process.)

Primary colors. Any three colors that can be combined to produce all colors of the spectrum.

Polymer. A molecule with high molecular weight created by joining smaller molecules or condensation.

Polymer, cross-linked. A long-chain molecule having links to other chains.

Polymer, linear. A long-chain molecule without links to other chains.

Putty (lime putty). A mix of lime and water used for a finish coat.

Railroad. To apply wallcovering horizontally.

Relax. To expand wallcovering after the paste has been applied (or a prepasted covering has been dipped in water).

Retemper. To add water and remix patching material or mortar after it begins to dry or set.

Sashtool. A sash-and-trim brush with a chiseled shape and a width between 1 and $2\frac{1}{2}$ inches.

Saturation. The brightness of a color.

Secondary colors. Colors produced by combining equal parts of two primary colors.

Scratch coat. The second coat in a three-coat plaster system.

Self-priming. A topcoat that can be used as primer.

Self-protective. A metal whose oxide adheres tightly and protects from further corrosion.

Selvage. The unprinted edge found on certain wallcovering.

Shade. A color with black added.

Sizing. A liquid used to seal a surface before wallcovering is applied; also the act of sealing a surface.

Substrate. The solid surface that has or will receive the coating.

Subtractive (pigmentary) process. The rule governing interaction of pigments in paint (contrast to Additive Process).

Swatching. To apply thinned adhesive at the seam locations before the wallcovering is applied.

Tack rag. A sticky rag used to remove dust before finishing.

Thinner. A liquid in paint that dissolves or suspends the solids.

Thixotropic. A fluid whose viscosity is high when undisturbed and low when stirred or brushed.

Tint. A hue with white added.

Tooth. Roughness of the surface that allows paint to adhere mechanically.

Trowel-finish. A smooth plaster finish that is completed by making circular motions with a trowel.

Vertical pattern repeat (pattern repeat). The vertical distance between identical elements of a wallcovering design.

White-blasted. Steel that has been abrasive-blasted to remove all corrosion; the steel is more or less white in color.

Whiting. A filler material used in putty and filler.

INDEX